PROFILES IN AMERICAN HISTORY

Significant Events and the People Who Shaped Them

Volume 3: *Indian Removal to the Antislavery Movement*
(1825-1852)

Indian Removal
Black Hawk, John Ross, Winfield Scott

Industrialization
Samuel Slater, Eli Whitney, Harriet Hanson Robinson

Women and Reform
Sarah Grimké and Angelina Grimké Weld, Susan B. Anthony, Amelia Jenks Bloomer

Plantation System
James Henry Hammond, Harriet A. Jacobs, Mary Boykin Chesnut

Slave Resistance
Denmark Vesey, Nat Turner, John Quincy Adams

Antislavery Movement
David Walker, William Lloyd Garrison, Frederick Douglass, Sojourner Truth, Harriet Beecher Stowe

Volume 4: *Westward Movement to the Civil War*
(1829-1865)

Westward Movement
Christopher "Kit" Carson, Marcus Whitman and Narcissa Prentiss Whitman, John Augustus Sutter

Mexican War
José Antonio Navarro, Sam Houston, Zachary Taylor, John Charles Frémont and Jessie Ann Benton Frémont

Transcendental and Romantic Movements
Henry David Thoreau, Margaret Fuller, Nathaniel Hawthorne

Pre-Civil War Controversies
Stephen A. Douglas, Dred Scott, John Brown

Civil War
Abraham Lincoln, Robert E. Lee, William Tecumseh Sherman, Martin Robinson Delany, Anna Ella Carroll, Mathew B. Brady, Walt Whitman

(Continued on inside back cover)

Civil Rights Movement to the Present

1924
▼
The National Origins Act sets quotas on number of immigrants allowed into United States. Native Americans gain full citizenship.

1934
▼
Indian Reorganization Act encourages continuation of Native American cultures.

1962
▼
Andy Warhol creates a new art style, Pop Art.

1961
▼
Freedom rides dramatize unequal treatment of blacks in the South.

1954
▼
"Separate but Equal" doctrine is overturned by Supreme Court decision *Brown* v. *Board of Education*.

1942
▼
Migration Labor Agreement authorizes farm workers' *bracero* program.

1963
▼
Freedom Summer project attempts to register blacks to vote in the South. John F. Kennedy assassinated. Betty Friedan founds the National Organization for Women.

1964
▼
Civil Rights Act outlaws segregation in public facilities. Gulf of Tonkin incident escalates U.S. involvement in Vietnam. Free speech movement begins at University of California.

1965
▼
Malcolm X is assassinated. El Teatro Campesino is founded for migrant workers.

1968
▼
Students demonstrate at the Democratic National Convention in Chicago. Robert Kennedy and Martin Luther King, Jr., are assassinated.

1986
▼
Immigration Reform and Control Act gives amnesty to some undocumented immigrants

1973
▼
U.S. troops begin to be withdrawn from Vietnam. Indian groups and the military clash at Wounded Knee, South Dakota.

1972
▼
Gloria Steinem begins *Ms.* magazine.

1971
▼
Daniel Ellsberg releases the Pentagon Papers.

1969
▼
Counterculture concerts at Woodstock, Massachusetts, and Altamont, California, are staged. Corky Gonzales holds the National Chicano Liberation Conference.

PROFILES IN AMERICAN HISTORY

Significant Events and the People

Who Shaped Them

Civil Rights Movement to the Present

JOYCE MOSS

and

GEORGE WILSON

AN IMPRINT OF GALE RESEARCH INC.
AN INTERNATIONAL THOMSON PUBLISHING COMPANY

ℙROFILES IN AMERICAN HISTORY:

Significant Events and the People Who Shaped Them

VOLUME 8: CIVIL RIGHTS MOVEMENT TO THE PRESENT

Joyce Moss and George Wilson

Staff

Carol DeKane Nagel, *U•X•L Developmental Editor*
Thomas L. Romig, *U•X•L Publisher*

Christine Nasso, *Acquisitions Editor*

Shanna P. Heilveil, *Production Assistant*
Evi Seoud, *Assistant Production Manager*
Mary Beth Trimper, *Production Director*

Mary Krzewinski, *Cover and Page Designer*
Cynthia Baldwin, *Art Director*

The Graphix Group, *Typesetting*

Library of Congress Cataloging-in-Publication Data

Profiles in American history : significant events and the people who shaped them.

Includes bibliographical references and index.

Contents: v. 1. Exploration to revolution. 8. Civil Rights Movement to the Present.

1. United States—History—Juvenile literature. 2. United States—Biography—Juvenile literature. 3. United States—History. [JUV] 4. United States—Biography. [JUV] I. Moss, Joyce, 1951- . II. Wilson, George, 1920- .

E178.M897 1994 920.073 94-6677

ISBN 0-8103-9207-0 (set : acid-free paper)
ISBN 0-8103-9211-9 (v. 1 : acid-free paper)
ISBN 0-8103-9215-1 (v. 8 : acid-free paper)

∞™ This book is printed on acid-free paper that meets the minimum requirements of American National Standard for Information Sciences—Permanence Paper for Printed Library Materials, ANSI Z39.48-1984.

Printed in the United States of America

Published simultaneously in the United Kingdom by Gale Research International Limited
(An affiliated company of Gale Research Inc.)

I(T)P™ U·X·L is an imprint of Gale Research Inc.,
an International Thomson Publishing Company.
ITP logo is a trademark under license.

Contents

Reader's Guide

The many noteworthy individuals who shaped U.S. history from the exploration of the continent to the present day cannot all be profiled in one eight-volume work. But those whose stories are told in *Profiles in American History* meet one or more of the following criteria. The individuals:

- Directly affected the outcome of a major event in U.S. history
- Represent viewpoints or groups involved in that event
- Exemplify a role played by common citizens in that event
- Highlight an aspect of that event not covered in other entries

Format

Volumes of *Profiles in American History* are arranged by chapter. Each chapter focuses on one particular event and opens with an overview and detailed time line of the event that places it in historical context. Following are biographical profiles of two to seven diverse individuals who played active roles in the event.

Each biographical profile is divided into four sections:

- **Personal Background** provides details that predate and anticipate the individual's involvement in the event
- **Participation** describes the role played by the individual in the event and its impact on his or her life
- **Aftermath** discusses effects of the individual's actions and subsequent relevant events in his or her life
- **For More Information** provides sources for further reading on the individual

Additionally, sidebars containing interesting details about the events and individuals profiled, ranging from numbers of war casualties to famous quotes to family trees, are sprinkled throughout the text.

Additional Features

Maps are provided to assist readers in traveling back through time to an America arranged differently from today. Portraits and illustrations of individuals and events as well as excerpts from primary source materials are also included to help bring history to life. Sources of all quoted material are cited parenthetically within the text, and complete bibliographic information is listed at the end of the entry. A full bibliography of scholarly sources consulted in preparing the volume appears in the book's back matter.

Cross references are made in the entries, directing readers to other entries in the volume that elaborate on individuals connected in some way to the person under scrutiny. In addition, a comprehensive subject index provides easy access to people and events mentioned throughout the volume.

Comments and Suggestions

We welcome your comments on this work as well as your suggestions for individuals to be featured in future editions of *Profiles in American History.* Please write: Editors, *Profiles in American History,* U·X·L, 835 Penobscot Bldg., Detroit, Michigan 48226-4094; call toll-free: 1-800-877-4253; or fax: 313-961-6348.

Preface

"There is properly no History; only Biography," wrote great American poet and scholar Ralph Waldo Emerson. *Profiles in American History* explores U.S. history through biography. Beginning with the first contact between Native Americans and Vikings and continuing to the present day, this series offers a unique alternative to traditional texts by emphasizing the roles played by individuals, including many women and minorities, in historical events.

Profiles in American History presents the human story of American events, not the exclusively European or African or Indian or Asian story. The guiding principle in compiling this series has been to achieve balance not only in gender and ethnic background but in viewpoint. Thus the circumstances surrounding an historical event are told from individuals holding opposing views, and even opposing positions. Slaves and slave owners, business tycoons and workers, advocates of peace and proponents of war all are heard. American authors whose works reflect the times—from Walt Whitman to John Steinbeck—are also featured.

The biographical profiles are arranged in groups, clustered around one major event in American history. Yet each individual profile is complete in itself. It is the interplay of these profiles—the juxtaposition of alternative views and experiences within a grouping—that broadens the readers' perspective on the event as a whole and on the participants' roles in particular. It is what makes it possible for *Profiles in American History* to impart a larger, human understanding of events in American history.

Acknowledgments

For their guidance on the choice of events and personalities, the editors are grateful to:

Jonathan Betz-Zall, Children's Librarian, Sno-Isle Regional Library System, Washington

Janet Sarratt, Library Media Specialist, John E. Ewing Junior High School, Gaffney, South Carolina

Michael Salman, Assistant Professor of American History, University of California at Los Angeles

Appreciation is extended to Professor Salman for his careful review of chapter overviews and his guidance on key sources of information about the personalities and events.

For insights into specific personalities, the editors are grateful to Robert Sumpter, History Department Chairman at Mira Costa High School, Manhattan Beach, California.

Deep appreciation is extended to the writers who compiled data and contributed the biographies for this volume of *Profiles in American History:*

Diane Ahrens
Erika Heet
Lisa Gabbert
Robert Sumpter
Colin Wells

The editors also thank artist Robert Bates for his research and rendering of the maps and Robert Griffin at U•X•L for his careful copy editing.

Introduction

The 1960s saw a growing number of citizens demand basic changes in American society, and an explosion of protest movements ensued. Sparking all struggles was the civil rights movement for blacks. People marched on the streets and suffered beatings and sometimes death to win black equality.

In 1964 and 1965 the U.S. government adopted far-reaching legislation that assured blacks equal access to public facilities and the freedom to exercise their voting rights. Also, for the first time in American history, the United States declared a war on poverty in the nation. At the beginning of the decade, President John F. Kennedy had spoken of a need to reaffirm basic American values. His successor, Lyndon B. Johnson, was determined to accomplish this and turn the nation into the "Great Society" it had set out to be.

By the mid-1960s a few goals had been reached. The Civil Rights Act of 1964 guaranteed the rights of blacks and other minorities, and other groups won separate victories. Chicano farm workers, after organizing into a union, won protection from abuses that for years had been committed by farm owners. Native Americans began to play a greater role than ever in government programs that concerned them, and a growing number of women won admission to professions and schools once reserved for males. A 1965 immigration law opened the nation's borders to Latin Americans and Asians who had formerly been turned away.

But along with these gains came disappointments, and these were sometimes followed by riots. Despite the new civil rights laws and the war on poverty, segregation persisted and the jobless rate remained higher among blacks than whites. Contributing to the tension, the United States sent troops into Vietnam to fight a war over the form of government there. In time, Americans began to wonder whether it was proper for them to be fighting in Vietnam. A rising tide of antiwar protest helped spur the United States to pull out of the war in 1973. But public confidence in American leaders suffered in the process. There was evidence that the public had been fed false reports about the war, in which many young Americans had died or had been maimed. Discovering the lies, citizens grew less trusting of American leaders.

Discouraged by the difference between their nation's ideals and practices, young people rebelled. Some of them formed a mass student movement. Working within the system, the students aimed to bring about changes that would help Americans live up to their basic ideals of liberty, equality, and justice for all. Others formed a counterculture movement, whose members turned away from the system and its values. Counterculture youth rejected standard dress and lifestyles. Criticizing the nation largely through music and art, they held up a mirror to society and helped stimulate change.

While all these movements became highly visible in the 1960s, they were not new to the United States. Blacks, Chicanos, Native Americans, and women began their movements in earlier decades. There were also cultural rebels, the beatniks, who preceded the counterculture. The reason why all the discontent reached a climax in the 1960s remains open to debate. It is clear, however, that the burst of activity was due to the efforts of determined men, women, and young people. Propelling the movements were individuals, from Fannie Lou Hamer to César Chávez to Betty Friedan, whose activities stimulated progress for their own groups and in general. Progress has slowed in later decades, and there is less mass participation in social movements. Yet efforts continue, with Americans settling down to resolve questions such as how to integrate the schools in their society and how to avoid war.

Picture Credits

The photographs and illustrations appearing in *Profiles in American History: Significant Events and the People Who Shaped Them,* Volume 8: *Civil Rights Movement to the Present* were received from the following sources:

On the cover: **Courtesy of the Library of Congress:** César Chávez, Martin Luther King, Jr.; **AP/Wide World Photos:** Gloria Steinem.

AP/Wide World Photos: pages 4, 20, 61, 65, 81, 93, 109, 133, 136, 139, 145, 157, 164, 172, 175, 226, 237, 241, 248, 257, 263, 276; **courtesy of the Library of Congress:** pages 9, 27, 37, 49, 117, 205; **courtesy of *Los Angeles Times* Photographic Collection, University Research Library, Department of Special Collections, University of California at Los Angeles:** pages 12, 25, 105, 120, 153, 187, 201, 211, 221, 231; **courtesy of the United States Information Agency:** page 18; **courtesy of the United States Army:** page 77; **courtesy of the United States Air Force:** page 96, 126; **©1994 The Andy Warhol Foundation for the Visual Arts, Inc.:** pages 149, 151; **courtesy of the *Texas Christian Herald:* page 190;** courtesy of Arté Publico Press: **page 217;** courtesy of Denver Public Library, Western History Department: **page 253;** courtesy of Stephen Lehmer: **page 254;** courtesy of *Arizona Highways* magazine: **pages 269, 273.**

Song Credits

Permission to cite Bob Dylan's song lyrics were received from the following sources:

Page 137: **"Blowin' in the Wind":** © 1962 Warner Bros., Inc. Copyright renewed 1990 by Special Rider Music.

Page 138: **"Masters of War":** © 1963 Warner Bros., Inc. Copyright renewed 1991 by Special Rider Music; **"Let Me Die in My Footsteps":** © 1963, 1965 Warner Bros., Inc. Copyright renewed 1991 by Special Rider Music; **"Talking John Birch Paranoid Blues":** © 1970 Special Rider Music.

Page 139: **"With God on Our Side":** © 1963 Warner Bros., Inc. Copyright renewed 1991 by Special Rider Music.

Page 140: **"My Back Pages":** © 1964 Warner Bros., Inc. Copyright renewed 1992 Special Rider Music.

Page 141: **"Rainy Day Women #12 & 35":** © 1966 Dwarf Music; **"The Times They Are a Changin'":** © 1963, 1964 Warner Bros., Inc. Copyright renewed 1991 Special Rider Music.

Civil Rights Movement

1910–1950s
National Association for the Advancement of Colored People (NAACP) brings civil rights cases to court.

1954
In *Brown* v. *Board of Education,* Supreme Court overturns "separate but equal" doctrine.

1961
Civil rights workers conduct Freedom Rides through the South.

1960
Black students conduct peaceful "sit-ins" in the South. Student Nonviolent Coordinating Committee (SNCC) is formed.

1956
J. Edgar Hoover submits report on "Racial Tension and Civil Rights."

1955
Martin Luther King, Jr., leads Montgomery bus boycott.

1962
Robert Kennedy sends federal troops to escort James Meredith into the University of Mississippi.

1962
Fannie Lou Hamer attempts to register to vote in Mississippi.

1963
Hamer suffers beating in jail. King leads protest in Birmingham, Alabama; brutal police treatment is televised.

1963
King leads civil rights march on Washington, D.C. **Malcolm X** criticizes King. NAACP organizer Medgar Evers is killed.

1971
In *Swann* v. *Mecklenburg Board of Education,* Supreme Court approves busing to desegregate public schools.

1968
King is assassinated. Congress seats rebel delegation of Democrats from Mississippi.

1965–1968
Riots erupt in ghettos of major cities.

1965
Malcolm X is assassinated; Congress passes Voting Rights Act of 1965.

1964
Congress passes Civil Rights Act of 1964. Civil rights workers Andrew Goodman, Michael Schwerner, and James Chaney are murdered during Freedom Summer.

CIVIL RIGHTS MOVEMENT

The struggle for African American civil rights reached a climax in the 1960s. Until then, it had centered mainly in the courts and in a push for laws against practices such as segregation (the separation of races). There were a few successes. In 1948, for example, segregation was outlawed in the military. Yet it remained common in the nation and was required by local law in the South. Blacks and whites attended separate schools, lived in different neighborhoods, and, in the South, were separated on buses and elsewhere.

A few citizens, blacks and whites, began to defy local laws in the South. In Montgomery, Alabama, Rosa Parks refused to give up her seat on a bus to a white man. She was arrested, after which blacks conducted a community-wide bus boycott (1955). Led by the black reverend **Martin Luther King, Jr.,** the boycott ended in success. The court outlawed segregated buses in Montgomery, and King went on to become leader of the American civil rights movement, using a creative strategy of nonviolent resistance to segregation.

In conducting the bus boycott, blacks had taken direct action. Lawyers meanwhile continued taking legal action to win civil rights. In two *Brown* v. *Board of Education* cases (1954 and 1955), the Supreme Court called for an end to segregation in public schools with all deliberate speed. But

1

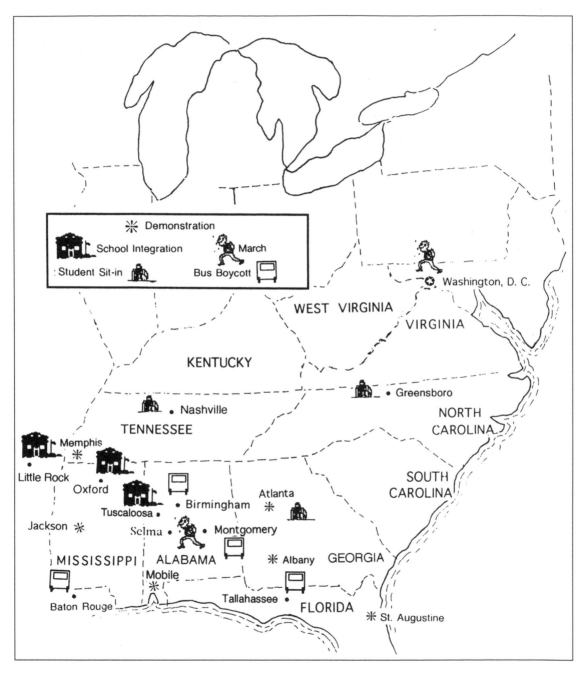

▲ Major events of the early Civil Rights Movement

by 1960 only about 10 percent of southern school districts had heeded the order. Protesters responded by forming more civil rights groups, whose members set out to take direct action to desegregate the South.

As it had for decades, the National Association for the Advancement of Colored People (NAACP) continued bringing cases to the courts. Other groups took different forms of direct action. College students, for example, began sitting next to each other at segregated lunch counters in the South. Started in 1960, the Student Nonviolent Coordinating Committee (SNCC) was founded to coordinate these "sit-ins."

Major Civil Rights Organizations	
Organization	**Date Founded**
National Association for the Advancement of Colored People (NAACP)	1910
Congress of Racial Equality (CORE)	1942
Southern Christian Leadership Conference (SCLC)	1957
Student Nonviolent Coordinating Committee (SNCC—pronounced "snick")	1960

Year	Nonviolent Direct Action
1960	Sit-ins at segregated lunch counters and restaurants
1961	Freedom Rides on segregated interstate buses
1963	Protest marches in Birmingham, Alabama
1963	Mass march for civil rights bill in Washington, D.C.
1964	Freedom Summer—voter registration efforts in Mississippi
1965	Protest march from Selma to Montgomery, Alabama

At the sit-ins, blacks and whites would occupy "whites only" lunch counters and other public places, refusing to move until arrested. Thousands were jailed. "Freedom Rides," conducted by CORE with the help of SNCC, were interstate bus trips on which blacks and whites sat next to each other on buses heading south, breaking local laws that the Supreme Court had already said were not constitutional. Stopping at bus terminals along the way, riders were greeted by angry whites who pelted their buses with stones. They suffered beatings, bombings, and bus burnings.

Local police stood by without trying to stop the violence, and federal authorities failed to come to the rescue at first. **J. Edgar Hoover,** long-time head of the Federal Bureau of Investigation (FBI), refused to defend civil rights workers, in part because he felt the FBI had no right to interfere with local problems.

Hoover, however, was in the awkward position of reporting to an attorney general, **Robert Kennedy,** who disagreed with the FBI's hands-off policy. In 1962 Kennedy and his brother, President John F. Kennedy, ordered federal troops to Mississippi to protect James Meredith, a black student who, the Supreme Court said, must be allowed to attend the all-white University of Mississippi. The controversy prompted a riot that claimed two lives.

More violence followed. In April 1963, King organized peaceful protests against segregation in Birmingham, Alabama. This struggle, he believed, would be the toughest so far, but victory here could affect public opinion across the nation. King proved right. Led by Eugene "Bull" Connor, Birmingham police mistreated the civil rights protesters in front of a wide-eyed television audience. To the horror of viewers, city officials used high-pressure fire hoses, police dogs, and electric cattle prods on the protesters. The sight sent shock waves through the nation, making southern white officials seem wild and unreasonable when compared with the calm-looking, nonviolent protesters, whose image soared.

Violence increased after Birmingham. In Mississippi Medgar Evers of the NAACP was murdered in his own driveway. President Kennedy called for a new civil rights bill that would ban segregation in all public places. To persuade Congress to pass the bill, King and others organized a march on Washington in 1963. Over 250,000 marchers participated, and King moved the nation with his famous "I Have a Dream" speech. Perhaps due partly to the marchers, President Lyndon B. Johnson pushed Congress to pass the 1964 Civil Rights Act,

◄
Martin Luther King, Jr., and Malcolm X at the Capitol Building, March 26, 1964

which finally outlawed racial discrimination in restaurants, hospitals, and other public places.

In politics, however, local officials continued to prevent blacks from registering to vote. A southern black woman became a leader in the effort to register. **Fannie Lou Hamer** marched into a Mississippi office and took the required test only to find that it was designed to make her fail. She would try again, meanwhile drawing more blacks into politics. During the summer months of 1964, which came to be called Freedom Summer, Hamer and others conducted a campaign to register voters in Mississippi. Again their efforts met with violence. They suffered church bombings, beatings, and murders. Three of the civil rights workers—James Chaney, Michael Schwerner, and Andrew Goodman—were killed.

Fearful but determined, the civil rights workers pressed on. They started the Mississippi Freedom Democratic Party, a mixed-race alternative to Mississippi's old Democratic Party, whose representatives were all white. But in the end the old delegates were sent to the 1964 national convention. It was a crushing blow to civil rights workers who were trying to create changes in America by working within the system. Some workers afterwards turned to violent tactics.

In 1965 King, still a champion of nonviolence, led a march from Selma to Montgomery, Alabama, in which protesters suffered brutal beatings. More of them abandoned nonviolence. With President Johnson's urging, Congress passed the 1965 Voting Rights Act, giving federal officers the power to register voters in areas where local officials made this difficult. Within a year, 400,000 more blacks had registered. White candidates started showing concern for black interests, and some blacks were elected to office. But none of this prevented riots from erupting in cities across the nation.

By 1965 many protesters had begun to lose faith in King's nonviolent approach. Though segregation had been overturned by law, it continued to exist *de facto,* or by custom, throughout the nation. In the North, blacks lived in poorer neighborhoods, and had fewer, less attractive job opportunities, and their children attended worse schools. What was the point of an end to legal segregation, blacks wondered, without equal opportunities in work, school, and housing? The civil rights movement seemed not to address these less visible types of inequality in the North. Tensions grew among its members. Civil rights workers began to disagree over whether to use violence, whether whites should be banned from their groups, and which leader to follow.

While King was a Christian leader based in the South, **Malcolm X** was a Muslim leader based in the North. A fiery speaker, he argued that the days of nonviolent resistance were over, and groups such as SNCC agreed. No longer willing to work with whites for civil rights, SNCC instead turned to militant, all-black action. Its new leader, Stokely Carmichael, urged blacks to carry weapons for self-defense and called for "black power" instead of freedom.

Riots broke out in cities across the nation, fueled by unequal conditions of life for blacks and whites in American cities. In 1965 thirty-four people were killed in a riot in Los Angeles, California. Over the next three summers, other riots followed in Cleveland, Ohio; Chicago, Illinois; Detroit, Michigan; Newark, New Jersey; and Jacksonville, Florida. King's murder in 1968 sparked riots in 125 cities.

In the 1970s, the courts turned their attention to the North. They approved the method of busing students to schools outside their neighborhoods to achieve integration. Many parents objected. In 1974, twenty years after the *Brown* decision had called for desegregating schools, northern whites hurled stones at some of the buses and enrolled their children in private schools to escape busing. In the North, as in the South, it would take more than a court order to restructure American society. Still, the civil rights movement had resulted in some major successes, inspiring the rise of other minority movements in the nation.

Martin Luther King, Jr.

1929-1968

Personal Background

Martin Luther King, Jr., was born on January 15, 1929, in Atlanta, Georgia. His forefathers were deeply rooted in the Southern Baptist tradition. As he later said, he was "the son of a Baptist preacher, the grandson of a Baptist preacher and the great-grandson of a Baptist preacher" (Carson, p. 1). His father, Michael Luther King, arrived in Atlanta as a poor, uneducated young man. He worked his way through high school, determined to become a Baptist minister. In 1926 he married Alberta Christine Williams, whose father, A. D. Williams, was pastor of the Ebenezer Baptist Church, one of the city's leading black churches. A popular minister and black activist, Williams treated King like a son, and King took over the church after his father-in-law's death in 1931.

"Love was central." Michael and Alberta King's first child, a girl they named Willie Christine, was born in 1927. Michael Luther King, Jr., followed in 1929, and another brother, Alfred Daniel (A. D.), a year later. In 1934 Michael King, Sr., changed his and his son's first name to Martin. Friends still usually called them both "Mike" or "M. L."

Family life in the King household was warm and close. As the younger M. L. later recalled, "love was central," though "Daddy King" could be stern and sometimes gave the boys whippings if he

▲ **Martin Luther King, Jr.**

Event: Nonviolent protests against racial segregation and discrimination.

Role: From 1955 to his assassination in 1968, Martin Luther King, Jr., led blacks in a series of stubborn but peaceful protests against segregation laws and racial hatred. A Baptist minister, King was strongly influenced by the ideas of Indian leader Mahatma Gandhi. King added elements of Christian love and forgiveness to Gandhi's strategy of nonviolent resistance.

thought they deserved them. Usually it was M. L. who got the whippings, because he stood up to his father more often than A. D. did.

Shock. At about age six, M. L. found out for the first time what it meant to be black in the white man's South. His best friend was a white boy from the neighborhood. They had played together for three years. Now the boy was entering school, which was segregated, and his father had forbidden him to play with M. L. anymore. Upset, M. L. went to Daddy King, who explained about racial segregation. "I was greatly shocked," said M. L. later in life, "and from that moment on I was determined to hate every white person" (King in Carson, p. 31). His parents told him it was his duty as a Christian to love even those who might treat him unfairly. Yet being judged only by the color of his skin seemed too unfair. M. L. could not help feeling as if he hated whites, who would break up his friendship just because of his skin color.

Background of racism. Because of segregation, M. L. rarely encountered whites in his day-to-day life. All in all he enjoyed a happy and normal childhood. A good student, he skipped ninth grade at age thirteen and entered tenth grade at all-black Booker T. Washington Public High School. He skipped once more, this time twelfth grade, then graduated at age fifteen.

In his last year, M. L. experienced another difficult racial incident. He was traveling with his teacher on a bus back to Atlanta after a state public-speaking contest. The white driver demanded that he and the teacher give up their seats for two white passengers who were getting on board. Though M. L. resisted at first, the teacher persuaded him to stand up. They proceeded to stand in the aisle for the next few hours as the bus rode on to Atlanta. "It was the angriest I have ever been in my life," M. L. later recalled (King in Garrow, p. 35). The incident was especially upsetting because of his topic in the public-speaking contest. Ironically, he had just spoken on "The Negro and the Constitution."

Morehouse and Crozer. At fifteen, M. L. entered Morehouse College, a well-respected black college in Atlanta that both his father and Grandfather Williams had also attended. He maintained average grades, becoming increasingly involved in activities outside class. M. L. sang in the Glee Club and the chorus, served on the student council, and joined the college chapter of the National Association for the Advancement of Colored People (NAACP). His feelings about religion meanwhile deepened. By the end of his senior year, when he was nineteen, he had committed himself to a future in religion. After much thought, Martin Luther King, Jr., had decided to follow his father into the ministry.

On graduating from Morehouse, King spent three years at Crozer Theological Seminary in Chester, Pennsylvania. As a graduate student, he could no longer devote so much time to social activities. Instead he pushed himself to study harder; his academic record improved until it became excellent.

Questioning peace. His studies of Christianity led King at first to think of religion as a powerful tool for social change, a way to improve society by encouraging justice and harmony within it. Soon, however, his readings led away from this hopeful view. Influenced by writers like Reinhold Niebuhr and Karl Marx, King began to reject his earlier belief in peaceful change. He wrote a paper criticizing pacifism (the belief in peace) and arguing that Gandhi's success with peaceful resistance in India would not necessarily work elsewhere. As he would later say, at this point in his life he thought that the only way America could solve its problem of segregation was an armed revolt.

President. Many southern whites attended Crozer. Though one of only a handful of blacks there, King was elected president of the student body in his final year. His high marks and public-speaking skills led to his being selected as class valedictorian, the student chosen to give the farewell address. With this honor, he also won the school's major prize, $1,200, to pursue his studies after graduation. Though his father hoped he would return as co-pastor at Ebenezer, King was now seriously interested in a life of scholarship and ideas. His next step was Boston University, to earn a doctoral degree in philosophy.

Coretta Scott. As in past summers, King returned briefly to Atlanta to assist his father at Ebenezer before setting out for Boston. He left in September 1951, driving north in a new green Chevrolet, a gift from his parents for his performance at Crozer. King worked hard in Boston but found time for socializing. He

▲ King speaking from the pulpit on civil rights

enjoyed going out on dates, his suits sharp, his manners smooth
and charming. In particular, he began seeing a beautiful young
Alabama woman named Coretta Scott, who was in Boston studying
at the New England Conservatory of Music. The first thing she
noticed about him, she later remembered, was his size. He
impressed her as a short, little man. Yet as he spoke, he seemed to
grow. "When he talked, he just radiated so much charm" (Garrow,
p. 45). The two married in 1953 and spent King's last year in Boston
in an apartment on Northampton Street.

Participation: Nonviolent Protests against Racial Segregation and Discrimination

Dexter. Soon after arriving in Boston, King had decided not to become a scholar. He still wanted to win his doctorate but had concluded that he was better suited to life as a minister, working with people in a congregation. He wanted to be pastor of a church, a large Baptist church in the South. That, he told Coretta, was where he was needed. He received job offers from many churches, preaching at several different ones to get a feel for the church and its congregation.

He finally accepted an offer from Dexter Avenue Baptist Church in Montgomery, Alabama. Both his father and Coretta were against his accepting it. His father wanted him to be co-pastor at Ebenezer, while Coretta wished to pursue her music career in the North. But they could not change his mind. In April 1953, King formally accepted the pastorship at Dexter. That summer the couple packed their belongings into the Chevrolet and headed south. Within a year, they were well settled in Montgomery. A daughter, Yolanda, was born in November 1955. (Over the next few years, she would be joined by two brothers and a sister: Martin III, Dexter, and Bernice.)

Boycott. Just a few weeks later, Rosa Parks was arrested and taken to jail for refusing to give up her bus seat for a white passenger. The next day, black community leaders met in Dexter's large basement meeting room. The brick building stood on a square in central Montgomery, just opposite the state capitol. King had preached there every Sunday for over a year, becoming a prominent voice in the community. Segregation on the city buses had become a major issue for Montgomery's blacks. They had to sit at the back, while whites sat in the front. In the middle was the "neutral zone," where blacks could sit unless a white needed the seat. In this case, they had to give up their seats and stand. The idea of a boycott—of deliberately refusing to ride the buses until segregation was ended—had been discussed many times. Now, with the arrest of a well-respected citizen such as Mrs. Parks, everyone agreed it was time. The boycott began. For one day, Monday, December 5, 1955, community leaders would try to get as many blacks as possible to stay off the buses.

begun to embrace nonviolent protest as a powerful tool. The Kings visited India in 1959, and King met with Indian Prime Minister Nehru, a follower of Gandhi's. To Gandhi's ideas, King added the Christian idea of loving one's enemies. He called on fellow blacks to fight white ignorance rather than fighting whites themselves.

Sit-ins. King's growing commitment to nonviolent protest profoundly shaped the emerging civil rights movement. Students and other young people, inspired by a leader who himself only turned thirty in 1959, took up King's call for peaceful protest. In January 1960, four black students in Greensboro, North Carolina, staged a "sit-in" at a lunch counter reserved for whites. They were refused service, but they simply sat there, peacefully and politely, until arrested. The sit-ins quickly spread, propelled by students who were already members of the NAACP and by young black ministers from King's SCLC. With King's aid, the students themselves founded the Student Nonviolent Coordinating Committee (SNCC).

By late spring, the sit-ins had spread to cities like Nashville, Tennessee; Montgomery, Alabama; and Orangeburg, South Carolina. Young black and white antisegregation protesters were refilling the lunch counters as fast as the police could arrest them. The thousands of arrests only helped fuel their cause because of the national publicity. King himself was arrested while joining an Atlanta sit-in.

Freedom Ride. Another example of nonviolence in action was the "Freedom Ride," an idea hatched by James Farmer, head of the Congress of Racial Equality (CORE). Farmer, a minister, had helped found CORE in 1942, basing the organization on ideas of nonviolent protest. In 1961 and 1962, CORE and then the SNCC conducted Freedom Rides through the South, in which blacks, as passengers on interstate buses, exercised their right to sit wherever they wanted. Despite the fact that federal law was now on their side, the Freedom Riders were attacked by white mobs over and over again, with little or no protection by the local police. Sometimes the police even arrested the riders, as in Birmingham, Alabama.

In Montgomery, the Freedom Riders in Reverend Abernathy's First Baptist Church were surrounded by a mob. In Chicago when they heard, Abernathy and King flew into Montgomery at once and made their way to the church, escorted by federal marshals to protect them from the crowd. As night fell, the angry crowd outside swelled to thousands. Rocks crashed through the stained-glass windows, and shouted threats to burn the building were hurled at those inside. King spoke inside, calming the civil rights workers and leading them in singing. Only under pressure from Attorney General Robert Kennedy did the governor of Alabama send in the National Guard to break up the racist crowd.

Birmingham. In 1963 King and the SCLC launched a well-planned series of boycotts and demonstrations in Birmingham, Alabama, by then the symbol of southern segregation. It was Birmingham's tough, thick-set sheriff, Eugene "Bull" Connor, who had arrested the Freedom Riders. If they could beat segregation in the toughest southern city, King reasoned, they could beat it in the rest of the South. Most important, King believed conflict in Birmingham would force the federal government to intervene more strongly in local affairs to protect civil rights. It was a dangerous gamble, but it paid off.

"Freedom!" Blacks made up 40 percent of the city's population, so black shoppers had heavy economic influence. For months, they boycotted segregated department stores. They marched peacefully on such places as city hall and were repeatedly arrested by Connor. King himself was arrested on Good Friday.

By May thousands of protesters crowded the jails, but the marchers now included students and children. Their cry was "Freedom! Freedom!" The police let dogs loose on the protesters, and many were badly bitten. Also, Birmingham's white firemen sprayed people with high-pressure hoses, sweeping them from the sidewalks. Newspaper photos and television news footage of the events threw the nation into turmoil. Finally, with Birmingham's business leaders as well as federal officials pressuring them, city officials agreed to end segregation in Birmingham. Once again, King's strategy of nonviolent protest had prevailed.

Letter from Birmingham Jail

While in jail in Birmingham, King wrote a reply to eight white Birmingham ministers who thought that the protesters should be more willing to wait for changes they wanted. "We have waited for more than 340 years for our constitutional God-given rights. The nations of Asia and Africa are moving at jet-like speed toward political independence, while we creep at horse-and-buggy pace toward gaining a cup of coffee at a lunch counter." (King in Patterson, p. 106)

▲ The March on Washington for Jobs and Freedom, August 28, 1963

March on Washington. In the wake of Birmingham, President Kennedy announced that he would introduce a major civil rights bill into Congress. The new federal law would end segregation in all public places. To show Congress all the public support for the bill, A. Philip Randolph, King, and other leaders planned a "March on Washington for Jobs and Freedom." It was to be a huge demonstration in support of black people's desire for equal treatment.

On August 28, 1963, some 250,000 Americans of all races and religions gathered in Washington from around the country. Assembling at the Washington Monument, they marched to the Lincoln Memorial. Senators, famous movie stars and musicians, leaders from religious and political organizations, and common people who had given up a day's work to be there—all listened in the heat of the day as the long series of speeches began, introduced by Randolph. In late afternoon, as the cooling shadows were beginning to lengthen, Randolph introduced the day's last speaker, Martin Luther King, Jr.

"I have a dream." King had prepared a special speech for the occasion. "I started out reading the speech," he recalled later, but "the audience response was wonderful that day—and all of a sudden this thing came to me that I have used ... many times before, that thing about 'I have a dream'—and I just felt that I wanted to use it here" (King in Garrow, p. 283). Though he'd used the words before, this time the occasion and his rhythmic, commanding delivery raised them to a new level.

> ### From King's Speech at the March on Washington (August 28, 1963)
>
> "I have a dream that one day this nation will rise up and live out the true meaning of its creed—we hold these truths to be self-evident, that all men are created equal.
>
> "I have a dream that one day on the red hills of Georgia, the sons of former slaves and the sons of former slave-owners will be able to sit down together at the table of brotherhood.
>
> "I have a dream that my four little children will one day live in a nation where they will be judged not by the color of their skin but by the content of their character. I have a dream today!" (King, *I Have a Dream*, pp. 101-6)

As the speech rose to a climax, the crowd's excitement rose with it, until at the end, dripping with sweat, King received a deafening roar of applause. His words had caught the hopes of all those who had come to Washington, and of millions more who could not come. His speech that hot afternoon stands as one of the most famous in history.

Nobel Peace Prize. King called 1963 "the most decisive year in the Negro's fight for equality" (King in Patterson, p. 126). Early the next year, *Time* magazine named him Man of the Year, recognizing his contribution to that extraordinary twelve months. In July 1964, the civil rights bill was passed, making segregation in public places illegal under federal law. And in December, King received the Nobel Peace Prize, at age thirty-five becoming the youngest person ever to be so honored.

Selma. Just before going to Norway to accept the prize, King was approached by black leaders from Selma, Alabama, who asked

him to support their voting rights campaign. Despite the Civil Rights Act of 1964, blacks were still, for one reason or another, being kept from voting in the South. Throughout January of 1965, King and others led peaceful marches in Selma. On February 1, he and many others were arrested while leading a march to register for the vote. He was released on bail on February 5. Through February and March, police violence against the marchers increased until President Johnson, calling for a voting rights act, warned state authorities not to interfere in the peaceful protests. Again King's strategy of forcing the federal government to play a direct role in local affairs had worked. President Johnson's Voting Rights Act of 1965 was passed in August, making it illegal for state officials to stop people from registering to vote.

Aftermath

Changing times. By 1965, despite such victories, many young blacks were losing faith in nonviolent protest. Militant leaders like Malcolm X had begun calling for change even if it had to be achieved through violence (see **Malcolm X**). While the civil rights movement had involved many whites in the past, the militants now wanted whites excluded from the movement. At the same time, King's own ideas had changed. He began to put greater stress on everyday economic factors—jobs, wages, and the like—in his vision of social equality. Also, in 1967 he began to speak out against the U.S. war in Vietnam. His antiwar position, along with his other activities, led to his being harassed by the FBI (see **J. Edgar Hoover**). His hotel rooms were always bugged, for example. His staff got used to looking out for the listening devices.

Troubles. To some bystanders, King seemed at times to be a lonely man. The man appeared to be surrounded by people but had few close friends. Exhausted from his heavy schedule and the constant strain of trying to please all of his supporters, he began to feel depressed and put on weight. His relationship with Coretta also suffered, for she was not happy with his desire that she remain in the

◄
King delivering his "I Have A Dream" speech during the March on Washington

▲ King's funeral procession

background. After the March on Washington, for example, she grew furious when he refused to take her along to meet President Kennedy. He spent little time at home and began seeing other women.

To the mountain top. In late 1967, King announced the Poor People's Campaign, a planned series of demonstrations to bring attention to the harsh conditions suffered by the poor. In March of the next year, he went several times to Memphis, Tennessee, where mostly black sanitation workers were striking for better wages. On his way again to Memphis on April 3, his plane was delayed by a bomb threat. That evening he spoke to the sanitation workers at a public meeting, telling them about the bomb threat. Exhausted, he was uncertain about the future:

> Well, I don't know what will happen now. We've got some difficult days ahead. But ... I've been to the mountain top. And I don't mind. Like anybody, I would like to live a long life.... But I'm not concerned about that now.... I've seen the promised land. I may not get there with you. But I want you to know tonight, that we as a people will get to the promised land. And so I'm happy tonight. I'm not worried about anything. I'm not fearing any man. (King in Garrow, p. 621)

The next morning, April 4, 1968, as he stood on the balcony of his motel in Memphis, Martin Luther King, Jr., was shot to death by an assassin. He was thirty-nine years old.

For More Information

Carson, Clayborne, ed. *The Papers of Martin Luther King, Jr.* Berkeley: University of California Press, 1992.

Garrow, David J. *Bearing the Cross: Martin Luther King, Jr., and the Southern Christian Leadership Conference.* New York: William Morrow, 1986.

King, Martin Luther, Jr. *I Have a Dream: Writings and Speeches That Changed the World.* San Francisco: HarperSan Francisco, 1992.

King, Martin Luther, Jr. *Stride Toward Freedom: The Montgomery Story.* New York: Harper and Brothers, 1958.

Patterson, Lillie. *Martin Luther King, Jr. and the Freedom Movement.* New York: Facts on File, 1989.

J. Edgar Hoover

1895-1972

Personal Background

Early life. John Edgar Hoover was born January 1, 1895, in the still-struggling town of Washington, D.C. Devoutly religious, his mother, Annie M. Scheitlin, ruled the family with a strict hand. His father, Dickerson Hoover, Sr., held a minor government position, chief of printing for the geodetic survey department. John Edgar, known simply as Edgar for most of his life, was their fourth child. Fifteen years older, his brother had arrived first, followed by two sisters. One of the sisters died at the age of three.

By the time Edgar was of school age, the other children were independent. He was the only one left to care for his parents (his father had become an invalid by then). In his mother's eyes, his main responsibility at this point was to excel. Edgar did so, achieving high grades in school while working to help raise funds for the family. At age twelve, he discovered that he could earn money carrying bags of groceries home from the store for the neighborhood women, then realized that he could earn more if he made deliveries. He began to deliver on the run, which, he claimed, was how he earned the nickname "Speed." A schoolmate explained this lifelong nickname another way: "We called him Speed Edgar because he talked fast. He was so fast, talked fast, thought fast" (Summers, p. 20).

Finishing elementary school in 1909, Edgar enrolled in the

▲ J. Edgar Hoover

Event: The civil rights movement.

Role: Director of the Federal Bureau of Investigation (FBI) for forty-eight years, J. Edgar Hoover shaped it into one of the most powerful U.S. organizations. He reluctantly became involved in the civil rights issue under presidents Dwight D. Eisenhower and John F. Kennedy. Only under Lyndon B. Johnson did Hoover willingly participate in the movement. Over the years, his FBI conducted operations against civil rights workers, Ku Klux Klan members, and black power groups.

From John E. to J. Edgar

It was during the war, in 1918, that Hoover first changed his signature to J. Edgar instead of John E. Hoover. The reason is uncertain, although perhaps he was imitating the head of the Bureau at the time, who signed his name A. Bruce Bielaski.

hardest classes offered at Central High School. It required two years of math. Edgar took math for four years. The same applied to history. His electives included physics and Latin. Still he found time to be active in jujitsu, wrestling, boxing, and baseball. He also became captain of the ROTC unit, which trained students to be army officers. Under Hoover, the unit did so well that it was invited to march in President Woodrow Wilson's inaugural parade.

In 1913 Edgar graduated with honors and was named valedictorian of his class. He earned a full scholarship to the University of Virginia, but his father, always weak and sickly, suffered a nervous breakdown that year. The family could not afford room and board in a distant college. Edgar would have to settle for working by day and studying law at George Washington University by night. He took a job as a clerk in the Library of Congress, a fortunate choice, since he learned the library's filing systems, which later helped him set up one of the most complex filing systems in the world.

Hoover earned his bachelor of law degree in 1916 and his master's degree in 1917. He soon became involved in World War I, not as a soldier, but as part of Washington's Justice Department. His first job was in the mail room, but, with the help of his cousin, a judge, he soon got transferred to the War Emergency Division. His job there was deciding what to do with suspect Germans and other aliens in the United States.

"Red raids." In 1919 Hoover became a special assistant to Attorney General Mitchell Palmer, his job being to gather evidence on revolutionary groups in the United States. A communist takeover of Russia's government had recently succeeded, causing great fear in the United States.

The fear spreading, Attorney General Palmer and his assistants went on a rampage of "Red raids" that resulted in the arrest of about 2,500 suspected leaders of the communist movement in America. These people were to be investigated, then brought to trial or shipped back to Europe. It was Hoover's job to prepare the legal

▲ A young Hoover as an attorney for the Department of Justice

cases against the 2,500 suspects and see that they were tried justly. Outraged about mistreatment of the suspects, the newspapers spoke of beatings by government officials. Hoover, however, appeared beyond reproach. Even the opposing attorneys applauded his careful preparation of cases and his show of courtesy.

27

Hoover did, however, use his assignment to spy on lawyers who either defended the suspects or protested the abuse of civil rights. One prominent lawyer, Felix Frankfurter, even argued that Hoover was deeply involved in these Red raids. Among his victims was the black leader Marcus Garvey, who advocated independence for blacks. Hoover hounded Garvey, then played a major part in getting him jailed and deported.

Early Klan pursuit. In 1921 a new attorney general took office, and Hoover joined the Bureau of Investigation (BI), where he would remain until the end of his life. The bureau had been formed thirteen years earlier because the Justice Department, whose job it was to prosecute dangerous criminals, needed a way to investigate the charges against them. Beginning with twenty-four investigators, the bureau was soon regarded by politicians as a source of jobs that could be handed out to their friends. The number of BI men grew to more than 300, mostly political cronies with no training in law or law enforcement. By 1921 the BI was such a disgrace that there was talk of disbanding it. Hoover began, in this atmosphere, to conduct careful investigations.

One of his 1920s investigations was of the Ku Klux Klan. An organization of white racists, the Klan had taken the law into its own hands in Louisiana. Blacks were beaten or disappeared just for being "insolent" to Klan members. The organization had grown so large and powerful that the governor of Louisiana, John M. Parker, was powerless to act against it. Planning carefully, Hoover found a legal way to involve the federal government in the state's affairs. He had Parker ask the president for federal help, then prepared a case that resulted in the arrest and conviction of a sheriff and two deputies who had participated in the beatings.

Bureau director. President Calvin Coolidge, who took office in 1923, inherited a government in disgrace. Needing badly to restore confidence, he appointed the highly respected Harlan F. Stone attorney general. Stone, in turn, appointed a new head of the Bureau of Investigation, J. Edgar Hoover, known for his carefulness, knowledge of law, and integrity. When Stone asked him to take over the bureau, Hoover accepted the appointment on two conditions: (1) that he have full rights to hire and fire within the department, and (2) that he report not to a lower authority but directly to the attorney general (for most of his career Hoover would, in fact, bypass the attorney general and report directly to the president). Stone agreed, and Hoover became director of the bureau, a position that he would hold for the next forty-nine years. Delighted, his mother gave him a star sapphire ring studded with diamonds, which he would wear for the rest of his life.

In 1935, after a decade with Hoover as director, the name of the organization was changed to the Federal Bureau of Investigation (FBI). By that time, he had built the bureau into one of the most respected organizations in the world.

Building the bureau. Hoover began to rid the bureau of crooked agents and political appointees. He instead hired new recruits, aged twenty-five to thirty-five, with a background in law or accountancy. Then he began a fingerprint division, the first attempt to centralize fingerprinting in the nation. Hoover persuaded local police forces and later all federal employees and U.S. soldiers to send in their fingerprints. He also created a crime laboratory, which developed into the most advanced in the world, hiring experts to analyze bullets, poisons, hair strands, and more. To train his investigators, he opened the FBI National Academy, before the United States had any official police-training programs.

To prove to Congress that there was a real need for the bureau, Hoover kept files on its activities and reported on them regularly to the attorney general and to Congress. Some congressmen helped publicize his fingerprinting effort by adding their own prints to the bureau files, and very soon his idea for a central fingerprint file paid off, leading to many more arrests and convictions of criminals than before.

Organized crime. Through the 1920s, Hoover and his staff continued to build respect while contending that it was not the bureau's responsibility to investigate local crimes. Meanwhile, the number of local crimes grew. In 1931, 282 kidnappings were reported—none of which, according to the law of the time, were under FBI jurisdiction. The kidnapping of Charles Lindbergh's son in 1932 changed this; afterward, Congress passed the Lindbergh Law, which made it a federal crime to send ransom notes or kidnapping threats through the U.S. mails. The bureau was now authorized to investigate many crimes committed by organized gangs. And there was much to investigate. Banks were being robbed at the rate of two a day, and gunfights occurred daily.

Gang leaders such as Pretty Boy Floyd, Machine Gun Kelly, and John Dillinger stole the headlines with their antics. In June of 1933, Pretty Boy Floyd and his gang killed a bureau agent and three police officers. Afterward, congressional bills authorized the bureau to investigate a wider range of crimes. One by one, the gang leaders were tracked down and arrested, or, if they resisted, shot down.

Personal life. Outside work, Hoover would develop three major interests—attending baseball games, going to the horse races, and filling his large home with Asian art. Before joining the bureau, he had planned to marry a woman who was romancing another man, an army officer, at the same time that she was seeing Hoover. The unhappy outcome (she chose the army officer) may help explain why Hoover never married. He became close with a few women in his life, including Helen Gandy, his secretary for over fifty years, and the actress Dorothy Lamour. His closest companion, however, was a man, FBI assistant director Clyde Tolson. Five days a week for more than forty years, the two ate lunch at the Mayflower Hotel (Hoover usually ordered a hamburger and vanilla ice cream) and dinner at Harvey's Restaurant (where he often ordered steak and green turtle soup). Saying he placed women on a pedestal, Hoover harbored a strong dislike for men who were unfaithful to their wives. He lived with his mother until her death and then by himself for the rest of his life.

Growing independence. Meanwhile, Hoover continued to build up the reputation of the FBI with careful investigations, reports to the attorney general, and more files. As the bureau grew, so did Hoover's power. He began to divide his files. Some were secret; others were used to publicize the efforts of the bureau. There were temporary files, kept only for six months and then destroyed. Other files were kept permanently in Hoover's office and used only by him.

Over the years, the FBI became politically important. Hoover developed a reputation as a man who never admitted he was wrong, and the public came to believe this too. Fearing or hoping to use the bureau files, government leaders began to ask Hoover for advice and information about their foes. Under Franklin Roosevelt, Hoover started reporting to the president directly rather than through the attorney general. Meanwhile, his FBI files on U.S. citizens grew and grew.

Participation: Civil Rights Movement

Efforts under Eisenhower. *Brown* v. *the Board of Education,* a 1954 Supreme Court ruling, outlawed segregation in public schools. In 1955 a second Brown decision directed schools to desegregate "with all deliberate speed," but southerners resisted. Eisenhower instructed Hoover to study and report on relations between blacks and whites in the region. Submitted in 1956, his report, "Racial Tension and Civil Rights," described an atmosphere that was growing tenser everyday. "The potential for serious outbreaks of violence," his report concluded, "is ever present" (Hoover in Powers, p. 28).

Personal views. Hoover was born in an era when blacks were expected to remain servants. He attended a whites-only high school and is said to have inherited the prejudices of his place and time. He was reluctant to hire black FBI agents; the few who worked for the bureau around the mid-1900s drove cars and performed other services. As late as the 1960s, Hoover found it strange to call a black man "mister" rather than "boy." It would take daily pressure from Robert Kennedy, once he became attorney general, for Hoover's FBI to hire more black agents. By the end of 1962, the total rose to ten in a force of several thousand. A decade later, at his death, there were seventy.

President Kennedy. Few people knew what was in the FBI files except for the information that Hoover wanted to make public. He insisted that if his men were asked to investigate any crime or person, they must be allowed to do so without interference from anyone else in government. Given this policy, many feared what might be in the FBI files. Hoover turned into one of the most powerful men in the nation.

Leaders found Hoover sometimes helpful, sometimes threatening. For either reason, the chain of presidents kept him in office even though there was almost always someone who believed he should be replaced. In 1961 President John F. Kennedy kept Hoover in office despite thinking that the director, then sixty-six, had grown too old for the job. Hoover secured his position by quietly sending Kennedy reports about his affairs with women, though Hoover was no longer to contact the president directly. The current attorney general, Robert ("Bobby") Kennedy, changed back to having Hoover report to him. Bobby had strict instructions from his brother, the president, to keep Hoover under control, but Hoover kept trying to gain the upper hand. Practicing a type of blackmail, he passed Bobby information about the private lives of both Kennedys until the attorney general tired of accounts of affairs with women and other such information. The FBI file on the president grew to more than 300 items.

Kennedy vs. Hoover. Hoover was in his sixties and his boss, Bobby Kennedy, was just thirty-five. The two men disliked each other and repeatedly disagreed during the civil rights movement. As civil rights protests grew in the 1960s, Hoover's FBI at first took little interest. It could not legally, in Hoover's view, become involved in actions within a single state. Each state must ask for federal help in tense situations, as Louisiana had done in the 1920s pursuit of a few Klan members. By the 1960s, as Hoover had predicted in his report for Eisenhower, there was more racial tension. In 1961 civil rights workers known as Freedom Riders traveled south. They purposely broke state laws that segregated the races and were no longer legal, according to the federal government. Attacked by local townspeople, the Freedom Riders received no protection from FBI agents, who did not even alert the U.S. Justice Department.

Bobby Kennedy, who as attorney general was head of the Justice Department, thought the FBI should be active in protecting the civil rights workers. Pressed by Kennedy and others, Congress passed a civil rights act in 1964 that finally drew the federal government and the FBI into the movement.

Hoover was already approaching the movement from another angle. Interested in protecting the government from threats of rebellion, he added to his files information about any civil rights leader who might be an enemy of the government.

Monitoring King. Hoover targeted the black civil rights leader Martin Luther King, Jr. He informed his superior, Bobby Kennedy, that King was under communist influence and began to monitor King's movements. Deeply involved in the anticommunist hysteria that had gripped the nation, Hoover had formed an FBI counterintelligence program called COINTELPRO-CPUSA (Counterintelligence Program—Communist Party USA). Under this program, he started to investigate King. Earlier attorney generals had approved the FBI's bugging of telephone conversations to further their investigations. After a great deal of pestering from Hoover, Kennedy too gave his approval, within limits that the FBI chief would ignore.

Hoover suspected that two aides to King were communists and began watching all King's movements to be sure that he was not influenced to try to overthrow the government. The FBI file on King grew to more than 600 items, including his affairs with women. Undaunted at first, King hinted that Hoover was too old for the job and that he had "apparently faltered under the awesome burden ... and responsibilities of his office" (King in Theoharis and Cox, p. 356).

At one point, angry that the FBI was not lending badly needed support to the civil rights movement, King suggested that most FBI agents in the South were racist southerners. This was not so, but King may have meant that they behaved like many southerners in their thoughts and actions. In any case, Hoover took offense and denounced King as "the most notorious liar in the country" (Hoover in Demaris, p. 190).

Face-to-face. Finally the two men held a meeting to settle their differences. FBI agents had discovered that King and the civil rights movement were *not* controlled by communists. So Hoover switched tactics, trying to bring down King with information about his affairs with women. Hoover hinted to King that the FBI knew secrets about him, which, if released, could greatly harm the civil rights movement. Anxious about this, King grew sleepless and depressed for a time, then decided not to give in to the strong-arm tactics.

Breaking the Klan. After Lyndon Johnson became president, Hoover had him listen to some of the tapes on King. Nothing, however, could sway Johnson from furthering civil rights. In 1964 three civil rights workers (two black and one white)—Andrew Goodman, Mickey Schwerner, and James Chaney—were killed in Mississippi. President Johnson, who had been Hoover's neighbor for some twenty years and got along fine with the FBI director, pressed him into action. The FBI soon found the killers, all Klansmen, as suspected.

Johnson set out to enforce civil rights laws and put a stop to terrorism against blacks in the South, calling on Hoover's FBI to achieve this goal. Under Johnson, Hoover directed an investigation that destroyed the deadly network of Klans in the South. Flying to Jackson, Mississippi, he personally opened a new FBI office there and sent in 153 agents, a display of his full commitment to the war against racial terror. Hoover actually did believe in putting down white lawlessness.

The FBI began a counterintelligence program against the Klan, COINTELPRO—White Hate Groups. Beyond investigating the breaking of federal laws, the FBI program conducted secret, illegal break-ins of private property for evidence to destroy these hate groups. Some 2,000 FBI spies joined the Klan, whose total was about 10,000 members. These FBI men engaged in counter-Klan activities, spreading rumors, for example, to create hard feelings between Klan members.

The FBI and black power groups. After 1964 riots grew more and more common in cities across the United States. Johnson pressed Hoover for information on the urban disorders. Was it a plot? The FBI began a Ghetto Informant Program that replied "no." Still there was great fear over the riots. So, using the same type of tactics it had against the Klan, the FBI set out to prevent a coalition of militant black groups and disrupt their operations, focusing mainly on the Black Panther party. Another counterintelligence program, COINTELPRO—Black Nationalist Movement, was formed by Hoover's bureau against these militant groups.

Aftermath

Hoover influence. As Hoover grew older, several attempts were made to investigate his direction of the FBI or to reduce the power of that organization. Senators organized committees to review FBI actions and files, and Hoover started to spend more and more of his time defending the bureau and his direction of it.

By 1968, when his friend Richard Nixon was elected president, Hoover had developed such detailed files that almost everyone in government feared to offend him. Reappointed by Nixon at age seventy-three, he remained a powerful figure in government until his death on May 2, 1972.

Containing the FBI. By then Congress was watching the FBI. In 1966 the Freedom of Information Act gave access to more FBI files to news reporters and scholars. In 1975 congressional investigations showed that Hoover had tried to win favor with presidential and congressional candidates by investigating their opponents. Attorney General Edward Levi issued new guidelines to govern FBI investigations, but debate continued about the function of the FBI. Its role wavered for a while but was restored by President Ronald Reagan, who resumed FBI investigations of radical political leaders and groups. Reagan's attorney general, William F. Smith, abolished the limits that Levi had placed on the FBI.

For More Information

Demaris, Ovid. *The Director.* New York: Harper's Magazine Press, 1975.

Donner, Frank. *The Age of Surveillance.* New York: Knopf, 1980.

Murray, Robert K. *Red Scare.* Minneapolis: University of Minnesota Press, 1955.

Nash, Robert J. *Citizen Hoover.* Chicago: Nelson-Hall, 1972.

Powers, Richard Gid. *Secrecy and Power: The Life of J. Edgar Hoover.* New York: Free Press, 1987.

Summers, Anthony. *Official and Confidential: The Secret Life of J. Edgar Hoover.* New York: G.P. Putnam's Sons, 1993.

Theoharis, Athan G., and John Stuart Cox. *The Boss: J. Edgar Hoover and the Great American Inquisition.* Philadelphia: Temple University Press, 1988.

Robert Kennedy

1925-1968

Personal Background

Robert Francis Kennedy was born on November 20, 1925, in Brookline, Massachusetts, a suburb of Boston. He was the seventh of Rose Fitzgerald and Joseph Patrick Kennedy's nine children, and the smallest and shyest of the four boys. Rose Fitzgerald Kennedy was the daughter of one of Boston's most colorful mayors, John Francis "Honey Fitz" Fitzgerald. Joseph Kennedy, grandson of middle-class Irish Catholic immigrants, had made a fortune in shipbuilding, movie distribution, and other investments beginning in the years after World War I. While never holding elective office, he was active in politics. For example, he supported Franklin Roosevelt's successful 1932 presidential campaign, and in 1937 Roosevelt appointed him ambassador to Great Britain. Wealth and power were permanent guests in the Kennedy household.

The family. Joseph and Rose Kennedy drove their children hard, pushing them to achieve their best. The measure of a man's success in life was not the amount of money that he earned, their father loved to say, but the kind of family that he raised. Full of ambition for his boys, he demanded toughness and competitiveness from them. He wanted them always to do their best to win. "We don't want any losers around here," he told them (Schlesinger, p. 15). Yet winning, though important, was not the final test. The boys

▲ **Robert Kennedy**

Event: Civil Rights Act of 1964.

Role: As attorney general during the presidency of his older brother, John Kennedy, Robert Kennedy was the government's strongest champion of civil rights. Under his leadership, the Justice Department fought to ban segregation, protect blacks' voting rights, and integrate schools and other public facilities, despite the opposition of southern white local officials.

knew their father would be satisfied as long as they had done their best.

Joe Kennedy, Jr., the tall, handsome, and athletic oldest brother, was the family star. Two years younger was John, called Jack. Then came four girls: Rosemary, Kathleen, Eunice, and Patricia. Robert, or "Bobby" as he was called, came next, born eight years after Jack. He was followed by another sister, Jean, and a four-years-younger brother named Edward, called Ted. The family divided most of its time between two large and comfortable houses, a mansion in Bronxville, New York, and a rambling summer estate in Hyannis Port, Massachusetts, overlooking Cape Cod. They also enjoyed a large ocean-side villa in Palm Beach, Florida.

Struggle. Bobby was smaller than his brothers. Lacking Joe's strength and Jack's cool wit, he found at an early age that he had to work hard for things that came easily to the older boys. Also, as he later said, "I was the seventh of nine children, and when you come from that far down, you have to struggle to survive" (Kennedy in Schlesinger, p. 25). He was always getting into scrapes in his struggles to prove himself. When he had trouble learning to swim, he simply threw himself off a boat into deep water, figuring he would have to learn that way or drown. He was four. As Jack commented, the act showed either a lot of guts or no sense at all, depending on how a person looked at it.

School, war, and tragedy. Bobby had just turned sixteen when the United States entered World War II. A poor student despite his best efforts, he had had a restless career, attending six schools in ten years. Finally, in 1942, his father decided to send him to Milton Academy in Massachusetts, where his grades slowly improved. He also insisted on playing football, though his small size and merely average coordination meant frequent and painful bruises.

Meanwhile, Joe and Jack were beginning their service in the navy. Jack was given command of a PT boat in the South Pacific in 1943, which was rammed and sunk by a Japanese destroyer. Despite a back injury, Jack led the survivors on a long swim to safety, towing an injured man by holding the strap of the man's life jacket in his teeth. Bobby longed to be a war hero like his brother, and even before graduating from Milton he enlisted in the Naval Reserve and reported for training. Then, in August 1944, Joe Jr. was killed when the experimental plane he was piloting blew up in the skies over England. A few years after the war, Kathleen Kennedy, Robert's pretty and charming older sister, died in a plane crash in Europe. The two tragedies would haunt the family for years.

Politics and Harvard. Joseph Kennedy, Sr., had made no secret of wanting a political career for his oldest son. With Joe Jr. dead, their father's ambitions focused more keenly on Jack and Bobby. In 1946, after his discharge from the navy, Bobby helped with Jack's first campaign, to represent a Boston district in the U.S. House of Representatives. Then, in September, Bobby returned to Harvard, where he had enrolled while in the Navy Reserve during the war. His main interest in college was football, where his determination made up for his lack of size and weight. Kenny O'Donnell, a close friend from the team, remembered his refusal to give up:

> He'd come in from his end like a wild Indian. If you were blocking Bobby, you'd knock him down, but he'd be up again going after the play. He never let up.... He just *made* himself better. (Schlesinger, p. 72)

Both his older brothers had also played football at Harvard, but neither had won a varsity letter, given to those who played in the big game against Yale. Bobby won his letter by persuading the coach to send him in near the end of the game. He had broken his leg during practice a few weeks earlier and still had the cast on. But he played anyway, winning his letter, a feat not achieved by either Joe or Jack.

Justice Department. After graduating from Harvard in 1948, Bobby traveled in Europe and the Middle East, where Jewish leaders were in the process of forming the state of Israel. He wrote several articles on the political situation there for the *Boston Post*. On returning, he enrolled at the University of Virginia Law School, earning his law degree in 1951. He got a job as an investigative lawyer for the Justice Department.

Marriage. In 1949 Bobby had fallen in love with Ethel Skakel, a pretty, lively, and athletic young midwesterner. They married in 1950, making Kennedy the second child in the family to do so

(Kathleen had married an Englishman during the war). A year later, the young couple produced the first Kennedy grandchild, Kathleen Hartington, named for Bobby's dead sister. They would have eleven children in all.

Senate campaign. In 1952 Jack decided to run for the Senate against popular Republican Senator Henry Cabot Lodge, Jr. Bobby persuaded his friend Kenny O'Donnell to help with Jack's campaign, but O'Donnell was discouraged by its lack of organization. He, in turn, persuaded Bobby to come up to Massachusetts from Washington and be Jack's campaign manager. Bobby was angry— he loved his job at Justice and did not want to leave it. In the end, though, he came. Working eighteen-hour days, he whipped the campaign into shape. He also won the nickname "ruthless Bobby" for his tough attitude toward local Democratic leaders, old-timers who liked to sit around the office and talk. Bobby wanted everyone to put out 100 percent for Jack at all times. Jack won the election by 70,000 votes.

Investigator. In 1953 Bobby returned to his Washington career as an investigative lawyer, working for Senator Joseph McCarthy's Senate Committee on Investigations. Six months later, however, he resigned in protest over the methods used by McCarthy and his helpers in their hunt for "communists" in the government. Late the following year, after McCarthy's spectacular downfall, he returned as the committee's chief counsel (head lawyer). For six years, he worked on exposing organized crime's grip on the labor unions. He focused on the Teamsters (truckers) union, winning a conviction against Teamsters leader Dave Beck. Beck's successor, Jimmy Hoffa, was more difficult to pin down, and his duel in the courts with Kennedy became the subject of many newspaper stories. Kennedy was convinced that Hoffa was a crook but had trouble finding witnesses willing to testify.

Participation: Civil Rights Act of 1964

1960 presidential campaign. In 1960 Bobby managed Jack's successful bid for the presidency, again putting in long hours and inspiring comments about his "ruthlessness." (His "ruthless" image had been strengthened by Bobby's long, single-minded pursuit of Hoffa.) There is no doubt that, at thirty-four, Bobby was now a master political organizer. Reporters began writing about the "well-oiled Kennedy machine" (Schlesinger, p. 207). Harris Wofford, however, said that the brothers' campaign worked "not because of a great machine but because they released energy in a lot of directions and sort of trusted that ... the general goal was right" (Schlesinger, p. 207).

Wofford was the campaign's coordinator on civil rights, an issue that neither brother had thought much about. They were not in favor of segregation, but neither had they been much concerned with the situation of blacks and other minorities in American society. Along with the rest of the country, they were, however, awakening to the anger built up in black Americans by hundreds of years of racial discrimination.

Famous phone calls. In October 1960, at the height of the campaign, police in Atlanta, Georgia, arrested black civil rights leader Martin Luther King, Jr. A white judge sentenced him to four months' hard labor, and in the middle of the night King was taken in chains from jail to a prison camp deep in the Georgia countryside. King's wife, five months' pregnant, feared for his safety in the hands of racist officers and convicts. Wofford and others urged John Kennedy to call her and offer his comfort and support. John agreed. When Bobby found out, however, he was furious. "You bomb-throwers probably lost the election," he said, meaning that the radical civil rights supporters had cost John the votes of white southerners (Kennedy in Schlesinger, p. 234). Getting John Kennedy elected came first, and John—Catholic, northern, and liberal—needed all the help in the South he could get.

Yet when he learned that the judge had refused to grant bail for Dr. King, Bobby was equally furious. He himself turned around and called the judge, complaining that King's rights had been violated. To Wofford and the others, he explained that he made the call not as John Kennedy's campaign manager but simply as a lawyer. The next day, after both calls were widely reported in the newspapers, King was released. John Kennedy may have lost some white votes in the South, but he won the black vote, largely because of the two famous calls. And the black vote may well have won him the race, which was the closest presidential election in American history yet.

Attorney general. John Kennedy chose his brother to serve in the cabinet as attorney general. The thirty-five-year-old attorney general took charge of the Justice Department, in which he had worked years before. It was the first time a president's close relative had been appointed to a cabinet position, and the appointment drew some criticism in newspapers and from Republican leaders. But John wanted someone he knew well to become part of the cabinet. Aside from serving as the highest law officer in the land, Robert Kennedy would be his brother's closest adviser on both foreign and domestic policy.

Enforcement. "I won't say I stayed awake nights worrying about civil rights before I became attorney general," Bobby—white, wealthy, and privileged—said later (Kennedy in Schlesinger, p. 286). But the issue would come to weigh heavily on him during his time in office. As black protest and white reaction mounted in the South, the question of civil rights grew more and more urgent. The brothers decided against trying to push a civil rights bill through Congress right away, however. Its passage would be difficult, if not impossible. John had won the presidency by only a narrow margin, which made his influence in Congress weak. Instead, they focused first on trying to make sure the civil rights laws that already existed were fully enforced.

Freedom Rides. It would be Bobby's responsibility, as attorney general, to carry out the federal laws. Bobby chose Burke Marshall, a young Washington lawyer, as assistant attorney general for civil rights. Other key civil rights aides were John Siegenthaler and Nicholas Katzenbach (Kennedy's successor as attorney general).

It was Siegenthaler whom Kennedy sent to Montgomery, Alabama, to greet the Freedom Riders there. The white and black riders were taking a well-publicized bus trip through the South to exercise the blacks' right to sit anywhere on the buses. In town after town, they were beaten by white crowds, as police stood by. In Montgomery, as he helped a young white rider to safety, Siegen-

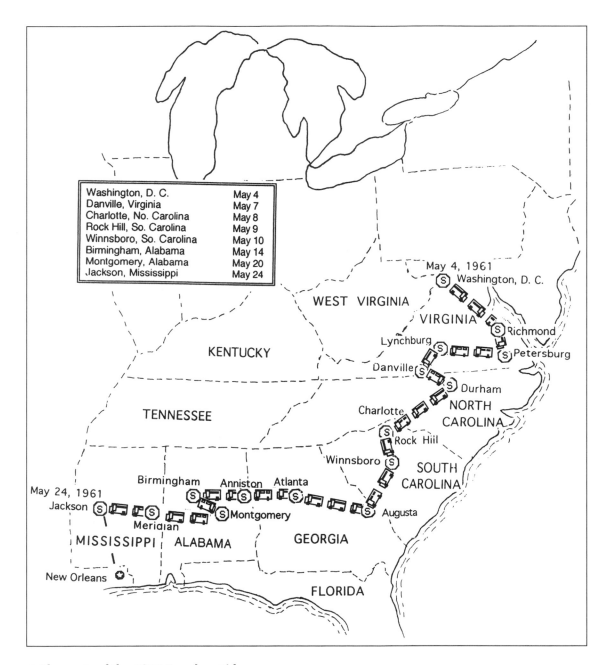

Washington, D. C. — May 4
Danville, Virginia — May 7
Charlotte, No. Carolina — May 8
Rock Hill, So. Carolina — May 9
Winnsboro, So. Carolina — May 10
Birmingham, Alabama — May 14
Montgomery, Alabama — May 20
Jackson, Mississippi — May 24

▲ **The route of the 1961 Freedom Rides**

thaler was clubbed over the head from behind and left unconscious on the ground. Kennedy sent 500 federal marshals to Montgomery. There, reinforced by state troopers and the National Guard, they

43

broke up a violent white crowd that had surrounded Martin Luther King's Dexter Avenue Baptist Church (see **Martin Luther King, Jr.**).

Schools. Like Siegenthaler, Nicholas Katzenbach also faced danger when Kennedy sent him to Mississippi. A court order had commanded the University of Mississippi to allow a black student, James Meredith, to enroll in classes. Katzenbach was assigned to take charge of his entrance into the university. As expected, violent white crowds turned out to threaten Meredith. Kennedy had to send federal troops to stop a riot in which two marshals were killed. Meredith, protected by the army, registered the next morning.

Voting rights. Kennedy pushed for desegregation in schools and transportation. Like King, however, Kennedy thought that the most important job was protecting blacks' right to vote. In many southern areas, blacks had long been prevented by local officials from registering. The situation was complicated. Kennedy promised to support black organizations that were conducting voter registration drives in southern states but was unsure of what legal right the government had to act as a police force over local organizations. As he said in 1964:

> Careful explanations of the historic limitations on the federal government's police powers are not satisfactory to the parents of students who have vanished in Mississippi or to the widow of a Negro educator shot down without any reason by night riders in Georgia. (Kennedy in Schlesinger, p. 328)

He was right. His own explanations about limits on federal powers did not satisfy civil rights leaders, either. Some began saying that the Kennedys' commitment to civil rights was all for show.

New laws. In June 1963, President Kennedy sent a bill to Congress that would ban segregation in all public places. Attorney General Kennedy took the lead in talking to as many senators as he could to try to win support for the bill. In August, black leaders organized the March on Washington, in which over 250,000 people gathered to demonstrate their support for the bill. The crowd heard Martin Luther King deliver his famous "I Have a Dream" speech, after which the leaders met with the Kennedys at the White House. There was direct pressure from the people to pass the bill. Yet as the brothers had feared, the bill was soon stalled in Congress by southern senators.

It took the tragedy of John Kennedy's assassination, on November 22, 1963, for the opposition in Congress to soften. Under President Lyndon Johnson, Congress passed the Civil Rights Act of 1964 and the Voting Rights Act of 1965. The Civil Rights Act banned segregation in all public places, and the Voting Rights Act gave the government the powers that Bobby had been unsure the federal government had a right to use. It allowed the government to step in and protect the voting rights of all citizens if local authorities were blocking those rights.

> ## Always "Bobby"
>
> Robert Kennedy's campaign for senator was marked by the crowds of children that never failed to show up when he was appearing. One day in 1967, even before the campaign was under way, Kennedy and Jacob Javits, the other senator from New York, were visiting a tenement building on New York's Lower East Side. As usual, a crowd of children was waiting for him to come out of the building. Someone came up and asked the kids what they were waiting for. Communicating how strangers responded to Kennedy, a young Puerto Rican child of about ten referred to him, as many others did, by his nickname: "Senator Javits and Bobby are inside the house." (Newfield, p. 49)

Aftermath

Senator from New York. For months after the assassination, Robert Kennedy suffered feelings of loss and despair. It was the darkest period of his life. He and Lyndon Johnson had never gotten along well. In July 1964, President Johnson told Kennedy that he would not choose him to run as vice president in the upcoming presidential election. Soon after that, Kennedy announced that he would run for one of New York's two Senate seats in the fall. He won easily, despite attacks against him for becoming a candidate in a state where he did not really live. After the election, he and Ethel took the children to New York City, where they moved into an apartment overlooking the East River.

A new politics. Great changes were taking place in America during the three years (1965-68) that Robert Kennedy served in the

Senate. It was a period of frightening social unrest. The hope of the early civil rights movement was dissolving into bitterness, with riots sweeping through American cities summer after summer in the mid-1960s. In the South, progress had been made in civil rights by changing laws. In northern cities, the frustration and poverty of black ghettos and slums would be more slippery to handle. Beginning in late 1965, in his speeches Kennedy began to talk more and more about the problems faced by those who lived hopeless lives of poverty. The following year, he announced a program to fight poverty in one terrible slum, the Bedford-Stuyvesant area of New York. Intended as a model for other such programs, his plan mixed corporate and federal funding to provide money for local businesses and social organizations.

As President Johnson pushed through Congress new programs to fight poverty, Kennedy pressed for yet more. In particular, he took up the causes not only of blacks, but of other minorities such as Puerto Ricans, Mexican Americans, and Native Americans. In his three years in the Senate, Kennedy became a champion of the powerless.

The war. Hesitantly at first, he also began to attack Johnson's escalation of the war in Vietnam, begun in 1965. Gradually the war was beginning to replace civil rights as the single issue that dominated American politics. As Kennedy had reacted to the horror of the ghettos, he also reacted to the bombing of Vietnamese villages by American planes. In 1965 and 1966, he questioned whether the war was right. He was, by 1967, openly condemning it as wrong.

The campaign. In early 1968, the war's unpopularity had led many to wonder if Kennedy would challenge Lyndon Johnson for the Democratic presidential nomination. For three years, Kennedy had been drawing large and enthusiastic crowds at his appearances. With his unruly hair and youthful appearance, he had become a hero to many of the young. Yet some blamed him for waiting too long to run. Senator Eugene McCarthy, a Democrat, announced that he would enter the race against Johnson as an antiwar candidate. After McCarthy scored surprisingly well against Johnson in the New Hampshire primary, Kennedy finally announced that he would run. McCarthy supporters were furious. Now that McCarthy had showed Johnson's weakness, they thought, Kennedy was using his famous name to step in and take advantage of the situation.

Assassination. Johnson withdrew from the race at the end of March 1968, two weeks after Kennedy announced that he would run. After winning primaries in Indiana, Nebraska, and the District of Columbia, Kennedy lost to Eugene McCarthy in Oregon. The next primary was in California on June 4. To stay in the race, Kennedy would have to win in California. From mostly white Oregon, Kennedy traveled to California with its black and Latino voters, its poor city dwellers, and its farm workers—groups that he had championed for three years.

Kennedy won the California primary, but shortly after giving his victory speech at Los Angeles's Ambassador Hotel, Robert Kennedy was fatally shot. He died twenty-five hours later, early in the morning on June 6, 1968.

> ## Kennedy Listens
>
> Kennedy campaigned among black militants in Oakland, California. They hurled names at him and blame at white leaders in general. Afterward Kennedy said, "I'm glad I went.... They need to know somebody who'll listen. After all the abuse the blacks have taken through the centuries, whites are just going to have to let them get some of these feelings out if we are all really ever going to settle down to a decent relationship." (Kennedy in Schlesinger, p. 909)

For More Information

Epperidge, Bill, and Hays Gorey. *Robert Kennedy: The Last Campaign.* New York: Harcourt Brace, 1993.

Newfield, Jack. *Robert Kennedy: A Memoir.* New York: Plume, 1988 [1969].

Schlesinger, Arthur M. *Robert Kennedy and His Times.* Boston: Houghton Mifflin, 1978.

Fannie Lou Hamer

1917-1977

Personal Background

Sharecropper by birth. Little is known about Fannie Lou's ancestors, except that her grandmother was a slave taken by ship from Africa to America. Two generations later on October 6, 1917, Fannie Lou Hamer was born in the racially segregated county of Montgomery, Mississippi. Her parents, Jim and Ella Townsend, were two hardworking sharecroppers whose earnings barely kept their huge family fed. Fannie Lou was the twentieth child in the family.

Sharecropping was the system that replaced slavery after the Civil War. A landlord normally advanced farm tools, food, and clothing to sharecroppers, who worked portions of a plantation. In return, the sharecropper took directions from the landowner about what to grow and "paid" the landowner, usually with half the harvest. Like most sharecroppers, the Hamers struggled to make ends meet.

Hardships of childhood. Fannie Lou was never a stranger to hardship, even as a child. At the age of six, she was tricked into picking cotton for a white plantation owner. As she played by a dusty road in the Mississippi Delta area, the landowner approached her, bribing her with candy and gingerbread from the local store. That week she picked 30 pounds of cotton for him. The next week

▲ Fannie Lou Hamer

Event: The civil rights movement.

Role: Fannie Lou Hamer was a key member of the civil rights movement in Mississippi. Active in politics, Hamer challenged segregation, helped make voting rights a reality for blacks, and ran for public office. Her efforts extended beyond politics to employment for blacks through a business venture called the Freedom Farm Cooperative.

she picked 60 pounds. And by the age of thirteen she was picking 200 to 300 pounds. At the time there were no laws to protect children from working, so she continued to do so throughout her entire childhood.

Between the months of December, when the cotton had been harvested, and March, when it was time to plant again, Fannie Lou went to school. She was allowed to attend only up to sixth grade, often going to school shoeless and with a stomach that rumbled with hunger. In the short time she spent there, she learned to read, write, win spelling bees, recite poetry, and sing. Very religious, Fannie Lou liked Bible study best. She joined a Baptist church, where she read the Bible regularly, continuing her education in this way after leaving school. When the time came to read and recite Scriptures, Fannie Lou would often burst into some southern Christian gospel song in one of the most beautiful voices heard from a young girl. Her belief in God and her singing, she would later remark, had kept her going strong in almost impossible times.

Fannie Lou was forced to rely on her faith quite often during her childhood. By the time she was thirteen, she and her family had been subject to some of the worst racist acts imaginable. She was pelted with racial slurs while picking as much as 200 to 300 pounds of cotton a week, mostly for the benefit of the white plantation owner. When her parents finally made extra money one year and bought their own mules, cows, farm tools and a car, a white man they had never seen before came to some land they had rented on their own and poisoned all the animals. The incident knocked the Townsends back down, and they never fully recovered from the loss. Fannie Lou learned early that Mississippi whites did not want blacks to be self-sufficient. However harsh, these experiences fueled what would become Fannie Lou's lifelong quest for racial equality.

Plantation life. After her mother went blind from an accident on the plantation several years later, Fannie Lou vowed to try and make life better not only for her family but also for other blacks in America. She later described her feelings about the life of blacks on the plantations of the South: "I began to get sicker and sicker of the system there.... I always said if I lived to get grown ... I was going to try to get something for my mother and I was going to do something for the black man of the South if it would cost my life" (Hamer in Mills, p. 13).

In the meantime, Fannie Lou had to work. After her mother's accident (her father had since passed away), Fannie Lou labored in the fields from sunrise until sunset picking cotton. She picked cotton for years, never making more money than it took to clothe and feed her mother and herself.

When she turned twenty-seven, Fannie Lou married a tall, strong sharecropper named Perry "Pap" Hamer. The newlyweds moved to yet another plantation to pick cotton for the white owner. Their life was hard, but not desperate: Pap started a little juke (juke box) joint—where blacks could gather socially. They would drink, dance, and talk of better days to come until the early hours of the morning, when it was time to head for the cotton fields again. Often the conversation revolved around the trouble both inside and outside the South. World War II was in full force at the time. At the juke joint, the thought of black Americans fighting for a country that gave them few, if any, civil rights was enough for customers to fill the air with their anger.

Anger. Fannie Lou Hamer had plenty to be angry about. Not only was it practically impossible for blacks to vote, despite the Fifteenth Amendment to the Constitution that had been in effect for over fifty years, but black people were also being lynched, their homes burned and shot at, their opportunities whisked away by a racist society. Hamer thought she had seen too much when she realized that the plantation owner's dog had its own indoor bathroom. A private bathroom was a luxury the owner would not afford the Hamers, who had to use a rickety old outhouse. She observed, "Negroes in Mississippi are treated *worse* than dogs" (Hamer in Mills, p. 14).

Such events were but the beginning of an angry fire that burned within Hamer. In 1961 Hamer went to a doctor for an operation to remove a cancerous tumor from her uterus. The doctor sterilized her, taking away her ability to bear children, without her knowledge or consent. His reasoning was that at forty-four she did not want or need any children, although she hadn't had any yet. She and Pap were outraged, but there was nothing they could do. Trying to find a white lawyer to take action against a white doctor at that time would surely have resulted in further danger, or even death, to Hamer.

The Freedom Riders. A year after Hamer was sterilized, talk of achieving equal rights for African Americans was brought to Mississippi by the Freedom Riders. They were a group of people—blacks and whites—who wanted civil rights for all Americans. The Freedom Riders traveled on buses across state lines in segregated parts of the South, purposely breaking local laws that called for segregation but had been declared illegal by the U.S. Supreme Court. Besides the Freedom Riders, groups like the Student Nonviolent Coordinating Committee (SNCC)—pronounced "snick"—and the Southern Christian Leadership Conference (SCLC) came to the Hamers' hometown of Sunflower County, Mississippi, to urge all black citizens to try and register to vote. They explained that if blacks insisted upon their voting rights, they could vote the segregationists out of office and make life better for themselves by voting in people who would support equal rights for all. Hamer grew interested, and at a Monday night church meeting, when the reverend asked for volunteers to come forward and try their luck at registering, one of the first hands that shot up was hers. Although Pap supported his wife, he was extremely afraid for her. White policemen, county workers, and citizens threatened blacks who tried to sign up for voting with fates as horrible as death.

Hamer would not back down. From her point of view, she had lost so much to the American system that there seemed to be nothing else to lose and precious freedom to gain. Taking only a pair of extra shoes to wear in case she got arrested, Hamer left her husband to tend the cotton crop and their two adopted children and boarded a bus headed for the courthouse in Indianola County, Mississippi. The forty-five-year-old black woman did not know it yet, but her attempting to register would set off a series of events that would permanently alter her life's course.

Participation:
The Civil Rights Movement

Registering to vote. When the bus pulled up to the courthouse on August 31, 1962, the eighteen passengers inside froze for a moment. Outside, they were faced with the immense hostility that a bus full of out-of-town blacks could draw from white locals in the South. All eyes were focused on the bus, while in the hands of those staring were guns and leashes leading to their protective dogs. The stalemate had to end sometime. Brave enough to break the deadlock by stepping off the bus, a stocky, determined black woman walked straight up the courthouse steps. She limped badly, either because of polio or a childhood accident. In any case, neither the limp nor the local white "reception party" stopped her. The woman was Hamer, completely focused on getting the right to vote.

Once inside the courthouse, Hamer was treated with hostility when she stated the group's intentions. The clerk told her only two of them could come in at a time, so Hamer and a gentleman stayed to take the required literacy test. They filled out the detailed applications and were then given a section of the Constitution to interpret. Hamer's section dealt with the complicated notion of de facto laws—laws by custom. Like most Americans, Hamer was not well schooled on the purpose of de facto laws, and the clerk flunked her.

The clerk could pass or fail whomever he wanted. In the South, that meant whites almost always passed and blacks almost never did. Rejected but not defeated, Hamer got back on the bus and headed homeward. It would take another year, but she would finally succeed at registering to vote.

Trouble going home. While Hamer and the rest of the group were riding home, a policeman pulled their bus over and arrested the driver for driving a bus of the wrong color. He said that because it was yellow it looked too much like a school bus. The driver was hauled away, and Hamer and the others were left to sit and await

> ### What Made Hamer Flunk
> "That literacy test was rough. The registrar, Mr. Campbell, brought this big black book over there, and pointed out something for me to read. It was the 16th section of the Constitution of Mississippi ... dealing with *de facto* laws. I knowed as much about a *de facto* law as a horse knows about Christmas Day. And he told me to read it and copy. Then ... give a reasonable interpretation. So you know about what happened to me. Well, I flunked the test." (Hamer in Rubel, pp. 54-55)

their fate. As the rest of the passengers grew frightened and fidgety, Hamer calmed them down by singing gospel songs. Her strong, beautiful voice soon filled the bus and soothed the nerves of the passengers.

After paying a large fine to the authorities, the driver was allowed to take the passengers home. By the time Hamer got there, her boss had been called and informed of her attempt to register to vote. He confronted her and demanded that she take her name off the list at the courthouse or her whole family would have to leave the plantation, losing their home and jobs. Hamer answered him by saying, "Mr. Dee, I didn't go down there to register for you, I went down to register for myself" (Hamer in Mills, p. 38). It was a bold retort and one she would repeat to others. Afterward the owner dismissed them from his plantation, then reconsidered and asked them back. The Hamers refused and left for a new town that same evening, never to return. Hamer had simply come too far to go back to her life the way it was.

Brutality and jail. Because of Hamer's brave attempt at registering and her unbending spirit, civil rights workers began to recognize her as a leader. She had already toured the country with SNCC members to raise money for the civil rights efforts. When the SCLC asked her to attend a civil rights program in South Carolina in 1963, Hamer accepted without hesitation.

At a stop on the way home from the conference, a few of the civil rights workers sat down at a segregated lunch counter in Columbus, Mississippi. The cafe owners and waitresses grew angry, refused to serve them, and told them to leave immediately. Hamer was still on the bus, resting. Suddenly she heard the commotion of the black civil rights workers being arrested outside. When she asked the policemen what they wanted, one of them kicked her and threw her in a police car. The next thing she knew, she was in Winona in a Montgomery County jail cell.

The worst abuse Hamer had ever suffered was beginning. In the cell, the law officers and police drilled her with personal questions and called her hateful names. They would not tell her why she had been arrested. As she sat quietly in the corner of her cell, she heard footsteps coming toward her. A highway patrolman and some officers took her into another cell known as the bull pen. The patrolman ordered the other prisoners, who were black, to beat Hamer, threatening them with abuse if they didn't follow his orders. She looked into the eyes of the inmate standing above her and asked, "You mean you would do this to your own race?" (Hamer in Mills, p. 60). He said nothing, and began beating her with a blackjack (a strip of leather) until he was exhausted and could not continue. Then another black prisoner took over.

> ### Hamer Suffers a Beating
>
> "One of the men told me, 'Get up from there, Fatso,' and he carried me outa that cell.... They had me to lay down on this bunk bed with my face down.... And I heard the highway patrolman tell that black man [another prisoner], said, 'If you don't beat her, you know what we'll do to you.' And he didn't have no other choice."
> (Hamer in Rubel, pp. 72–73)

When they were finished, Hamer was put into a cell with some people from her group, a few of whom had also been beaten and were bleeding very badly. Hamer suffered too—she had a high fever, high blood pressure, and a severe headache, and her body was terribly swollen and bruised from the blows. A friend who was in the cell with her remembered: "She really suffered in that jail from that beating. I mean, her body was so black and her skin felt ... rough, it was like raw cowhide" (Mills, p. 61). All Hamer could do to live through the pain was sing. Just as it had calmed the busload of frightened activists before, her voice filled the whole jail and brought a measure of peace to its inmates. In the other room, she could hear the law officers planning to kill her and the rest of the civil rights workers. But she could sing louder than the officers could speak, and she did.

The workers' lives were spared, partly due to help from the SNCC. SNCC representatives found out where the workers were being held and flooded the jailhouse with calls. They also alerted newspapers of the arrests. Enough publicity was generated to prevent another batch of lynchings. A few days later, all of the workers were released after being charged with disorderly conduct and resisting arrest. Hamer refused to let her family see her in such a sorry state. Spending a month in Atlanta, she recovered from her wounds but suffered permanent kidney damage and a blood clot in her left eye that limited her sight.

No justice. The beatings that the workers received in jail immediately became the basis for both civil and federal cases against the law officers and the county. All of these cases charged that the victims' civil rights were violated by those officers who arranged the beatings. The Federal Bureau of Investigation (FBI) came to Hamer's house to question her about the incident. Refusing to photograph her back, where she was beaten, they instead took photographs of her arms and hands, which showed minor bruising.

The trials took place in the last months of 1963. In the courtroom crowd were white students waving old Confederate flags. On every charge, the officers were found not guilty of violating Hamer's civil rights.

Politics. Though Hamer never fully recovered from the beatings she received that day in jail, she continued her struggle against civil rights violations. At the end of 1963, civil rights leaders Robert Moses and Allard Lowenstein created the Mississippi Summer Project. The next year, the project would bring an army of volunteers to Mississippi to educate blacks as voters and organize a more representative Mississippi political party—the Mississippi Freedom Democratic party. In the planning meetings, which Hamer attended, there was a complaint that whites, who made up about 20 percent of the staff workers, should be less involved. There was danger, went the complaint, of their taking over the project. Hamer objected, as did Moses. "If we're trying to break down this barrier of segregation, we can't segregate ourselves," she reasoned (Hamer in Rubel, p. 89). Singing and tutoring, Hamer helped prepare the volunteers. She taught them how to reach the people with whom they were about to live and work.

In December 1964, Hamer ran for a seat in the Mississippi Congress as a member of the Mississippi Freedom Democratic Party (MFDP). She lost, undoubtedly because only 1 percent of the black population was allowed to register to vote in Mississippi at the time, as opposed to 80 percent of the white population. She fought against this imbalance by accusing the state of not allowing blacks to vote and demanding a new election. The election was held, but she lost it too. Still, Hamer pressed on, touring the country and urging blacks to register and fight for their civil rights. She was becoming a national voice in this fight. In 1964 she also testified before the Democratic National Convention in an attempt to get MFDP delegates seated as the representatives of Mississippi instead of the regular state Democratic party delegates. Broadcast over television, her testimony included her description of being beaten in jail, moving viewers and helping bring to light conditions in the South for those unaware.

As a politician, she drew respect from some of the most famous figures of the day. She appeared with Malcolm X, who held her in high regard, more than once at civil rights meetings. Also, she marched with Martin Luther King, Jr., in a voting rights march, and he joined her in singing gospel songs.

A step toward victory was achieved with the passage of the Voting Rights Act of 1965. The act set up new laws and programs to make it easier for blacks to register. Satisfied only with the idea, Hamer was dismayed at the slow pace with which these rights were administered. It took several years before restrictions on voting even began to disappear.

Meanwhile, Hamer endured much personal misfortune. Her daughter Dorothy died because she would not be treated by any white doctor in the area and there were no black doctors to choose from. She was hemorrhaging badly after childbirth, and passed away on the road to the only hospital that would treat her, 127 miles away. Added to this loss were the assassinations of her friends Malcolm X and Martin Luther King, Jr.

Despite these tragedies, Hamer carried on long enough to witness some triumphs. She saw the first black legislator in Mississippi, Robert Clark, being sworn in after a 1968 election. And that same year her political party, the MFDP, finally won all the seats for their state in the 1968 Democratic Convention. Hamer attended. She would remain active in the Democratic Party for the rest of her life, serving on its ruling committee from 1968 to 1971.

Aftermath

Still working for the vote. By the early 1970s, Hamer's health was not good (she suffered from diabetes, high blood pressure, and breast cancer), so she shied away from politics and concentrated on running Voter Education Project drives. Although conditions were changing, Mississippi still had its share of corrupt practices when it came to giving blacks their voting rights. She toured from county to county, lecturing people on what they needed to know to get around these obstacles.

Freedom Farm Cooperative. In 1969 Hamer purchased the first 40 acres of a project that became the passion of her later years. Over 5,000 people raised their own food on a farm whose size multiplied into 680 acres, but weather conditions along with other setbacks resulted in its failure. By 1974 the farm had shrunk back to its 40-acre beginning. That same year Hamer suffered a nervous breakdown.

The last years. It seemed Hamer was uncomfortable with the idea of ever settling down, but her weakening body forced the issue. On some days, she had trouble doing anything for herself. Her husband would be right by her side to help her whenever possible. Still, she was lonely for days on end while Pap went to work for at least twelve hours a day to support their family and try to pay for her medical bills.

Pap Hamer was disgusted at people's treatment of his wife during her last years. Used to being surrounded by people and helping her friends, she rarely had visitors. The woman who cared for so many others couldn't even lift her arms to take care of herself. June Johnson, a civil rights worker who was jailed with Hamer, was one of her only visitors in the last months of her life. Pap Hamer declared, "My wife loved people, but people didn't love her back" (Mills, p. 303).

Apparently, some people did love Hamer back, though, for she received scores of awards and honorary degrees from civil rights groups and universities. In Ruleville, Mississippi, a Fannie Lou Hamer Day was declared in 1976. During the celebration, young blacks were urged to vote, for the sake of Hamer's efforts of the past and their hopes for the future. Civil Rights leader Charles Evers raised more than $2,000 for Hamer's hospital bills.

After telling Johnson to "remember her and to keep up the work," Hamer died in a Mississippi hospital on March 14, 1977 of heart failure. SNCC leader and black activist Stokley Carmichael spoke at the memorial service, calling her "the very best of us" (Mills, p. 310).

For More Information

Belfrage, Sally. *Freedom Summer*. Charlottesville: University Press of Virginia, 1990.

Mills, Kay. *This Little Light of Mine: The Life of Fannie Lou Hamer*. New York: Penguin, 1993.

Rubel, David. *Fannie Lou Hamer: From Sharecropping to Politics*. Englewood Cliffs, New Jersey: Silver Burdett, 1990.

Malcolm X

1925-1965

Personal Background

Malcolm X was born Malcolm Little, in Omaha, Nebraska, on May 19, 1925, the fourth of eleven children. His father, Earl Little, was a Georgia-born Baptist minister and a supporter of Marcus Garvey, the founder of modern black nationalism. Earl Little had joined Garvey's movement soon after marrying Louise Norton, a black woman from the West Indies, in 1919. The two settled in Philadelphia but soon moved to Omaha, where Little headed the local chapter of Garvey's organization, the Universal Negro Improvement Association (UNIA). A big, dark-skinned man, Earl Little was known as a powerful speaker on behalf of blacks' rights. Louise Little, well educated and intelligent, reported on local UNIA activities for the organization's newspaper, the *Negro World*.

Death on the tracks. White racist groups targeting the outspoken Little hounded him and his growing family in Omaha and later burned down the house they moved into on the outskirts of Lansing, Michigan. In 1931, when Malcolm was six, his father's body was found crushed by the wheels of a Lansing trolley. Louise Little and other blacks thought he had been beaten by whites and left on the tracks to die, but nothing was ever proven. Three of Earl Little's brothers—Malcolm's uncles—had died violently at the hands of whites.

▲ Malcolm X

Event: Rise of militant black nationalism.

Role: For more than a decade (1952–63), Malcolm X was the leading voice of the Nation of Islam (also called the Black Muslims), an African American religious cult that considered whites to be "devils." Malcolm X struck off on his own as a black leader in 1964, abandoning such anti-white racism. Yet he continued to criticize white society, integration, and nonviolence. He was assassinated in 1965, before his changing ideas could fully develop.

Black Nationalism

Black nationalism is the name given to organized self-reliance and unity among blacks in the face of white racism. It emphasizes blacks' African origins and black pride, and often includes a call for a separate black nation either in America or Africa. While several black leaders contributed to the growth of such ideas, Marcus Garvey's "Back to Africa" movement of the 1920s was the first to gain wide support among American blacks.

Mother's breakdown. The family slowly began to fall apart after Earl Little's death. Louise Little had trouble supporting her many children, and her mental health began to suffer under the strain. Whenever an employer found out who her husband had been, she lost her job. Welfare injured her pride and did not go far toward feeding eleven children. The Littles often suffered hunger. Already shaken by his father's death, Malcolm now saw his mother getting worse and worse. She began talking to herself or just staring into space for long periods of time. Disturbed by the situation at home, Malcolm began causing trouble in school, and state officials placed him with a foster family and then in a reform school. Soon after, when Malcolm was fourteen, his mother was committed to a mental institution in Kalamazoo, Michigan.

"Be realistic." For several years, Malcolm struggled to be as "white" as possible, to please the white people—state officials, the couple who ran the reform school, teachers—who now controlled his life. One day a teacher asked him about his plans for the future. Malcolm replied that he wanted to be a lawyer. The teacher's response bothered him:

> We all here like you, you know that. But you've got to be realistic about being a nigger. A lawyer—that's no realistic goal for a nigger. You need to think about something you *can* be. You're good with your hands—making things.... Why don't you plan on carpentry? (Malcolm X, pp. 41–42)

Yet he had often heard the teacher encouraging others to pursue professional careers. And Malcolm, recently elected class president by his all-white classmates, was one of the brightest students. "It was then that I began to change—inside," he explained. "I drew away from white people." He saw for the first time that, despite his intelligence, white society would always limit him because of his skin color. Soon after that, at age fourteen, he dropped out of school.

Boston, Harlem, and prison. Malcolm moved to Boston, where he lived with his older sister, Ella. Over the next six years, he pursued a series of "hustles," first in the Boston area and then in Harlem, where he moved in 1942. Soon picking up the slang of the street, he "ran numbers" (took bets for an illegal lottery), pushed drugs, and "steered" customers to prostitutes. He wore a zoot suit. Popular in the 1940s, these suits featured full-legged, tight-cuffed trousers and a long coat with padded shoulders. Malcolm also "conked" (straightened) his hair, the reddish color of which led to his nickname, "Detroit Red." He began using drugs, too, smoking "reefers" (marijuana cigarettes) and sniffing cocaine. After organizing a burglary ring near Boston, Malcolm was arrested in 1946 and sentenced to eight to ten years in prison. He was twenty years old.

Participation:
Rise of Militant Black Nationalism

"Fish." Malcolm was sent to Charlestown State Prison in Massachusetts. There, as a "fish," or new inmate, he was introduced to a whole new series of activities. He learned to get high on substances available in prison, then started buying reefers and other drugs from corrupt guards. He got into as much trouble as he could—dropping his tray in the dining hall or refusing to answer when his number was called, for example—and spent long hours in "solitary." He liked solitary, passing the time by pacing "for hours like a caged leopard" (Malcolm X, p. 167).

Bimbi. Things began to change when he met a prisoner called Bimbi, however. Like Malcolm, Bimbi was tall and light-skinned with reddish hair. Other prisoners respected Bimbi because he knew so much. He would start talking about subjects like religion or history, and soon a group of listeners would gather around him. He would hold even the prison guards spellbound. One day Bimbi told Malcolm that he had brains and ought to use them by taking correspondence courses and checking out books from the prison library. Malcolm signed up for a course in English and checked out some books, reading them with difficulty. Gradually, though, his letters to his brothers and sisters improved.

Norfolk. In 1948, with his sister Ella's help, Malcolm was transferred to the Norfolk Prison Colony, also in Massachusetts. Set in the countryside, Norfolk had luxuries like toilets that flushed and individual rooms, without bars, for each inmate. It also had an outstanding library.

Nation of Islam. While in prison, Malcolm had been writing to his brothers and sisters and had regularly received letters from them. Four of them, Wilfred, Hilda, Philbert, and Reginald, had been spending time together in Detroit. They told him about a new influence that had changed their lives. They had come to believe, they told him, in what they called "the natural religion of the black man" (Malcolm X, p. 171). Led by a man who called himself Elijah Muhammad, the "Lost-Found Nation of Islam" taught that blacks were the "Original Man" and that in ancient times a black scientist had created white devils to enslave the rest of black humanity. It was now time, Elijah Muhammad said, for the blacks to rise up as a race and overthrow the devilish whites.

"White society's crime." To Malcolm, in the white man's jail for breaking the white man's laws, such beliefs made sense. They certainly made more sense to him than Christianity, which seemed to teach blacks to "turn the other cheek"—that is, not to fight against white oppression. Like his brothers and sisters, Malcolm adopted the beliefs of the Nation of Islam. He began writing a page-long letter every day to Elijah Muhammad, who lived in Chicago. Muhammad wrote back, as he did to many black prisoners. He said that Malcolm's imprisonment "symbolized white society's crime of keeping black men oppressed and deprived and ignorant, and unable to get decent jobs, turning them into criminals" (Malcolm X, p. 184). Malcolm had finally found something to believe in. He spent hours studying Elijah Muhammad's face in the photographs sent to him by his brothers and sisters.

"My alma mater was books." Malcolm began reading more and more, especially books on history and philosophy. He also learned about slavery, discovering that European whites had dominated darker-skinned peoples around the world, in places like India, China, and Africa. To help himself read, he improved his vocabulary by slowly copying out every page in a dictionary, from *A* to *Z*. Reading, he said, changed his life:

▲ **Malcolm X speaks at a Black Muslim rally in Harlem**

I have often reflected upon the new vistas that reading opened to me. I knew right there in prison that reading had changed forever the course of my life.... My homemade education gave me, with every additional book that I read, a little more sensitivity to the deafness, dumbness and blindness that was afflicting the black race in America.... You will never catch me with fifteen minutes in which I'm not studying something I feel might be able to help the black man.... I don't think anybody ever got more out of going to prison than I did. (Malcolm X, pp. 195–96)

Islam and the Black Muslims

Islam is a major world religion, founded in Arabia in the 600s by Muhammad. Followers of the religion are known as Muslims. They believe that God, whom they call Allah, chose Muhammad as his prophet. In their view, Jesus Christ was one in a long series of prophets that began with Abraham and ended with Muhammad.

A black man named Wallace Fard (Wali Farad) founded the Black Muslim religion in America in 1930. After his disappearance in 1934, it was headed by Elijah Muhammad (formerly Elijah Poole), who led it until his death in 1975. His son and successor, Wallace Dean Muhammad, later changed the Black Muslims' official beliefs to fit in more closely with those of other Muslims. A splinter group, headed by Louis Farrakhan, kept the old beliefs.

Minister. Malcolm spent almost seven years in prison, winning parole in 1952, when he was twenty-seven. After spending his first night of freedom with his sister, Ella, he caught a bus for Detroit. There he moved in with his brother Wilfred, centering his life around the Nation of Islam, or the Black Muslims (followers of Islam are called Muslims). While still in prison, Malcolm, like other Black Muslims, had dropped his "slave name" Little, taking "X" instead as a symbol of the African name that his family had lost.

Malcolm became a minister for the Nation of Islam, traveling around the country organizing Black Muslim temples and trying to win new black followers. The most energetic of the Nation's ministers, he spoke on street corners, "fishing" for new followers, and found buildings that could be rented to serve as temples. Mostly because of his efforts, by the early 1960s the Black Muslims had grown from only a few hundred to nearly 4,000.

Confrontation in Harlem. In April 1957, a confrontation with police in Harlem, New York, brought the Black Muslims to the attention of the black community. A Black Muslim named Johnson Hinton had protested when two policemen beat a black man on the sidewalk. One of the policemen grabbed Hinton and started to beat him, too, and the other officer joined in. Clubbed over the head with the officers' nightsticks, his scalp split open. The bleeding Hinton was taken to a nearby police station.

Hearing of the arrest, Malcolm organized a group of about fifty Black Muslim men, marched them in formation to the police station, and had them stand at attention outside. A crowd gathered, following the men as they marched. Malcolm went in. Though the police at first denied that Hinton was there, Malcolm insisted on seeing him. He then demanded that Hinton be taken to a hospital, where his injuries were found to be so severe that surgeons needed to put a steel plate in his skull. Word spread on the street of these Black Muslims, who had faced the police and made them back down—an unheard of victory in Harlem.

Marriage. In January 1958, Malcolm married Sister Betty X, whom he had met through the church. He was organizing a temple in New York at the time, and the two moved into an apartment in Queens. They would have six daughters: Attalah, born in 1958; Qubilah, born in 1960; Ilyasah, born in 1962; Amilah, born in 1964; and twins, Malaak and Malikah, born after Malcolm's assassination in 1965.

"Hate That Hate Produced." In 1959 television reporters Mike Wallace and Louis Lomax asked Malcolm if they could do a story on the Nation of Islam. Malcolm told them to ask Elijah Muhammad, who agreed. The reporters came and filmed meetings, classes, and speeches and interviewed Black Muslims as well as other blacks. The show aired later that year. While not inaccurate, its scenes were chosen for shock value.

Titled "The Hate That Hate Produced," the program showed Black Muslim men talking angrily about white racism, and classes of Black Muslim children learning a version of history that portrayed all whites as evil oppressors. The Flower of Islam, young men who served as bodyguards for Black Muslim officials, were shown performing martial arts training. The documentary brought the Black Muslims to immediate national attention. Suddenly people across the country were asking about the angry-sounding blacks who called themselves the Nation of Islam.

Voice of the Black Muslims. Elijah Muhammad's health was fragile. He could not speak for long without dissolving into a fit of violent coughing, so he relied on his ministers to do most of his speaking for him. Malcolm's abundant energy, wit, forcefulness, and ironic humor made him a natural speaker. By the time "The Hate That Hate Produced" was aired, he had become the Black Muslims' main spokesman to the outside world. Aroused by the program, the media naturally focused its intense curiosity on him. Malcolm's answers did little to calm nervous whites who read his statements in the newspapers or saw him speak on television. Nor did his answers reassure black leaders such as Martin Luther King, Jr., who were leading nonviolent protests against segregation in the South (see **Martin Luther King, Jr.**).

"By any means necessary." As a minister of the Nation of Islam, Malcolm presented Black Muslim beliefs in direct language that pulled no punches. Even toward whites, he was friendly and joking in private life, his tall frame often shaking with laughter. But when speaking in public, he burned with anger. Integration, he said, was foolish. White racism would not go away, and blacks should therefore be separate from white society rather than trying to fit into it. Equality should be taken, not politely asked for, Malcolm claimed, scorning the nonviolent sit-ins and Freedom Rides of King and others. "We are humbling ourselves," he declared, "sitting-in, and begging-in, trying to unite with the slave master!" (Malcolm X in Myers, p. 118).

Instead, he argued, blacks must take equality "by any means necessary," including violence, if whites continued to deny blacks their rights. There could be no middle ground, he said. "Revolution is bloody, revolution is hostile, revolution knows no compromise, revolution overturns and destroys everything that gets in its way" (Malcolm X in Myers, p. 107).

"Farce on Washington." One complaint that Malcolm had about the civil rights movement was that it was actually controlled by whites, who used black leaders as "puppets" (Myers, p. 131). In 1963 black leaders organized the "March on Washington," a massive demonstration of support for the civil rights movement. Approximately 250,000 people met at the rally, where they heard speeches by civil rights leaders. Most famous was Martin Luther King's "I Have A Dream" speech. Malcolm, however, called the event the "Farce on Washington." White participation, he said, changed the "original 'angry'" protest into "an outing, a picnic" (Malcolm X, pp. 305-6). Malcolm was especially outraged when white clergymen, protesting the strong language of one young black leader's speech, forced the speech to be changed so it would be less offensive to whites.

Break with Elijah Muhammad. For twelve years, Malcolm X had made his statements in the name of the Nation of Islam, and especially in the name of its leader, Elijah Muhammad. When interviewed by reporters, he mentioned "the Honorable Elijah Muhammad," constantly downplaying his own role as a leader and giving all credit to Muhammad. But Malcolm nevertheless become a powerful figure in his own right, and other Black Muslim ministers began growing jealous of his influence.

In 1963 Malcolm's faith in Elijah Muhammad was shattered when it was discovered that Muhammad had been involved sexually with a number of his young female secretaries. Such affairs were absolutely against the strict moral code that Muhammad preached. Tension grew between Malcolm and Muhammad. In December 1963, Muhammad suspended Malcolm from the Nation of Islam. Three months later, Malcolm left the group completely.

> ### Malcolm and the March on Washington
>
> "The morning of the March, any rickety carloads of angry, dusty, sweating small-town Negroes would have gotten lost among the chartered jet planes, railroad cars and air-conditioned buses. What originally was planned to be an angry riptide, one English observer aptly described now as 'the gentle flood'…. The marchers had been instructed to bring no signs—signs were provided. They had been told to sing one song: "We Shall Overcome." They had been told how to arrive, *when, where* to arrive, *where* to assemble, when to *start* marching, the *route* to march. First aid stations were strategically located—even where to *faint!"* (Malcolm X, p. 306)

Pilgrimage. During those months, Malcolm had continued to claim publicly that he still accepted Black Muslim beliefs. Later that spring, however, he made a journey that changed his life as much as the Nation of Islam had changed it twelve years earlier. On April 13, 1964, Malcolm flew from New York to Cairo, Egypt. He had decided to undertake the *hajj,* or pilgrimage to the Muslim holy city of Mecca, Saudi Arabia. In Cairo he joined thousands of other Muslim pilgrims on the *hajj,* a religious journey that every Muslim is supposed to make at least once in his lifetime.

On the trip to Mecca, Malcolm learned not only about true Islam but also that he was famous throughout the Muslim world. Furthermore, he met white Muslims who embraced him as a brother. He traveled on to other sites in the Middle East and Africa, where he was also welcomed as a famous figure. On his return, in May, he announced his conversion to orthodox Islam. He said that he had given up the anti-white racism of the Black Muslims, and later accused Elijah Muhammad of "religious fakery" (Malcolm X, p. 459).

OAAU. Although he now accepted that some whites might be good human beings as individuals, Malcolm continued to condemn the racism of white society in general. Before the *hajj,* he had already formed his own group, the Muslim Mosque, Inc. After his return, though, he wanted to reach a wider audience than just the former Black Muslims who, with him, had left the Nation of Islam. Accordingly, in June he formed the Organization of Afro-American Unity (OAAU). Its purpose was to unite people of African descent around the world. Malcolm also declared his willingness to work with other black groups.

Death threats. Most black leaders welcomed Malcolm's statements, but the Black Muslims reacted with bitter attacks, many of which were printed in their newspaper, *Muhammad Speaks.* Malcolm began receiving death threats, which he believed came from members of the Nation of Islam. There were several attempts on his life by mysterious attackers, and on February 14, 1965, his home was firebombed while he, Betty, and their four daughters were asleep inside.

Assassination. Malcolm took the death threats seriously. He had bodyguards protecting him around the clock and kept a loaded rifle in his home. Still, he knew that determined assassins would be able to kill him if they wanted.

A week after the firebombing, on February 21, 1965, Malcolm X was shot to death as he spoke to an OAAU meeting in the Audubon Ballroom in New York City. He was thirty-nine years old. Three Black Muslims were later convicted of the crime.

Aftermath

Legacy of militant nationalism. Unlike leaders such as Martin Luther King, Jr., who had been working mostly to end segregation in the South, Malcolm X had spoken for the poor, urban blacks of the northern ghettos. Their first concern was not whether they could vote or sit on any seat of a bus, but whether they had access to good jobs and decent housing. By the mid-1960s, many younger blacks had begun to lose faith in nonviolence, which seemed to achieve integration without social equality. After Malcolm's death, a new generation of black leaders arose. These leaders—Stokely Carmichael, H. Rap Brown, Huey Newton, and others—used slogans like "Black Power" and "Black is beautiful." In their anger and pride, they drew inspiration from the legacy of Malcolm X.

For More Information

Malcolm X, with Alex Haley. *The Autobiography of Malcolm X.* New York: Ballantine, 1965.

Myers, Walter Dean. *Malcolm X: By Any Means Necessary.* New York: Scholastic, 1993.

Vietnam War

1945
▼
Ho Chi Minh declares independence in Vietnam, struggles against French forces. United States supports France.

1954
▼
Conference in Geneva temporarily divides the nation of Vietnam. United States supports South Vietnam's government.

1965
▼
Johnson sends U.S. combat troops to Vietnam. **James Stockdale,** his aircraft shot down, is imprisoned.

1964
▼
President **Lyndon B. Johnson** gets Congress to pass Tonkin Gulf Resolution, which allows him to wage war in Vietnam.

1963
▼
President John F. Kennedy increases number of U.S. advisers in South Vietnam to more than 16,000.

1956
▼
The French leave Vietnam; President Dwight D. Eisenhower raises number of U.S. advisers there to about 680.

1967
▼
In New York City, 300,000 U.S. citizens protest U.S. involvement in the war.

1968
▼
North Vietnam launches Tet Offensive. Johnson does not seek reelection. U.S. troop strength peaks at 543,000.

1969
▼
President **Richard M. Nixon** begins secret bombing of Cambodia, renews bombing of North Vietnam, begins troop withdrawal.

1970
▼
News of My Lai massacre and Cambodia invasion lead to further antiwar protests.

1976
▼
Vietnam is formally unified under communist rule.

1975
▼
South Vietnam surrenders. Emergency airlift rescues U.S. embassy workers out of Saigon.

1973
▼
Congress passes War Powers Act. United States signs cease-fire agreement with North Vietnam.

1971
▼
Daniel Ellsberg turns over Pentagon Papers to the *New York Times*.

VIETNAM WAR

America's most deadly conflict of the Cold War era occurred in a nation-state of Southeast Asia called Vietnam. The conflict began slowly, growing out of the ashes of World War II. During that war, Japan occupied French colonies in Indochina—the peninsula of Southeast Asia that includes Vietnam, Cambodia (now Kampuchea), and Laos. The French fled the region during the war while Ho Chi Minh, a Vietnamese communist, led a continuing effort to resist the Japanese.

In 1945 Japan lost the world war, and Ho declared Vietnam an independent republic. The French, however, wanted to return to their colonial rule of Indochina. They attracted support from the United States, now involved in a U.S.-Soviet contest for world supremacy (the Cold War). France, weakened by World War II, needed help to defeat Ho, and America aimed to stop the spread of communism. So President Harry Truman decided in 1947 to aid France in Vietnam. Ho, in turn, received aid, first from the Soviet and later from the Chinese communists.

Soon the United States was supplying most of the money for the French effort. The French fared poorly. There was popular support for Ho among the Vietnamese, while support for the French-backed government was relatively weak. Badly

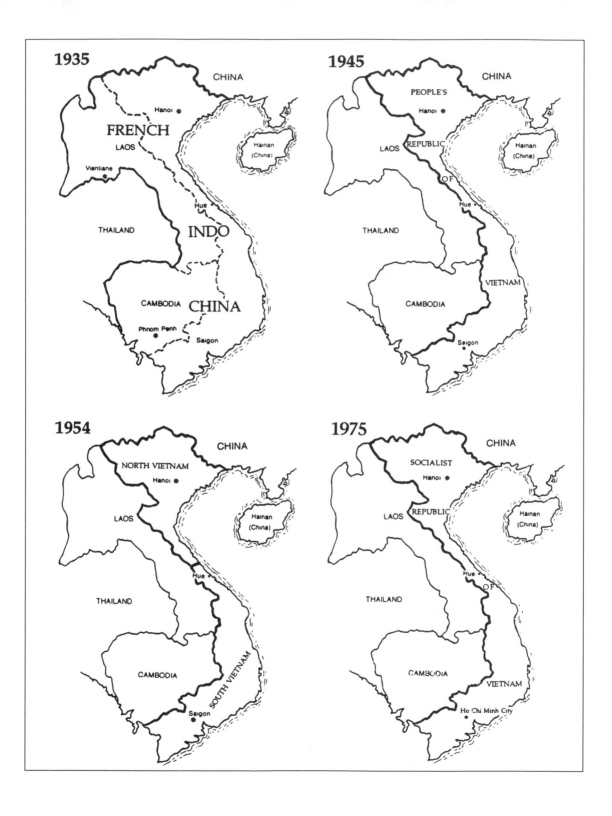

defeated at Dien Bien Phu in 1954, France began to withdraw from Vietnam. The land remained in turmoil, its government uncertain. Ho was strongest in the north, and the United States backed Ngo Dinh Diem, an anticommunist, in the southern city of Saigon. A world conference held in Geneva, Switzerland, divided Vietnam into two zones around the seventeenth parallel latitude. Meant to be temporary, the division became long-term as the land split into two countries: North Vietnam, led by Ho, and South Vietnam, led by Diem. Elections were planned for 1956 to determine which one would be Vietnam's leader, but Diem, fearful that Ho would win, refused to hold them. America backed his refusal.

Number of U.S. Advisers and Troops in Vietnam*			
1961	675	**1967**	485,000
1963	16,000	**1968**	543,000
1965	184,000	**1972**	39,000
1966	385,000	**1973**	0

*1961–63 = number of U.S. advisers;
  1965–73 = number of U.S. troops

Diem's rule was not popular even in the south. President Dwight D. Eisenhower, however, believed that if Vietnam fell to communism, so would nearby Burma, Thailand, and Indonesia. Furthermore, he believed that Ho had close ties to the Soviet Union, though he did not. Later U.S. presidents shared these beliefs and acted accordingly. During the 1950s, Eisenhower increased American aid to Diem's government. Besides money, he boosted the number of U.S. military advisers to help Diem fight communists in South Vietnam. Called the Viet Cong, these southern communists were backed by the north and its Soviet and Chinese allies. In 1961 President John F. Kennedy sent Diem more U.S. advisers.

Kennedy's successor, **Lyndon B. Johnson,** dramatically changed the nature of U.S. involvement in Vietnam. South Vietnam's government was on the brink of collapse. Not wanting to go down in history as the president who lost Vietnam to communism, Johnson made a drastic change. He involved the United States fully in the war. In 1965 Johnson began to step up, or escalate, U.S. military activity. He sent U.S. soldiers to fight the Viet Cong, breaking an election promise not to do this. By 1968 nearly 600,000 American soldiers were fighting in Vietnam.

A few Americans questioned the wisdom of escalation almost as soon as it began. Should they be fighting communism even if it meant sacrificing American ideals? Was it not an American belief that a nation should be left alone to decide its own form of government? Students asked such questions at "teach-ins" on college campuses beginning in early 1965. By 1967 as many as 300,000 marched in New York against the war. These antiwar protesters were viewed as troublemakers at first but in time won to their side a few government leaders who began doubting that the war could be won. After 1968 the number of U.S. officials against the war increased.

Yet Johnson doggedly continued his war effort, turning bitter against those who questioned his policy. Among them were several challengers for the Democratic presidential nomination of 1968, in which the war was becoming the major issue. Johnson's popularity had plummeted. Outside the White House, student protesters could usually be heard, chanting "Hey, hey, LBJ, how many kids did you kill today?" Antiwar candidate Eugene McCarthy nearly beat Johnson in the New Hampshire primary in March 1968. Another contender, Robert Kennedy, was also against the war. At the end of March, ruined by the war, Johnson announced a halt in bombing of North Vietnam and withdrew from the race for president.

The year 1968 brought assassinations, riots, and angry antiwar demonstrations. **Richard M. Nixon,** the Republican nominee, barely won the presidential election. Nixon had promised "an honorable peace" in Vietnam, but like Johnson he refused to be the president who lost Vietnam.

Known for being firmly opposed to communism, Nixon had his own ideas about how to proceed in the war. He wanted to train and supply the South Vietnamese, then let them do their own fighting. This would allow American sol-

▲ The U.S. military's weapons were far superior to those of the Vietnamese

diers to return home. Also, Nixon would try to isolate North Vietnam by becoming friendlier with the Soviets and the Chinese. Nixon's policy failed. The South Vietnamese army never did grow strong enough, despite American aid. And the North Vietnamese, stubborn and independent, would not be told what to do by either the Soviets or the Chinese.

The Americans had a huge advantage in technology. But their side did not move into the position of winning the war. The enemy seemed to be everywhere, and the South Vietnamese government, though backed by the Americans, failed to gain the support of its own people. In fact, there were villagers in the South who felt sympathy for the North. Their villages offered perfect cover for Viet Cong fighters, who would slip away when the Americans approached and then slip back in again. South Vietnam shared a long border with Laos and Cambodia on which the North Vietnamese set up bases that supplied the Viet Cong. U.S. forces tried but failed to interrupt the flow of supplies with bombings. Killing thousands of innocent civilians, the bombings made the war even more unpopular back in the United States.

Protesters called attention to the high number of ethnic Americans serving in Vietnam. As in past wars, the military offered many blacks, Chicanos, and other minorities better jobs and higher pay than they could find elsewhere in American society. Some enlisted for these reasons. Others were drafted. Students were excused from service if they attended college full time. But minority students were often too poor to meet this requirement and ended up in Vietnam. The many ethnic Americans who served in the war highlighted the unfairness of unequal racial conditions back home.

Nixon's policy meant withdrawal of American troops, which was supposed to lessen the protests at home. The protests continued, however, because Nixon was forced to take other measures to counteract South Vietnamese weakness. After Nixon ordered an invasion of Cambodia in 1970, six protesting students were killed by National Guardsmen and police at two universities, Kent State in Ohio and Jackson State in Mississippi. That same year, the public learned of the murder of more than 300 Vietnamese by U.S. troops in the village of My Lai. The troops had herded unarmed villagers—mostly women, children, and old men—into ditches and shot them. For some Americans, My Lai became a symbol of a brutal, pointless war.

Nixon, too, grew bitter and resentful of those who were against the war. In 1971 **Daniel Ellsberg,** a former government official, gave the *New York Times* a secret study of the war carried out by the Pentagon. Nixon tried but failed to prevent the newspaper from printing the study. Called the

Pentagon Papers, it showed how deception and poor planning had shaped American policy in Vietnam.

American soldiers in Vietnam suffered from low morale, or spirits, about the fighting. There were other problems too, such as the fate of prisoners of war (POWs). Commander **James Stockdale,** and others who were unlucky enough to be captured, endured torment. They were beaten, starved, and tortured for information. At home, their families felt that the public and government were ignoring their plight. Sybil Stockdale, James's wife, called attention to the prisoners, organizing their family members to pressure the U.S. government into protesting against POW mistreatment.

Finally, on January 29, 1973, Nixon's adviser Henry Kissinger signed a peace agreement with Le Duc Tho of North Vietnam. Though the war was not yet over, the men agreed to the release of American POWs and the withdrawal of American troops from Vietnam. The Americans pulled out in 1973. Just over a year later, South Vietnam fell to the northern forces.

The war left deep scars on all participants. Perhaps 3 million Vietnamese, Cambodians, and Laotians were killed, many of them civilians. And U.S. bombing and chemical warfare left much of the land in Vietnam poisoned, unsuitable for growing crops. American losses included 58,000 killed, more than 1,000 missing, and a great loss of confidence at home. Out of the war came a questioning attitude in America that has since continued. No longer is the American public so automatically trusting of its leaders as it once was.

Lyndon B. Johnson

1908–1973

Personal Background

Lyndon Baines Johnson was born on August 27, 1908, on his family's farm near Johnson City, in the "Hill Country" of west Texas. His parents, Sam Ealy Johnson, Jr., and Rebekah Baines Johnson, took three months to name him. Yet legend has it that long before that his Grandfather Johnson had decided on the boy's career. On hearing of his grandson's birth, Big Sam Johnson had galloped off on his favorite gray horse, Fritz, to share the news with friends and neighbors. "A United States Senator was born today—my grandson" (Steinberg, p. 12). Big Sam's prediction appeared likely to come true when, less than a year later, the Johnsons took baby Lyndon to a picnic. There he greeted each guest with a big smile and an attempt to climb from his father's arms into theirs. "Sam, you've got a politician there," one of them quipped. "I can just see him running for office twenty-odd years from now" (Dallek, p. 32).

Both sides. Politics ran on both sides of the family. Rebekah's family, the Baineses, had served in the Arkansas and Texas legislatures, and Sam Johnson, Jr., also served several terms as a state legislator. He made a name for himself as an enemy of the Ku Klux Klan and of the powerful business interests who tried to control state politics. At six, Lyndon himself started living up to the early predictions when he passed out campaign leaflets supporting the

▲ Lyndon B. Johnson

Event: "Escalation" of American military involvement in Vietnam.

Role: When Lyndon B. Johnson took over the presidency in 1963, U.S. troops in Vietnam were limited to about 16,000 "advisers." By 1968 more than 500,000 U.S. soldiers were fighting on the ground. Yet they were unable to gain victory for America's ally, the unpopular South Vietnamese government. The war appeared both wrong and unsuccessful as it progressed, forcing Johnson not to run for reelection in 1968.

candidate for governor that his father favored. And in his first-grade class, he showed a politician's flair for self-promotion.

Two large blackboards sat on either side of the doorway, and children who went to the restroom (a wooden outhouse) were supposed to write their names on one of the boards. Most children, embarrassed, wrote as small as possible. Not Lyndon. He would scrawl "Lyndon B." in the largest possible letters on one board, and "Johnson" on the other. Later, as the Democratic Senate majority leader under a Republican president, he would also work "both sides of the aisle," but in the usual sense of getting both parties to work together.

San Marcos. Not a very serious student, Lyndon clowned his way through school, always trying to be the most popular in his class and usually succeeding. He also set himself apart from his classmates by slicking back his hair and wearing fancy clothes (he often sported a bow tie). For three years after high school, he drifted through several part-time jobs, resisting his parents' pressures to go to college. He hitchhiked to California with friends but was unable to find the well-paying job he had imagined. Thumbing his way back, all the way to Texas, he returned exhausted and hungry after the 1,500-mile journey. His grandmother's patchwork quilt at the foot of his bed was "the prettiest sight I ever saw," he later said (Johnson in Dallek, p. 60). The trip ended his period of rebellion, and he agreed to enroll at the Southwest Texas State Teachers College in nearby San Marcos.

Assistant's assistant. The Johnsons were poor, despite his father's career in politics, so Lyndon pretty much had to pay his own way at San Marcos. His family helped when they could, and he found a job with the campus cleanup crew. Lyndon had better things in mind, however, and boldly approached the school president, Dr. Cecil Evans, asking for another job. Evans agreed to let him assist the janitor of the science building. Unsatisfied, Lyndon came back shortly after that and asked if he could be Evans's personal assistant. Evans politely pointed out that he already had a full-time assistant, one Tom Nichols. Unwilling to let a detail like that stand in his way, Johnson offered to help Nichols. Evans, worn down by Johnson's persistence, agreed.

That was all Johnson needed. He parked himself at the door of Evans's office, jumping up to greet all visitors. Soon faculty members began thinking they had to get approval from Johnson before seeing the president. Johnson also took messages to faculty members, and his lofty manner always made them think he was much more than a message boy. To the shock of faculty members, once he even greeted the dignified president with a slap on the back! "Lyndon," Evans said, "I declare you hadn't been in my office a month before I could hardly tell who was president of the school— you or me" (Steinberg, p. 37).

"Mister Dick." In 1930, after finishing college in just over three years, Johnson got a job teaching public speaking and debate at Sam Houston High School in Houston. He was meanwhile drawn to politics like a magnet, however, and by November 1931 the twenty-three-year-old Johnson was working for a congressional candidate named Richard Kleberg. Known as "Mister Dick," Kleberg came from one of Texas's wealthiest families. His father, Robert, owned the famous King Ranch in south Texas, one of the largest ranches in the state. Kleberg won the race, and in December 1931 he went to Washington, D.C., as a new member of the House of Representatives. With him went his new personal secretary, a gangly six-foot-three-inch-tall young Texan named Lyndon Johnson.

Early years in Washington. For the next four years, Johnson busily built up a network of friends and contacts in Washington. As earlier with Dr. Evans, he soon took over Kleberg's office. Johnson ran the office when the congressman took time off to golf, play polo, hunt, or play cards. Working long days, young Johnson soaked up experience. As a friend later remembered:

> [Johnson would] learn all he could and learn it fast. You never had to tell him anything a second time. This skinny boy was as green as anybody could be, but within a few months he knew how to operate in Washington better than some who had been here for twenty years before him. (Dallek, p. 97)

"Lady Bird." In 1934 Johnson married Claudia Alta Taylor, a young Texas woman known to family and friends as Lady Bird. (A childhood nanny had said she was "as pretty as a lady bird," and the name stuck.) A charming and graceful woman, Lady Bird Johnson would do much to support her husband's career. The Johnsons had two daughters, Lynda Bird, born in 1944, and Luci Baines, born in 1947.

NYA. When President Franklin D. Roosevelt began the historic reforms known as the New Deal, Kleberg's young secretary was one his most vocal supporters. In 1935 Roosevelt chose Johnson to head the Texas division of the National Youth Administration (NYA), a New Deal program providing educational and employment aid to young people. At twenty-six, Johnson was the youngest of the state NYA chiefs, and also (according to one NYA official) the most effective. He managed a large staff, distributed money to schools and educational projects, and created work programs. His efforts helped thousands of grateful voters, winning widespread public praise both in Texas and in Washington.

Congress. In 1937 Johnson ran for the U.S. House of Representatives in Texas's Tenth Congressional District. Against him were eight other candidates, five of them well-known older politicians. Yet they faced a hard race against Johnson. The young candidate was aided by his adviser Alvin Wirtz, an older political figure whose fatherly manner concealed real toughness and ambition. They planned to make it look as if Johnson were the only candidate who supported President Roosevelt, and as if a vote for one of the others would be a vote against the New Deal. Though the other candidates in fact publicly supported the New Deal, in his speeches Johnson claimed repeatedly that they did not. By campaigning harder than his opponents, he managed to drown them out. Giving the impression that he was Roosevelt's only real friend in the race, Johnson won by a comfortable margin.

To the Senate. Remaining in the House of Representatives for over a decade, Johnson worked hard to both serve the people of his district and advance his own political career. His talents for the favor-swapping that was common in Washington politics brought him quick assignments to powerful House committees. He continued to support Roosevelt and was rewarded by Roosevelt's public support in return. Both suffered a setback in 1941, when one of the two Texas seats in the Senate became vacant. For several years, opposition to Roosevelt had been growing among Texas Democrats. Roosevelt's backing failed to help Johnson win the seat, and anti-Roosevelt Democrats succeeded in putting W. Lee O'Daniel in the spot.

In 1948, however, Johnson ran again for the Senate. He won the Democratic nomination by only eighty-seven votes in a heated and controversial race, then went on to easily win the final election against his Republican opponent.

Majority leader. Johnson's political skill, which had quickly brought him juicy assignments in the House, served him equally well in the Senate. He immediately won a spot on the powerful Senate Armed Services Committee. In 1953 he was elected Senate leader of the Democratic minority. When the Democrats won back control of the Senate from the Republicans the following year, Johnson became the Senate majority leader. He held this influential position for six years, through the Republican presidency of Dwight D. Eisenhower.

Kennedy assassination. In 1960 Johnson ran for the Democratic presidential nomination, losing to John F. Kennedy, who then offered him the vice president's position on the Democratic ticket. Johnson accepted the offer, and with his help (attracting voters from Texas and the rest of the South) Kennedy won a close race against Richard M. Nixon. Three years later, on November 22, 1963, Kennedy was assassinated in Dallas. That afternoon on Air Force One, Lyndon Johnson, standing next to the widowed Jacqueline Kennedy, took the oath of office as the thirty-sixth president of the United States.

Participation:
Escalation of the War in Vietnam

Balancing act. Johnson faced a number of challenges when he stepped into office after Kennedy's assassination. The nation— and Kennedy's White House advisers—mourned the slaying of their handsome, princelike leader. Johnson had to deal not only with the unhappy public, but also with the president's family and staff. He knew that Kennedy's advisers, largely intellectuals from colleges in the Northeast, saw him as a country politician from Texas who did not really belong in the White House.

From moving the dead president's personal belongings out of the president's Oval Office to meetings with his family and staff,

Johnson had to be careful not to seem pushy, on the one hand, or unsure of himself, on the other. He faced a similar balancing act with the grief-stricken public. Rising to the occasion, Johnson delivered a calm and modest speech to Congress, televised a few days after the funeral, that won sympathy and support. He had carefully calculated exactly the right tone of calmness and modesty to make the speech a success.

Great Society. Johnson's success in assuming the presidency led to high popularity ratings, and a year afterward Johnson easily won reelection against Republican Barry Goldwater. Before the 1964 election, he had pushed major tax and civil rights laws through Congress. Afterward, with the weight of electoral victory behind him, he succeeded in getting Congress to pass more new laws.

These laws made up a program Johnson called the "Great Society." Altogether these laws placed Johnson second only to Roosevelt, his hero, in widening the government's role in people's daily lives, especially in helping minorities and the poor.

Seeds of trouble. Yet seeds of trouble were sprouting beneath these early victories. Johnson's civil rights acts and war on poverty failed to stop the explosion of summer riots that erupted in cities across America from 1964 to 1968. Meanwhile, in the background at first but looming ever larger, lay another unfolding disaster. But it was centered outside U.S. borders, in a far-off Asian country called Vietnam.

Dangerous legacy. Johnson inherited the problem of Vietnam from previous presidents Kennedy and Eisenhower. Since the 1950s, the United States had backed the South Vietnamese government of Ngo Dinh Diem in its war against the North Vietnamese communist government. Supported by China and the Soviet Union, North Vietnam hoped to take over South Vietnam. U.S. commitment to the south remained small under Eisenhower and Kennedy, beginning with a few hundred military advisers, along with financial aid to the Diem government.

Diem, a corrupt dictator, grew more and more hated among his people. In November 1963, just before Kennedy's assassination,

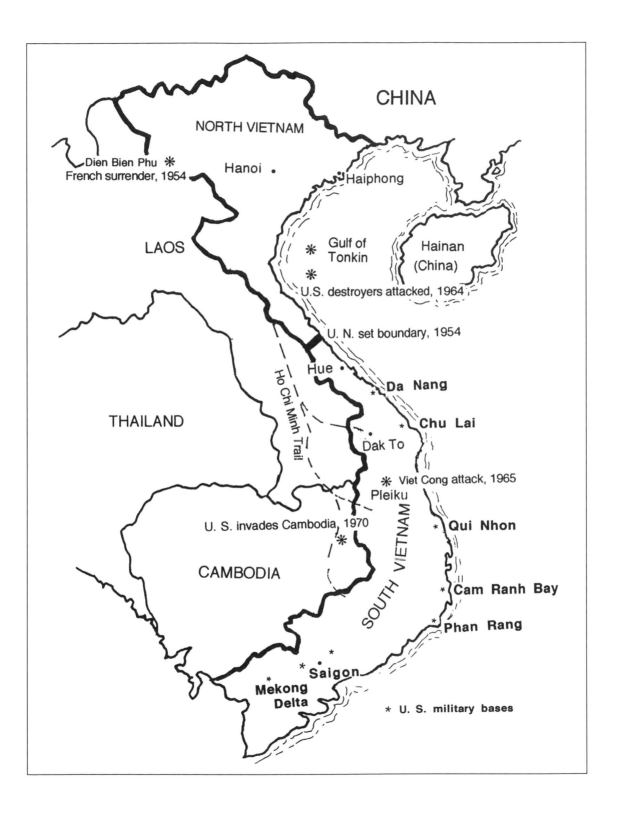

CHINA

NORTH VIETNAM

Dien Bien Phu ✳
French surrender, 1954

Hanoi ·

Haiphong

LAOS

✳ Gulf of
Tonkin

Hainan
(China)

✳

U.S. destroyers attacked, 1964

U. N. set boundary, 1954

THAILAND

Ho Chi Minh Trail

Hue ·

Da Nang

Chu Lai

Dak To

✳ Viet Cong attack, 1965

Pleiku

U. S. invades Cambodia, 1970

✳

Qui Nhon

CAMBODIA

SOUTH VIETNAM

Cam Ranh Bay

Phan Rang

✳ **Saigon**

**Mekong
Delta**

✳ U. S. military bases

Diem was himself overthrown and assassinated. The United States supported his overthrow, fearing that he would lose the war. Yet the situation worsened, with the weak South Vietnamese government becoming even more unpopular and unstable. North Vietnamese–backed guerrillas, called the Viet Cong, scored military successes in the south. More important, they won growing support among the South Vietnamese people.

Tonkin Gulf Resolution. Johnson had campaigned in 1964 on a promise to keep American soldiers out of the fighting. He was in fact looking for an excuse to do the opposite. Like Kennedy, Eisenhower, and others, Johnson believed in the Domino Theory, which said that if one country became communist, others nearby would fall like dominoes to communism as well. Johnson was determined not to be blamed for a communist victory in Vietnam. He waited for an opportunity to step up the action.

In August 1964, the opportunity came. Two American destroyers were reportedly attacked by North Vietnamese forces in the Tonkin Gulf, off the coast of North Vietnam. Johnson informed Congress of the attack, then requested wide presidential powers in responding to the North Vietnamese. With only two opposing votes, Congress obediently passed the Tonkin Gulf Resolution, giving Johnson power "to take all necessary measures ... to prevent further aggression" (Steinberg, p. 765). Later it became known that the United States had provoked the attack by invading North Vietnamese waters to aid South Vietnamese commando raids. Johnson also exaggerated the attack itself, which failed to harm the ships. He had actually prepared the resolution ahead of time and was only waiting for an excuse to use it.

Escalation begins. The Tonkin Gulf Resolution allowed Johnson to send American troops to Vietnam without an official declaration of war from Congress. In early 1965, seven Americans died during a Viet Cong raid on an American air base at Pleiku, in South Vietnam. Soon after, Johnson began large-scale escalation ("stepping up") of American involvement in the war. In Operation Rolling Thunder, the U.S. Air Force began massive and continuous bombing of North Vietnam in hopes of forcing it to try to arrange a peace settlement. Johnson also ordered U.S. ground troops into the fighting, increasing the number of American soldiers in South Vietnam from 25,000 in early

1965 to 184,000 by the end of the year. In 1966 that number grew to 385,000; in 1967, to 485,000; and in 1968, to 543,000.

Protest movement. Though at first there was wide support for the war, growing numbers of Americans soon began questioning the decision to escalate. The antiwar movement, led by young student protesters, gained ground on college campuses across the nation. College antiwar rallies captured headlines and appeared on the nightly television news. Glimpses of the war itself could also be seen on the news, which brought bloody scenes of violence and destruction into American living rooms.

Civil Rights Legislation

On the domestic front, Johnson remains one of the most effective presidents in American history. Aside from the Civil Rights Act of 1964, which banned racial discrimination in public places, he also proposed and won passage for the Voting Rights Act of 1965. Perhaps the most far-reaching law of the 1960s, the Voting Rights Act ended the literacy tests and other devices that southern states had long used to deny blacks the vote.

By early 1966, Johnson had begun dealing with opposition to the war in Congress, too. In February Senator William Fulbright's Foreign Relations Committee began nationally televised hearings on the war. By the end of the year, a majority of Democratic senators opposed Johnson's Vietnam policy. Johnson, however, held special bitterness for one opponent in particular—Senator Robert Kennedy. The late president's younger brother and the attorney general, Kennedy seemed to have inherited his older brother's magic in the eyes of the public.

"Credibility gap." From the beginning of the escalation, Johnson and his military advisors, especially General William Westmoreland, had promised that victory was just around the corner. Though Johnson's sunny predictions continued, it became increasingly clear that the Viet Cong, despite heavy losses, were nowhere near defeat. The difference between Johnson's version of the war and the version that appeared in the media became known as the "credibility gap"—in other words, the gap between Johnson's claims and what was credible, or believable. Beginning with the deception in the Tonkin Gulf, escalation was achieved by continuing to deceive the nation. In time, public trust in the president was damaged beyond repair.

Tet Offensive. The inaccuracy of Johnson's claims was dramatically shown in early 1968, when the North Vietnamese launched

War on Poverty and Great Society Programs

In 1965 Johnson won approval from Congress for Medicare and Medicaid, providing health care for the elderly and the poor. Other Johnson laws provided federal money for education and housing and created the Department of Housing and Urban Development and the Department of Transportation. Johnson also expanded the food stamp program, unemployment compensation, and youth employment aid. By the late 1960s, however, the expense of the war had cut deeply into the money available for such programs.

a strong offensive into South Vietnam. For three weeks, beginning on the Vietnamese New Year Holiday of Tet on January 30, Viet Cong and North Vietnamese forces attacked major South Vietnamese cities and towns. In Saigon, the South Vietnamese capital, the U.S. embassy itself came under fire. Though the Tet Offensive failed to win lasting military victories for the north, it came as a deep shock to the American public. Many of the targets had been thought of as well protected; by reaching them the Viet Cong scored a major propaganda victory. Becoming a major turning point in the war, Tet solidified American opposition to Johnson's policy.

"I shall not seek...." By early 1968, an election year, the atmosphere in the White House was one of a fortress surrounded by hostile forces. On most days, student demonstrators could be heard outside, chanting "Hey, hey, LBJ, how many kids did you kill today?" In March Democratic antiwar candidate Eugene McCarthy, a senator from Minnesota, won a shocking 42 percent of the vote in the season's first primary race in New Hampshire. Four days later, Robert Kennedy also entered the race for the Democratic nomination. On March 31, Johnson stunned the country—and his own advisers—in his conclusion to a speech that announced a pause in the bombing of North Vietnam: "I shall not seek—and will not accept—the nomination of my party for another term as your president" (Johnson in Califano, p. 270).

"A great American." The two announcements created a surge of popularity for the embattled Johnson. Newspaper and television commentators across the country praised him. The *Washington Post* said that Johnson had "made a personal sacrifice in the name of national unity that entitles him to a very special place in the annals of American history" (Califano, p. 270). Instead of protesters at his next public appearance, signs greeted him saying "LBJ IS A GREAT AMERICAN" (Califano, p. 271). Yet peace talks with North Vietnam in Paris made little progress, and the war continued, though Johnson stopped all bombing of the north in November. After the assassination of Robert Kennedy in August, the Democratic nomination went to Johnson's vice president, Hubert Humphrey, who lost to Republican Richard Nixon.

Aftermath

Retirement. Nixon, who had promised "an honorable end" to the war, found himself caught up in continuing it. Meanwhile, Johnson retired to his ranch near Johnson City (named after a relative). There he worked on his memoirs, which were published as *The Vantage Point: Perspectives of the Presidency, 1963–1968.* His health was fragile. He had suffered one heart attack in 1955, and his heart now troubled him regularly.

In 1970 he made a last visit to Washington, where he had lunch with a group of reporters from the *Washington Post.* How he had aged, thought the reporters. The tall, back-slapping Texan they remembered seemed smaller and fragile now. And he had grown his hair out in the style of southern senators, so that it was curly in back. Everyone talked quietly for a couple of hours about Johnson's current activities: working on the ranch when he was strong enough and writing his memoirs. Then the subject of Vietnam came up. "He began talking about Vietnam," one of the reporters wrote afterward, "and suddenly he was more vigorous and assertive. He folded and unfolded his napkin, began leaning forward, rocking back and forth in his chair, speaking first slowly and then loudly. Now he was, clearly, LBJ" (Harwood and Johnson, p. 162). For the next several hours he remained the LBJ they remembered, larger than life.

Lyndon Johnson died at his home on January 22, 1973.

For More Information

Califano, Joseph A., Jr. *The Triumph and Tragedy of Lyndon Johnson.* New York: Simon & Schuster, 1991.

Dallek, Robert. *Lone Star Rising: Lyndon Johnson and His Times, 1908–1960.* New York: Oxford University Press, 1991.

Harwood, Richard, and Haynes Johnson. *Lyndon.* New York: Praeger, 1973.

Steinberg, Alfred. *Sam Johnson's Boy.* New York: Macmillan, 1968.

James Stockdale

1923-

Personal Background

Parents. James Simpson Stockdale was born December 22, 1923, in Mt. Pleasant, Iowa, into a family that placed high value on a person's sense of duty and pursuit of perfection. His father, Vernon Stockdale, had left school to support his parents and sister at age sixteen. Three years later, he moved the family to Abingdon, working first in a brass-fixture factory, then in a pottery factory. In time, he would become a manager in one of the pottery works.

When she was nine, Jim's mother, Mabel Bond, moved with her family from a nearby farm to Abingdon. She attended school there through college, then left the state and taught in New Mexico and Montana. She returned to Abingdon in 1917 and renewed her acquaintance with "Stock," as Vernon was called. The budding romance was put on hold by World War I. Stock joined the navy, in two years moving up to the rank of chief petty officer. He returned to marry Mabel in 1919.

Early life. The values of hard work, reliability, and a sense of family were instilled in the young Jim. So was an obligation to become a high achiever. He participated in sports as much as possible, at the same time trying not to let his parents down. Although he was small and not too fast, he worked hard to play football in high school. He also competed on the track team—as a high hurdler. In

▲ James Stockdale is reunited with members of his family at Miramar Naval Air Station near San Diego, California, after being released by the North Vietnamese

Event: The Vietnam War.

Role: On duty as a navy pilot leading a raid over North Vietnam, James Stockdale was shot down and imprisoned. He was the senior officer in the prison and was, therefore, in charge of and responsible for the other American prisoners of war.

spite of his light weight, Jim eventually made the starting varsity football team as a guard. Many of his accomplishments on the athletic field stemmed from the encouragement of his father, who, according to Jim's later memory, never missed a practice or a game. Meanwhile, Jim studied hard to earn the high grades that were expected of him, and with all this activity still found time to have a reasonably lively social life.

Jim had long dreamed of joining the navy. In 1935 his father took Jim to hear a lecture at Iowa Wesleyan College. The speaker was Admiral Richard Byrd, just back from his Arctic exploration, looking proud and shiny in his navy uniform. A bit later, the family stopped at the U.S. Naval Academy at Annapolis while on vacation. Jim stood beside the school statue of the Indian leader Tecumseh and renewed his determination to become a navy officer. His father seemed to be telling him through these two trips that he would help if Jim worked hard. By the time Jim graduated from high school, his father had made the acquaintance of a local politician and been assured that if his grades were good enough, Jim Stockdale would have a nomination to Annapolis.

Annapolis and flight school. Now 170 pounds and still not swift, Stockdale tried out for the Annapolis football team. Every year he joined the squad and worked out but never played. Graduating after four years with high grades, he was sent for three years of sea duty. Stockdale applied for flight training at Pensacola during these years and was accepted. Now older and tougher, he was able to play on a first-string football team for the first time. Stockdale played guard for the Pensacola Goslings until he earned his wings in the summer of 1950.

Next Stockdale applied for test pilot school to learn how to fly the several kinds of airplanes used on the aircraft carriers. He was so successful in his studies that he graduated from test pilot school third in a class of seventeen and stayed at the school to teach for a while. A seven-month tour at a survival school followed, after which Stockdale found himself headed for sea duty. By 1964 he was squadron commander of Fighter Squadron Fifty—one aboard the aircraft carrier U.S.S. *Ticonderoga*. It was at this point in his career that trouble broke out in the Gulf of Tonkin near Vietnam.

The Tonkin Gulf affair. Since June 1964, navy aircraft had been making secret flights deep into Laos, Vietnam's neighbor to the west. The aircraft came from some carriers sailing just outside the Gulf of Tonkin near North Vietnam. Meanwhile, other navy ships had been cruising the waters near Vietnam to establish their right to sail the seas outside the Vietnam territorial limits. On August 2, the destroyer U.S.S. *Maddox* was cruising along the coast when some PT (patrol torpedo) boats hiding near an island off North Vietnam threatened to attack. Stockdale and three others were flying on practice flights at the time of the threats and were ordered to shoot the PT boats. Their U.S. aircraft sank one of four boats and seriously damaged the others.

Two days later, in the dark of night on August 4, their aircraft carrier received an alert from the *Maddox*. Now in the Gulf of Tonkin, it was again being attacked by North Vietnamese ships. Stockdale flew over the *Maddox* to help. He could see both the wake, or course, of the destroyer as it maneuvered to escape and its gunfire. Stockdale flew around the destroyer, firing wherever he saw its gunfire directed. In the darkness, he could not see the enemy boats from the air.

Three and a half hours later, Stockdale returned to the *Ticonderoga,* which had received some very confusing reports from the commander of the *Maddox.* The reports led Stockdale to believe that there had not really been any enemy ships threatening the *Maddox* that night.

The reports of the commander of the *Maddox* were sent on to Washington but apparently were not carefully studied there. President Lyndon Johnson was outraged that a second attack on American navy ships had been made by the North Vietnamese. He demanded that Congress pass a resolution giving him wide authority to respond in ways that would prevent any further threats to the United States (see **Lyndon B. Johnson**). With just two senators voting against it, the Tonkin Gulf Resolution passed both houses of Congress. The United States had been helping first the French and then the South Vietnamese since the presidency of Harry Truman. Now, for the first time, it passed a resolution that made official its own opposition to North Vietnam. This was as close to a declaration of war as the United States would come in the affair.

▲ **A U.S. Air Force plane downed by a rocket over Vietnam**

Soon American airplanes were conducting bombing raids from both sea and land against targets in North Vietnam. But Stockdale and his fellow fliers had already learned that this war would not be fought in standard military style. The day after the *Maddox* affair, President Johnson and Defense Secretary Robert McNamara had ordered raids on targets in North Vietnam to retaliate against or repay the North Vietnamese for the imagined August 4 attacks. The raiders were to destroy a PT boat base and oil storage tanks near the North Vietnamese city of Vinh. No one asked Stockdale or any of the other military leaders in the field for advice about these actions.

Just a week after the *Maddox* affair, the *Ticonderoga* was visited by two members of the Department of Defense. Alvin Friedman and Jack Stempler had been sent over to find our what really happened that night of August 4. In Stockdale's own words:

I could stand right there in the cabin and write the script of what was to come: Washington's second thoughts, the guilt, the remorse, the tentativeness [uncertainty], the changes of heart, the backout.

And a generation of young Americans would get left holding the bag (Stockdale and Stockdale, p. 36).

It was an accurate estimate of what was to come. American pilots were ordered to carry out massive bombing raids in North Vietnam against the advice of the field officers in the area. Targets were picked by McNamara's staff in Washington for political reasons rather than for military ones. American servicemen were pushed one way and then another by people in Washington who planned an action one day and changed their opinions the next. The American military was well trained and had superior weapons. Still, Stockdale guessed that the war would drag on for at least five more years. His main concern came to be the protection of his own fliers, not from the North Vietnamese but from the whims of Washington politicians. Still, his loyalty to his country did not waver.

Participation: Prisoner of War in Vietnam

Capture. The date was September 9, 1965. Commander Stockdale had already flown more than 200 sorties into enemy territory. Now from the deck of the U.S.S. *Oriskany,* he readied himself for his last flying day from a carrier. They were to destroy the Dragon's Jaw Bridge near the North Vietnamese town of Vinh. Weather changed their plans, however, as visibility at the bridge sank to zero. Stockdale took his men toward a secondary target, the railroads and trains near Tihn Gia about fifty nautical miles farther north. At 12:10 P.M., after a successful raid on a row of boxcars, Stockdale was struck by enemy antiaircraft missiles. Even as he parachuted to land, enemy riflemen began shooting at him. Stockdale landed in the middle of town.

Village strongmen jumped him immediately, pounding and twisting his body until police arrived. The beating now stopped, but villagers continued to strip him of his clothing and his emergency morphine and radio. While giving up his boots and watch, he realized that his left leg was broken and his shoulder was so crushed he could not raise his arm.

Stockdale was carried to the main north-south highway and thrown onto the canvas cover of a loaded truck. Some time later, a doctor examined the leg and indicated that he would need to amputate. Stockdale objected and was left to heal in his own way. (The leg was later put in a cast.) By September 13, his captors had driven him on various trucks to the North Vietnam capital, Hanoi. He spent a delirious month there on an old library table in a cell of the French-built Hoa Lo Prison. It was at this point that the enemy began questioning him and trying to make him betray his country.

He was treated with surgery to repair the broken left leg and then asked to mark navy refueling sites on a map. There were no such sites, but Stockdale's refusal to mark the map identified him as a stubborn prisoner. He was thrown into a cell equipped with a small bucket and a cement bed in a section of prison called Heartbreak Hotel. Here and in a neighboring area known as New Guy Village, he and other prisoners were beaten and tortured until they were willing to give answers to their guards. A particularly difficult form of torture was "the ropes." The torturers bound their prisoners tightly around the wrists and arms, painfully shutting off blood circulation. The prisoners were then pressed into agonizing positions until they were prepared to answer the questions. While the torturers might receive some answers, there was, of course, no guarantee that the answers were truthful.

Commander. The prisoners had already begun to develop ways to communicate. A prisoner whistled to warn others of approaching guards and whistled again to let the others know that the coast was clear. Single-handed sign language was invented to signal messages. There were other methods, too. The prisoners invented ways to tap messages on the walls or tied knots in threads pulled from pajamas to form Morse Code signals. Using these signals, Stockdale was able to learn the names of many of his fellow prisoners. He also learned that he was the senior officer among the prisoners and, therefore, in command.

The Code of Conduct. In the early 1950s, Americans had been involved in a war between North and South Korea. Prisoners in that war found themselves in unexpected situations without any military rules to guide them. They were told only what information they were allowed to give the enemy. Some of these prisoners weakened under pressure in ways that were felt by the military to be destructive to the army and navy. Consequently, the United States military came up with a Code of Conduct for prisoners of war in 1955. The code was used by the prisoners taken in Vietnam.

Commander Stockdale began to send messages around the prison camp in line with the Code of Conduct, his orders were tempered by the knowledge that few men could withstand the brutal treatment to which they were regularly subjected: "Don't bow in public." "Admit no crimes." "No early release; we will all go home together." "Unity over self." Issued by Stockdale, these rules bound the 300 to 400 prisoners together and gave them support. The commander made use of the various secret communications systems to build emotional strength among the prisoners.

This strength was tested severely. Few days passed in which no prisoner was taken to one of the special rooms for beatings or for torture with the ropes. Most of the prisoners were tortured until they were willing to make statements in answer to questions posed by the North Vietnamese. Apparently the torturers' main goal was not to gain information but to use the prisoners to deliver propaganda for North Vietnam to the world. The North Vietnamese planned, as one communist propagandist told Stockdale, to "defeat you on the streets of New York" (Stockdale, p. 187). This prediction nearly came true as people in America began to listen to the North Vietnamese and question U.S. involvement there. There were visits to North Vietnam by officials who

The Code of Conduct

I am an American fighting man. I serve the forces which guard my country and our way of life. I am prepared to give my life in their defense.

I will never surrender of my own free will. If in command, I will never surrender my men while they still have the means to resist.

If I am captured, I will continue to resist by all means available. I will make every effort to escape and aid others to escape. I will accept neither parole nor special favors from the enemy.

If I become a prisoner of war, I will keep faith with my fellow prisoners. I will give no information nor take part in any action which might be harmful to my comrades. If I am senior, I will take command. If not, I will obey the lawful orders of those appointed over me and will back them up in every way.

When questioned, should I become a prisoner of war, I am bound to give only name, rank, service number, and date of birth. I will evade answering further questions to the best of my ability. I will make no oral or written statement disloyal to my country and its allies or harmful to their cause.

I will never forget that I am an American fighting man, responsible for my actions, and dedicated to the principles which made my country free. I will trust in God and in the United States of America.

brought back tales of how well the U.S. prisoners were being treated and how misunderstood the North Vietnamese were. Senator James Fulbright, who had supported the Tonkin Gulf Resolution, was among those who began to question the American position.

Americans back home were turning against the war. They seemed also to be abandoning the soldiers and sailors in Vietnam. While this was another blow to the morale of the prisoners, most of them held to their resolve not to aid the government in Hanoi. Stockdale required his men to endure torture before surrendering to the demands of their captors. At least one prisoner obeyed the order in the code to try to escape and was beaten to death for his efforts. Still, most of the men held firm to their leader and to the rules he imposed.

Eventually Stockdale's signaled messages were discovered. He was brought into the punishment room and tortured to reveal all the methods the prisoners used to communicate. By that time, he knew what to expect. Stockdale had been punished many times before for his stubborn refusal to make propaganda reports and broadcasts. Of his seven years in prison, the commander spent four in solitary confinement for his uncooperative ways.

Sybil. All the while, the commander's wife, Sybil Stockdale, was caring for their three sons and traveling throughout the United States calling attention to the problems of the prisoners in Vietnam. She organized their wives into a strong union to pressure the government into protesting. North Vietnam had signed the Geneva Convention rules on dealing with prisoners and was now violating that agreement. With the aid of a navy officer, Sybil succeeded also in sending a coded message to her husband and he was able to respond. The message was coded into a short letter to her husband to be delivered by the Red Cross. It contained pictures, one of the family and one said to be of James Stockdale's mother. He could not believe how his mother had changed. In desperation he decided that the photo must be some sort of message and decided to soak it in water. Soon he was amazed to find that a message was fixed to the photo. It had been written with invisible carbon paper attached to the photo. Now the commander could send back secret messages that contained the names of men he knew to be prisoners. It was a great satisfaction to some of the families who had waited fearfully to find out what had happened to their warrior sons and husbands.

Nixon. By 1969 the United States was in complete disarray. President Johnson had committed 400,000 soldiers to the Vietnam effort, and the fight was still going poorly. At least part of the failure stemmed from blundering orders and counter orders issued by the Department of Defense and the Department of State in Washington. American citizens responded with civil disobedience, taking to the streets to champion their own causes. Antiwar protesters such as Abbie Hoffman planned to plant bombs if necessary to emphasize their position. Tom Hayden and others formed a committee to help the North Vietnamese. In the midst of all this chaos, President Johnson declared that he would not run again for the presidency.

Believing that Richard Nixon had a plan for ending the war, the Americans elected him to replace Johnson as president. Nixon did have a plan. He would step up the "Vietnamization" of the war by attacking the North Vietnamese supply lines, beefing up the South Vietnamese army, and ridding the villages of the Viet Cong (Vietnamese communists). The forces defending South Vietnam conducted a raid into Cambodia to cut the supply trails to their section of the country (where the North Vietnamese steadily denied they had any troops). Bombing of North Vietnam, which had been stopped by Johnson, was resumed, much to the delight of Stockdale and the other prisoners. (They were treated most cruelly when it appeared that American efforts in the war were weak, and more gently when the United States' resolve appeared greatest.) Still the war proceeded slowly. The North Vietnamese, winning the propaganda match, were slow to make such concessions as the safe release of prisoners. In 1972 heavy bombing of Hanoi was stepped up and the North Vietnamese agreed to peace talks. The United States would withdraw from South Vietnam as rapidly as the South Vietnamese could take over. Also, the prisoners would be released and separate North and South Vietnam governments would be left to work out their own differences. News seeped in to the prisoners of Hanoi that the war was over. Secretary of State Henry Kissinger signed a cease-fire with North Vietnam that took effect January 28, 1973, and shortly thereafter giant cargo planes began to shuttle out the American prisoners of war.

A last insult. The Code of Conduct required that no prisoners agree to an early release and that they follow a strict order of evacuation—those in prison longest were to be the first released. At least the second part of the rule would be violated. The prisoners got a taste of conditions back home as soon as they began being released. Now the United States took a turn seeking propaganda from them. Henry Kissinger flew into Hanoi and selected twenty men to return to America with him on a private jet. For publicity, he would break the country's own Code of Conduct. James Stockdale was outraged by this action, though, for the most part, those in prison longest were taken out first. In Hoa Lo Prison for seven years, Stockdale was among the first to be released.

Aftermath

Going home. Now a rear admiral, Stockdale was eager to resume his navy career, but, badly beaten, he had suffered physically from his experience. One knee was still weak and not healing well. His back had been broken. Smashed in the landing, his left shoulder had not been treated, and he had only limited arm movement. Still, he wanted to fly again and after much medical testing and retraining received permission from the navy. In April 1976, he was assigned to duty at the Pentagon. A year and a half later, he was commissioned a vice admiral and became president of the Naval War College. Six years after his return from prison, Admiral Stockdale retired from active service to become president of the Citadel, a military school in South Carolina. He soon left this position to teach and conduct research at Stanford University in California.

Awards for him and for her. Stockdale retired from the service with twenty-six combat decorations, including four Silver Star medals. He was awarded the Congressional Medal of Honor for his leadership in Vietnam.

While her husband was a prisoner, Sybil Stockdale had spent endless hours trying to make known the North Vietnamese violations of international law. At the risk of never hearing from her husband again, she had helped bring information about the prisoners to other Americans through the invisible carbon paper messages. She also lent emotional support to many of the prisoners' wives and families during the long wait for the men to return. For her tireless efforts, Sybil Stockdale was awarded the navy's highest civilian award, the Distinguished Public Service Award.

Protesters. Among the mass of Americans who protested the war, some appear to have been disappointed at its slow progress and therefore turned against it because they felt it would take too long to resolve. Others rebelled against the war to protest what they believed to be a corrupt and weak government in South Vietnam. Still others felt that if the United States would get out of the fray, South Vietnam and North Vietnam would resolve their differences and fewer lives would be lost.

This last argument proved partly right. The war did soon resolve the differences between the North and South Vietnamese. Supported by China, the North quickly overran the South and unified Vietnam. The northern soldiers then invaded Cambodia. Communists there took charge of the country and began a massive "reform" in which as many as 3 million Cambodians disappeared.

Politics. Admiral Stockdale continued to speak out about the issues of the war and particularly its prisoners. A handful of prisoners had sided with the North Vietnamese, and Stockdale tried for some time to bring these men to trial as traitors to the country. Americans of the time, however, were in no mood for trials of potential traitors in Vietnam. No action was ever taken to bring the prisoners in question to trial.

As time passed, Stockdale became convinced that moral rebirth in America would come only with reform in government. In 1992 he accepted an invitation to become a candidate for vice president of the United States. He ran as an independent alongside Ross Perot. Perot eventually withdrew from the election, and the presidency was won by Bill Clinton.

For More Information

Howes, Craig. *Voices of the Vietnam POWs.* New York: Oxford University Press, 1993.

Stockdale, James B. *Ten Years of Reflection: A Vietnam Experience.* Stanford, California: Hoover Press, Stanford University, 1984.

Stockdale, Jim, and Sybil Stockdale. *In Love & War.* New York: Harper & Row, 1984.

Daniel Ellsberg

1931-

Personal Background

Prologue. Armed troubles in Indochina had begun before World War II as the people of Cambodia, Laos, and Vietnam struggled to free themselves from French rule. In 1945 President Harry Truman assured the French that the United States would help in controlling Indochina. The next president, Dwight D. Eisenhower, kept this promise by sending weapons and military advisers to the French. During his presidency, John F. Kennedy increased the number of military "advisers" to about 30,000. His successor, Lyndon Johnson, further increased the number of American soldiers in Vietnam to more than 400,000. None of these presidents wanted to formally declare war in Vietnam, although Kennedy believed that it surely was a war.

Kennedy's secretary of defense, Robert McNamara, agreed that the United States should be involved. He chose, however, to direct the battles from Washington rather than to trust the actual fighting to the commanders in the field. Vital military targets were ignored because McNamara's advisers in Washington felt that attacking them might harm diplomatic efforts of the various leaders to reach a peaceful settlement. President Johnson's advisers ordered massive bombing of North Vietnam in spite of objections from the field commanders over the choice of targets. Largely

▲ Daniel Ellsberg

Event: The Vietnam War—the Pentagon Papers.

Role: In an attempt to bring the war in Vietnam to an earlier end, Daniel Ellsberg distributed materials from a top-secret Department of Defense file to eastern newspapers.

because of these political maneuvers, the fighting in Vietnam progressed poorly for the United States. Many in government and in the military began to call it "McNamara's War." Growing weary of the fight and perhaps concerned for his own place in history, Secretary McNamara directed his department to assemble all the documents related to the war and write a report, which was called "History of the U.S. Decision-Making Process on the Vietnam Policy 1945–1967." One of the writers on this project was a young researcher named Daniel Ellsberg.

Early life. The United States was in the throes of a great depression, and Harry Ellsberg numbered among the many unemployed when his son Daniel was born in Chicago on April 7, 1931. Daniel's parents were well educated. His father was a structural engineer and his mother, a musician. Yet the couple soon found it necessary to leave Chicago to find work. The family, which included Daniel and his sister, Mary (a third child would join the family later), moved to southern Illinois and then to Detroit, where Daniel lived until he was a teenager.

Daniel was so bright that his friends thought he could learn anything. At age six, he could recite Lincoln's Gettysburg Address and could as easily learn a sport or music. Daniel spent many hours practicing the piano while still in elementary school. All this practice time paid off, though he hated it. By his teen years, Ellsberg was good enough at the piano to play in concerts around Detroit.

When Daniel was fifteen, his mother died. He soon enrolled in Cranbrook School for Boys, which prepared high school students for college. Again Daniel performed outstandingly. On his application for admission to Harvard, the Cranbrook administration wrote "a brilliant superior student ... inclined at times to feel superior, but no recluse [loner]"(Ungar, p. 43). On the basis of his work at Cranbrook, he was awarded a full four-year scholarship to the university. The scholarship not only paid his way to Harvard but even provided an allowance for Daniel to travel home at each semester's end.

Daniel was not only interested in school during this period. At age nineteen, although he had never climbed mountains before, he decided that this would be an interesting challenge. So he trained himself for the activity, then went to Colorado to climb 14,000-foot Long's Peak.

Harvard. Ellsberg certainly proved to be "no recluse" at Harvard. While continuing to earn top grades, he managed to become president of the *Advocate,* an undergraduate literary magazine. He also served on the editorial board of the *Crimson,* Harvard's daily newspaper. For graduation, Harvard required students to write a thesis. Ellsberg's paper in 1952, an essay on economic game theory, earned him honors recognition and a fellowship for advanced study at Cambridge.

Meanwhile, in 1951 he courted and then married Carol Cummings, a sophomore from nearby Radcliffe. She was the daughter of a marine colonel who was to greatly influence the next few years of Ellsberg's life.

A year after graduating Harvard, Ellsberg returned there to work on a master's degree. Within a year, he had again graduated, this time with a rating from the faculty of Excellent Plus. He could have immediately become a member of the Harvard Society of Fellows, the most select group of candidates for the doctorate. Instead, perhaps influenced by his father-in-law, he went off to join the marines. He was a lieutenant when trouble broke out over the Suez Canal but, although sent to the Middle East, was not involved in combat.

The RAND Corporation. After two years, Ellsberg returned to Harvard to earn a doctorate. At the same time, he began working for the RAND Corporation, a company doing research for the U.S. Air Force. He also presented lectures in economics at the Boston Library and sometimes served as a military advisor to future president John F. Kennedy. As a researcher at RAND and an adviser to politicians, Ellsberg was called often to the nation's capital. He served as an aide to Assistant Secretary of Defense John McNaughton. He was in Washington during the Cuban Missile Crisis and also at the time of the "attacks" on American ships in the Gulf of Tonkin in Vietnam (see **Lyndon B. Johnson**). These so-called attacks triggered even deeper U.S. involvement in the war in Vietnam. President Johnson declared the attacks on two destroyers an act of violence against the United States. He asked Congress for a resolution that would empower the president to take necessary measures to prevent future attacks. The Tonkin Gulf Resolution was the nearest to a declaration of war that the country would see. It was passed by both houses of Congress on August 5, 1964. All but two congressmen voted for it.

Despite such broad approval, there was already some government and civilian debate about whether or not the United States should be in Vietnam. Chairman of the Senate Committee on Foreign Affairs William Fulbright, for example, was originally in favor of American involvement. By the mid-1960s, however, he had begun to question the value of American participation.

Even more Americans debated how U.S. involvement should be conducted. Within a few days of the Tonkin Bay incident, representatives from the Department of Defense were sent to Vietnam to determine if the military had reacted properly.

Family. A pivotal year in the Vietnam War, 1964 also proved to be a turning point in Ellsberg's private life. His family had grown to include two children, a daughter, Mary, and a son, David. Ellsberg and his wife divorced in 1964. Relations between Ellsberg and the two children remained good. A few years later, they helped him in his most daring endeavor.

War hawk to dove. At work, Ellsberg began to earn a reputation for being self-centered. One associate described him as "unable to put himself in other people's positions very well, he's so convinced of his rectitude [being right] and morality" (Ungar p. 46). Indeed, he did seem convinced that his military research was correct and that America's participation in Vietnam was also proper. The spring of 1965 found him lobbying for the war effort and requesting to be sent to Vietnam. By midyear he had won an assignment as an apprentice to Major General Edward Lansdale in Vietnam.

The sight of Vietnam and the Vietnamese villagers had a powerful effect on Ellsberg. The beauty of the country and the plight of its people moved him deeply. Ellsberg, who had been a strong supporter of the war, began to wonder if the price of destroying the land and its people was worth the potential gain.

▶

North Vietnamese villagers place bamboo punji sticks, perhaps poisoned, point up in a moat surrounding their village of Ap Ha in the Mekong Delta as a defense against enemy attacks

By that time, leaders of the Vietnam campaign had begun a plan of "Vietnamization." Rather than fight a general war that might grow into World War III, the army strategy was to take one town or village at a time, search out the dissenters and members of the enemy Viet Cong in or near it, make the region safe for South Vietnam-style democracy, and move on to the next town. Using this strategy, reasoned the policymakers, all of South Vietnam would be rid of the Viet Cong. The strategy, however, did not work. At night the Viet Cong reappeared and instilled fear in the villagers. The Americans left each spot eventually, and once a "purified" village had lost its American support, the Viet Cong stepped back in control. Ellsberg observed this failure and began to doubt the value of America's involvement. At the very least, it appeared that solving the problems in Vietnam would take a long time and result in a great loss of lives. He began to report the lack of military success to his friends in the United States. Again and again, he saw villages attacked and purified of Viet Cong. Then the enemy returned to harass the villagers. Ellsberg began to feel that the slaughter of villagers during all these changes was too costly for any gain that might be achieved by the United States. Ellsberg described his observations in a memo to the Harvard Fellows titled "The Day Loc Tien Was Pacified." The Vietnam experience had changed him from a hawk, a champion of the war, to one of the most outspoken doves, who wanted peace at any cost.

Ellsberg's tour of duty ended when he developed hepatitis. He returned to the United States and to the RAND Corporation. Shortly thereafter, Secretary of State Henry Kissinger asked Ellsberg to summarize President Richard Nixon's options in dealing with the war and to outline the probable consequences of each option. He was also to prepare a questionnaire about the war. It would be answered by different government agencies, and Ellsberg would analyze the responses. It was part of a project authorized by Secretary of Defense Robert McNamara. From time to time, Ellsberg was called on to help with other parts of the project. By now, even McNamara was beginning to question whether massive bombing would be effective in the jungles of North Vietnam.

The McNamara study of how U.S. involvement in Vietnam had begun and grown into full-fledged war would eventually require three dozen writers and fill forty-seven volumes with government documents relating to the war and comments about them. Leslie Gelb directed the research and writing. He and Daniel Ellsberg may have been the only two involved with the project who were allowed to see the entire set of books, which would soon become known as the Pentagon Papers.

Participation:
Public Release of the Pentagon Papers

The Pentagon Papers. To Ellsberg, the Pentagon Papers appeared to show a continuous plan for American treatment of Vietnam that was imperialistic (colony-seeking). The plan, he concluded, had been blindly followed by a string of presidents. All of these presidents—Harry Truman, Dwight D. Eisenhower, John F. Kennedy, Lyndon B. Johnson, and Richard Nixon—had, Ellsberg believed, involved the United States in a hopeless and unnecessary war. While working for the RAND Corporation on the papers, he grew to believe that if only the public could see these top-secret papers, public sentiment would bring an end to the struggles in Vietnam.

Plotting the release. By 1969 Ellsberg was helping to conduct a study of the Vietnam experience. He had asked for and been granted top-security clearance to read all the Pentagon Papers. He was allowed to take volumes of the Pentagon documents away from their security storage at the Department of Defense. In 1969 he traveled to Washington and returned to Santa Monica with eighteen of the volumes.

Now committed to somehow making the papers public, Ellsberg rented a copier. With the help of a friend and his two teen-age children he began to copy the eighteen volumes. Meanwhile, he tried to get the Pentagon Papers released through authorized government channels. Senator James Fulbright, chairman of the Senate Foreign Relations Committee had, like Ellsberg, begun to question American involvement in the war. Ellsberg visited Fulbright and showed him a sample of the papers, hoping that Fulbright would make them public through the records of the Senate. Fulbright, however, wanted to operate within the regular Senate proce-

What Was
in the Pentagon Papers?

The Pentagon Papers contain letters and reports between heads of various government agencies. These papers span the presidencies from Truman to Kennedy. An example of potentially explosive documents is a 1964 memorandum from Assistant Secretary of Defense for International Security Affairs John T. McNaughton. It gives his opinion about why the United States was staying in Vietnam:

70 percent—to avoid a humiliating U.S. defeat

20 percent—to keep South Vietnam territory from Chinese hands

10 percent—to permit the people of South Vietnam to enjoy a better, freer way of life.

(Adapted from Ungar, p. 13)

dures. Over the next year, he would several times ask the Department of Defense to release Pentagon Papers to his Senate committee. The Defense Department steadfastly refused these requests. Ellsberg, meanwhile, tried a new approach. He joined several other RAND researchers in writing a letter to the *New York Times* protesting American involvement in the war. The *Washington Post* joined in the protest. On October 12, 1969, the *Post* published a letter demanding that the United States get out of Vietnam. In May 1970, Ellsberg testified before the Senate Foreign Relations Committee, predicting doom for America if it continued in what he believed to be an evil war.

Releasing the Pentagon Papers. Ellsberg was now dedicated to finding a way to make the papers public. He suspected, however, that such action might make him a war criminal if he stayed in military research at RAND. At the very least, RAND's status as a research organization for the military would be put in jeopardy. Later that year, he resigned from the RAND Corporation and took a job as a research fellow at the Massachusetts Institute of Technology (MIT). This move, he thought, would allow him more freedom to speak out. Earlier in the year, President Nixon had sent army troops into Cambodia, Vietnam's neighbor. The action deepened Ellsberg's opposition to the war. He felt he must act immediately to try to stop the war.

About the same time that Ellsberg joined MIT, he married a long-time friend and supporter, Patricia Marx. She became Patricia Ellsberg on August 8, 1970, and continued to support Ellsberg throughout his future difficulties.

Early in 1970, Ellsberg wrote that the United States was in a quagmire in Vietnam and that the best the Americans could hope to achieve would be a stalemate. The United States was now wavering so much over the war that its goals changed. It no longer intended to win but was determined not to lose.

Vietnam in America. Ellsberg was certainly not alone in his view of the war. Several congressmen had become outspoken critics of U.S. involvement in Vietnam. Antiwar demonstrations spilled over onto the streets of America, in areas already wracked by demonstrations for civil rights.

In another attempt to enlist help from Congress, Ellsberg asked George McGovern to make the papers public. McGovern, who was preparing to run for the presidency, did not want to cloud his chances by doing so, however. He refused to help release the Pentagon Papers.

Some Outspoken Doves in Congress

For the United States to stay out of Laos
    John Cooper
    Frank Church

For total U.S. withdrawal from Vietnam
    George McGovern
    Mark Hatfield

For restricting the U.S. war effort to South Vietnam   James Fulbright
For a fixed date of U.S. withdrawal from Vietnam (1970)   Charles Goodall

The *New York Times*. Unable to rouse appropriate government officials, Ellsberg now took the task on himself. In March 1971, he visited Neil and Susan Sheehan. Neil was a reporter for the *New York Times* and Susan was a writer for the *New Yorker* magazine. Neil Sheehan immediately saw the news value of the Pentagon Papers and contacted the *Times* publisher. Executives at the *Times* were certain that releasing the papers would bring a strong government reaction, so they moved slowly. It took three more months before the newspaper began to publish parts of the secret Pentagon Papers. The first installment came in the *Times* edition of June 13, 1971. It was followed by two other installments before the government could get a court order to stop the publication. By this time, however, other newspapers had begun rewriting the *Times* articles and republishing them. Some of the first to do so were the *Washington Post,* the *Boston Globe,* and the *St. Louis Post-Dispatch*. It was an unexpected news scoop that soon created a tremendous reaction from newspapers around the world. The former Defense Secretary Clark Clifford described the reaction as "an event of outstanding significance. I came to Washington to stay in the spring of 1945. I had never seen anything like it in twenty-six years" (Ungar, p. 19).

Their release of the Pentagon Papers sent the *Washington Post* and the *New York Times* into court to defend themselves under the First Amendment to the Constitution, which guarantees freedom of the press. It also resulted in the indictment of Daniel Ellsberg in July 1971, accused of possessing Department of Defense documents (he had kept four volumes of the Pentagon Papers), theft of government property, and conspiracy against the government. Ellsberg thought he had performed a great but painful service for the American people. In an interview with Walter Cronkite, he stated his position: The American government "bears major responsibility for every death in combat in Vietnam in the last twenty-five years—and that's one to two million people" (Ellsberg in Ungar, p. 239).

Aftermath

The newspapers. The *New York Times* and the *Washington Post* appealed to the Supreme Court to lift the ban on publishing more of the Pentagon Papers. On June 30, 1971, the nine-member Court reached a decision. It released the Pentagon Papers from government restriction, and the publishing of them resumed. The judges voted six to three to allow the newspapers to continue but could not agree on the wording of the decision. Consequently, each of the nine judges wrote a separate opinion in the case.

Ellsberg on trial. Ellsberg knew that he had broken the rules of the RAND Corporation and the Department of Defense by copying the Pentagon Papers. Shortly after a grand jury indicted him for his actions, he told news sources that he was fully aware of what he had done and was prepared to accept responsibility for his actions. The grand jury, however, accused him not only of the expected charges but also of the much more serious crime of spying. Daniel Ellsberg and his partner in misdeeds, Anthony Russo, eluded the FBI for a time and then surrendered for trial. Ellsberg pleaded not guilty to the charges and a trial was set. It took place in the California court of Justice Matthew Byrne, from January to May 1973. Once more the confusion of the American people showed, as the first trial was declared a mistrial. A second trial was dismissed by Justice Byrne, with the government being accused of misconduct and wiretapping. In the process of gathering evidence against Ellsberg, government agents had broken into the office of his psychiatrist, Dr. Lewis J. Fielding, and tried to steal Ellsberg's records. Egil Krogh, Jr., Charles Colson, G. Gordon Liddy, and presidential aide John Ehrlichman were found guilty of the break-in. Ellsberg returned to his post as research fellow at MIT, regarding the outcome of the trial as a major accomplishment—the beginning of the "demystification" and "desanctification" of the U.S. presidency. It had grown removed from the people, who would no longer be so trusting that U.S. leaders could do no wrong.

The Vietnam War. Neither the bombing of North Vietnam nor the sending of troops to Cambodia had the desired effect on slowing the North Vietnamese penetration of South Vietnam. President Nixon prepared to withdraw American troops from Vietnam—slowly so he would not embarrass America by admitting defeat. Time was also needed to rescue some South Vietnamese military and government personnel, who would surely be put to trial by the communist forces for war crimes. Not until January 27, 1973, did the president announce that all fighting in Vietnam had stopped, and many more months passed before all American troops left that country.

The South Vietnamese government and army held some territory for a short time, but government corruption and military weakness finally gave North Vietnam control of a united Vietnam. Shortly thereafter, North Vietnamese soldiers entered Cambodia. An estimated 3 million Cambodians disappeared in a "reeducation" program that was conducted to orient the country to the new communist rule.

For More Information

Ginger, Ann F. *The Pentagon Papers Trial.* Dobbs Ferry, New York: Oceana, 1975.
Schrog, Peter. *Test of Loyalty.* New York: Simon & Schuster, 1974.
Ungar, Sanford J. *The Paper and the Papers.* New York: Dutton, 1972.

Richard M. Nixon

1913-1994

Personal Background

Richard Milhous Nixon was born on January 9, 1913, in the small farming town of Yorba Linda, California. His father, Frank Nixon, had run away from home at thirteen, working his way west from his native Ohio. In 1907, at twenty-eight, Frank was working as a train conductor in the small California town of Whittier, about twenty-five miles east of Los Angeles. There he met and married Hannah Milhous, the quiet, religious daughter of a prominent local family.

Quaker restraint. Like many in Whittier, the Milhouses were Quakers, and Frank too became a Quaker. He built a house in nearby Yorba Linda, where the Nixons raised lemons and ran a small grocery store. They had five sons, of whom Richard—named for King Richard the Lionhearted of England—was the second. Emotions were kept well under control in the strict Quaker household, except for Frank Nixon's occasional outbursts of bad temper. He was always sorry afterward. More than their father's anger, which passed quickly, the boys dreaded the restrained, pious lectures that came when their mother was upset. Also self-controlled when it came to affection, Hannah Nixon was not one to hug or kiss her children. Yet they never doubted her love. "I can never remember her saying to any of us 'I love you'—she didn't have to!" Nixon once remarked (Aitken, p. 15).

▲ Richard M. Nixon

Event: "Vietnamization"; invasions of Cambodia and Laos; Paris Peace Accords.

Role: Richard Nixon's Vietnamization policy, which helped him win the presidency in 1968, called for South Vietnamese troops to take over the fighting from American soldiers. Secretly Nixon ordered massive bombing of Cambodia, where the North Vietnamese had bases and supply routes. When revealed, the secret bombing shocked the American public. Later invasions of Cambodia and Laos, along with renewed bombing of North Vietnam, increased the war's unpopularity in the United States during Nixon's presidency.

"Slights and snubs." Richard, called Dick, worked hard in school, pushing himself to survive on little sleep. He would stay up doing schoolwork until midnight, then rise at four to drive into Los Angeles and pick the daily vegetables for the family's grocery store. In school, he especially made his mark as a debater, expressing himself best when on the attack with words. He was not a popular boy, which only made him work harder:

> What starts the process really are the laughs and slights and snubs [put-downs, insults] when you are a kid. Sometimes it's because you're poor or Irish or Jewish or Catholic or ugly or simply that you are skinny. But if you are reasonably intelligent and if your anger is deep enough and strong enough, you learn that you can change those attitudes by excellence. (Nixon in Aitken, p. 29)

Best student. Dick's hard work won him scholarships to Harvard and Yale, the famous universities back east in New England. The Harvard Club of California, in fact, had named him the state's "best all round student" in his senior year at Whittier High. But the year was 1929. It was the beginning of the Great Depression. Despite the scholarships, which would pay for classes, the Nixons couldn't afford to pay living expenses. Hiding his disappointment, Dick enrolled instead at nearby Whittier College.

"Coming back fighting." Dick tried to fit in with the crowd more in college than he had in high school. Though small and light, he insisted on joining the football team, where he and others like him were used as "cannon fodder" for the first-string players to practice on. "We were the two smallest guys on the squad," remembered a friend, "but we learned how to hang in there and smash the big guys back. I'll say this for Nixon. He had plenty of guts when it came to taking a beating, getting up off the floor, and coming back fighting" (Aitken, p. 34). His small size meant that Dick spent all four seasons on the bench, allowed to practice but not to play in games.

"Play to win." He was happy to do this, however, because he idolized "Chief" Newman, the coach. Newman disagreed with the old saying, "It's not whether you win or lose, but how you play the game that counts." "Nonsense," the Chief said to that idea. "You play to win. And if you don't win you kick yourself in the butt[ocks] and be sure you don't make the same mistakes again" (Aitken, p. 34). Another favorite saying was "Show me a good loser and I'll show you a loser" (Ambrose, p. 66). Nixon later wrote, "There is no way I can adequately describe Chief Newman's influence on me" (Nixon in Ambrose, p. 66).

School politics. At Whittier, Nixon continued to develop his debating skills and his interest in school politics. In high school, he had lost to a more popular boy in an election for student body president, though Dick was at first expected to win. Following Chief Newman's advice, Dick carefully analyzed his reasons for losing. He was not going to make the same mistakes again. Nixon won election as president of his college freshman class and then as student body president for the next three years.

Law school. Before graduating from Whittier College, Nixon saw a notice there offering scholarships to Duke University Law School in Durham, North Carolina. Nixon applied and easily won one. His record was outstanding; he graduated second in his class at Whittier in 1934. At Duke, Nixon lived a disciplined, almost monkish life. He had so little money that at one point he lived in an abandoned toolshed in the woods near campus. He spent almost all his time studying, and his efforts were rewarded when he graduated from the highly competitive law school third in his class.

Marriage. After law school, Nixon tried but failed—despite his excellent record—to find a job with a high-powered New York law firm. Moving back to Whittier in 1937, he joined a law practice in town and began taking part in community activities. He also taught Sunday school and joined a local theater group. There he met a beautiful young woman named Thelma Ryan, called Pat because she was born on St. Patrick's Day. Nixon fell in love at first sight, though Pat ignored him at first. He wouldn't give up, however, and she soon found herself attracted by his energy and enthusiasm. The two were married on June 21, 1940. The Nixons would have two daughters, Julie (who married David Eisenhower, President Dwight D. Eisenhower's grandson) and Tricia.

War service. The following year, the United States entered World War II. Nixon accepted a job in Washington for the Office of Price Administration, where he worked on the regulations that

▲ Nixon's political victories began in California

dealt with tire rationing. Because of the war, the government had begun to control many such aspects of daily life to make sure that there were enough supplies to go around. As a result of this experience, Nixon developed a disgust for large government organizations that would last the rest of his life. Seven months later, he joined the navy as a lieutenant and was posted to the South Pacific. There he worked as an operations officer in charge of cargo bases, airfields handling supplies for the war against the Japanese.

Invitation to politics. Even before the war, Nixon had come to the attention of Whittier Republican Party Chairman Herman Perry, the father of one of his high school friends. Perry, the town's leading banker, remembered Nixon from the young man's debating days at Whittier High. When the war ended, Perry and the Whittier Republicans were looking for someone to run against Democratic Congressman Jerry Voorhis, who had represented the area for five terms in Washington. They chose Richard Nixon and sent him a letter asking if he would be interested in running on the Republican ticket. After talking it over with Pat, who shared a streak of boldness and ambition with him, Nixon agreed.

Unseating Voorhis. An intelligent and amiable man, Jerry Voorhis was not much of a politician. His political views had fit the era of Roosevelt and the New Deal, but now the country was reacting against the New Deal ideas of expanding the government and regulating business. People were also starting to become nervous about communism, as President Truman led the United States into a competition called the "cold war" against the Soviet Union.

In his campaign, Nixon made clever use of these trends. He especially focused on communism, charging that Voorhis was supported by communists. In fact, Voorhis was opposed by the American Communist Party, which he had always voted against. But in 1946 Republicans were desperate. Democrats had controlled the government since the early 1930s, and communism looked like the issue that would help defeat them. Nixon was not alone in making charges of communist sympathies against his opponent that election year, but he was among the most effective. Fortunately for Nixon, Voorhis also made some mistakes in his campaign that helped him. Nixon won by a large margin. A Voorhis aide later accused him of lying during the campaign. "I had to win," he answered. "That's the thing you don't understand. The important thing is to win. You're just being naive" (Nixon in Ambrose, p. 140).

The Hiss case. Congressman Nixon went to Washington in 1947, along with many other victorious Republicans. He was assigned to the House Un-American Activities Committee (HUAC), a little-known committee that he himself would make famous the following year. In August 1948, Whittaker Chambers, an editor of *Time* magazine and a former communist, accused a one-time U.S.

The Checkers Speech

During the 1952 Eisenhower-Nixon campaign, Nixon was accused of having a "slush fund" of shady campaign money that he used for his own personal gain. The charges were untrue, but they caused enough uproar for Eisenhower to consider dropping Nixon from the ticket. Nixon saved himself by going on television and giving an emotional speech in his own defense. After making public all his finances, he went on to tell about the one gift he had accepted—the Nixons' little dog, Checkers, which an admirer had sent to the family. After the broadcast, over a million letters flooded in demanding that Nixon remain on the ticket. Eisenhower kept him on it.

official named Alger Hiss of helping him pass secret documents to the Soviet Union. Hiss was respected, and few believed the charges, but still there had to be an investigation by HUAC. Only one man on the committee, Richard Nixon, suspected that Hiss was lying when he claimed that he had never known Chambers. Despite some opposition from President Truman and many members of Congress, Nixon pursued Hiss. Hiss was later convicted of perjury (lying under oath), and Chambers produced evidence that suggested his guilt as a spy, though the actual truth is still disputed. Nixon, a freshman congressman, won national fame for his determined pursuit of Hiss.

"Tricky Dick." While some Americans applauded Nixon's performance, others believed Hiss had been treated unfairly. In any case, Nixon's fame after the Hiss affair gave him a chance to run for the Senate in 1950, against Helen Gahagan Douglas, a liberal Democratic congresswoman. It was a dirty campaign on both sides. Like Voorhis, Douglas hurt herself by making mistakes. Yet many observers saw Nixon's false charges that she supported communism as lower than the usual level of political mudslinging. While he labeled her "the Pink Lady" (linking her to the "Reds," or communists), she called him "Tricky Dick." Nixon's enemies—who now included news reporters—would make sure the nickname stuck.

Participation: "Vietnamization"; Invasions of Cambodia and Laos; Paris Peace Accords

Vice president. Now a famous senator in his early forties, Nixon was clearly on the rise. In 1952 Republican presidential nominee Dwight D. Eisenhower chose Nixon as his running mate. As Eisenhower's vice president for eight years, Nixon was unusually active, gaining more foreign policy experience than most vice presidents. He visited over fifty countries, among them Vietnam, Cambodia, and Laos, where U.S. aid was being given to the French in their efforts to keep communists from coming to power.

It was on this six-day visit in 1953, as he toured the battlefields, that Nixon had the first glimmer of an idea that would later shape his own Vietnam policy. He ate beef bourgignon and drank fine wine with the French officers, who, he noticed, looked down on the

Vietnamese soldiers serving under them. Nixon then spent equal time with the soldiers, dining on monkey stew in the Vietnamese tents. Afterward, he decided that the officers' scorn would cost them victory. "The French," he concluded, "if not losing the war, did not know how to win it" (Nixon in Aitken, p. 227). He came to believe that the Vietnamese needed to be shown how to fight for themselves, rather than be commanded by officers who had no respect for them.

Defeats and "retirement." In 1960 Nixon ran for president but lost to John F. Kennedy in the closest race in American history up to then. Two years later, Nixon ran for governor of California against Edmund G. Brown, losing by a wide margin. On the day following the election, Nixon appeared before reporters and gave a long, rambling press conference. Obviously exhausted, he also seemed bitter and hostile. Since the days of the Hiss case, he had thought the press treated him unfairly. Now he surprised them by announcing that they would not have Nixon to kick around anymore because this would be his last press conference.

Years of preparation. Reporters across the country wrote various versions of Nixon's political death notice. Such a statement must mean the end of his political career, they thought. Yet even as he drove home from his "last press conference," Nixon was already planning his comeback. He resumed his legal career but kept abreast of politics at home and abroad. Foreign leaders especially respected him for his deepening understanding of international events. French President de Gaulle, for example, said he expected that Nixon would someday win the American presidency.

Between 1963 and 1965, Nixon also made several more trips to Vietnam. Developing his ideas about the war there, he wrote articles for popular magazines such as *Reader's Digest* and academic ones such as *Foreign Affairs*. Meanwhile, President Lyndon B. Johnson increased America's commitment to the war (see **Lyndon B. Johnson**). There was discontent over this increase within the nation, however. A movement opposing the war slowly gained strength among the American public. In 1966 Nixon campaigned tirelessly for Republican congressional candidates across the country. The following year, he traveled around the world, cementing his already close ties with foreign leaders. By then, Vietnam had become the most important issue in American politics.

Taking over. In March 1968, President Johnson announced that, because of the war, he would not seek reelection. Nixon, who easily won the Republican nomination, went on to beat Vice President Hubert H. Humphrey in a close race. During the election, Nixon promised an "honorable peace" in Vietnam, skillfully attracting both those who wanted America to get out and those who wanted victory (Nixon in Aitken, p. 352). He put forward his "Vietnamization" plan for training and supplying the South Vietnamese to fight for themselves. Now in office, he had to put his plans into effect and deliver on his promises.

Domino theory. Despite his desire for peace, Nixon would not simply pull the American troops out of Vietnam. Like Johnson, he believed that America's image as a world leader depended on not abandoning U.S. allies. He also accepted the "domino theory," the widely held idea that if one country "fell" to communism, its neighbors would follow like dominoes in a row. Nixon refused to give in to communists, even though they were more popular among the Vietnamese people than the rulers installed by the United States.

Great powers. Along with Vietnamization, which Nixon hoped would strengthen the South, he also had a plan to weaken the North. With his adviser Henry Kissinger, he developed the strategy of negotiating not with the North Vietnamese but their communist allies, the Soviets and the Chinese. He hoped to get both countries to withdraw their support. This "great powers" approach to ending the war improved relations between the United States and the other two countries. However, U.S. relations with China did not affect the tough and stubborn North Vietnamese.

Secret bombing, invasion of Cambodia. Communist forces in South Vietnam had been supplied along the Ho Chi Minh Trail, which ran along the border areas of Laos and Cambodia. Soon after taking office, Nixon had ordered a secret bombing campaign in Cambodia, supposedly a neutral country. An unknown number of Cambodian villagers were killed, and the bombing had little effect on the supply trail. In 1970 U.S. forces invaded Cambodia and attacked points along the trail. The invasion soon ended but not before triggering massive unrest in the United States. Antiwar demonstrations erupted on college campuses, and 100,000 students marched on Washington in protest.

Laos. Nixon withdrew most of the U.S. ground forces, relying on air power. In February 1971, the South Vietnamese army, with U.S. air support, tried to cut off the Ho Chi Minh Trail by invading Laos. But without U.S. ground forces fighting alongside them, the South Vietnamese soldiers were badly defeated when they ran into communist opposition. Survivors turned and fled in disarray. The invasion, intended to show the success of Viet-namization, instead turned out to be an embarrassing failure. Still, Nixon continued bringing the U.S. ground forces home. By the end of 1971, there were fewer than 200,000 U.S. soldiers in Vietnam.

Christmas bombing. Peace talks were meanwhile making little progress. The North insisted on total U.S. withdrawal without any conditions. Nixon, for his part, wanted to leave under conditions that would ensure the continued existence of a noncommunist government in the South. After winning reelection by a landslide in November 1972, Nixon ordered further massive bombing of North Vietnam. In twelve days of bombing, nearly 2,000 civilians were killed and many more evacuated from northern cities.

Peace Accords, War Powers Act. In early 1973 both sides finally signed a peace treaty in Paris. Neither side kept to it, however, and Nixon continued bombing Cambodia. Later that year, however, Congress passed the War Powers Act, which limited the president's power to wage war without a declaration of war from Congress. Unless Congress declared war, U.S. troops sent abroad had to come back within sixty days. The War Powers Act meant the end of America's involvement in Vietnam.

Watergate, resignation. Nixon aides operated outside the law to achieve their goals. They placed wiretaps on telephones, conducted illegal break-ins, and stole or photographed documents

▲ **Trucks traveling the Ho Chi Minh Trail**

belonging to other Americans. Supposed to be a secret, the 1970 U.S. bombings of Cambodia, for example, had been made public by news reporters. Their phones were afterward tapped by the government in an effort to discover how they were obtaining secret information.

In 1973 Congress began investigating a burglary of the Democratic party headquarters at the Watergate apartment complex in Washington, D.C. The burglars were linked to the Committee to Reelect the President, the Nixon campaign organization. As America watched months of televised hearings in which Congress questioned Nixon's aides, it became clear that Nixon had tried to cover up or keep this connection secret by preventing the crime from being investigated. The scandal led to arrests and convictions for many of Nixon's aides. When it was clear that Congress would impeach him, Nixon resigned on August 9, 1974. He was the first American president to do so.

Aftermath

Elder statesman. Nixon left office in disgrace, though he was pardoned by President Gerald Ford, his successor, for any crimes he may have committed while in office. Over the next two decades, Nixon's reputation slowly began to improve. The abuses of Watergate and the wounds of war faded into the background while Nixon's achievements, especially in foreign policy, moved into the foreground. Nixon wrote several best-selling books of memoirs and political commentary. Leaders began seeking his opinions, especially during the Republican presidencies of Reagan and Bush.

During the early 1990s, as communism collapsed in the Soviet Union and Eastern Europe, Nixon began appearing frequently on television news programs or on the editorial pages of major newspapers. He called for strong financial support for the new democratic Russia, in order to avoid a return to dictatorship. His beloved wife, Pat, died in 1993. The following year, Nixon suffered a stroke soon after returning from a trip to Russia. He died a few days later, on April 22, 1994, with his daughters at his bedside.

For More Information

Aitken, Jonathan. *Nixon: A Life*. Washington, D.C.: Regnery Publishing, 1993.

Ambrose, Stephen. *Nixon: The Education of a Politician*. New York: Simon & Schuster, 1987.

Wicker, Tom. *One of Us: Richard Nixon and the American Dream*. New York: Random House, 1991.

Counterculture and the Student Movement

1960
College students organize Students for a Democratic Society (SDS).

1961
Allard Lowenstein supports Stanford University students in protest over campus government.

1962
Andy Warhol creates Pop Art image of Campbell's soup can.

1963
Bob Dylan emerges as a spokesman for his generation with his performance at the Newport Folk Festival.

1963
Dylan describes the generation gap in "The Times They Are A-Changin'."

1964
Free Speech Movement begins at University of California at Berkeley. Students conduct Freedom Summer in Mississippi.

1965
SDS sponsors first national demonstrations against the Vietnam War.

1968
Lowenstein organizes "dump Johnson" campaign against the president. Students stage over 200 antiwar demonstrations on school campuses.

1968
Student radicals attempt to disrupt the Democratic National Convention in Chicago.

1971
Twenty-sixth Amendment lowers the voting age to eighteen.

1969
300,000 young people gather at Altamont, California, to hear a Rolling Stones concert.

1969
400,000 "flower children" gather at Woodstock music festival. Militant group called Weathermen conducts an attack in Chicago.

COUNTERCULTURE AND THE STUDENT MOVEMENT

Young people showed disenchantment with conditions of life in the United States in the decades after World War II. In the 1950s, poet Allen Ginsberg and others formed the "beat generation," rebelling against mainstream customs and goals. Critical of society, which had became more consumer-driven than ever, the beats, or beatniks, as they were some-times called, chose to live in poverty. They disassociated themselves from what they saw as false values in American society, rejecting especially the goal of owning things. Instead the beats sought joy and insight through jazz music, sexual activity, alcohol, and drugs.

The next generation saw the appearance of another, much larger group of young rebels called the counterculture, Like the beats, the counterculture developed during wartime. The decade of the Korean War, the 1950s, gave way to the decade of the Vietnam War, the 1960s. Made up largely of young, middle-class whites, counterculture youth criticized the nation around them in discussion, art, and music.

Through their work, artists of the period shared with the public their comments on the times. **Andy Warhol,** for example, created pictures of Marilyn Monroe, Campbell soup cans, and dollar bills, his images holding a mirror up to American society, exposing its tastes and values.

Some Artists and Musicians of the Counterculture Era	
Artists	**Musicians**
Jasper Johns	Joan Baez
Roy Lichtenstein	Bob Dylan
Andy Warhol	Janis Joplin

Sometimes called "hippies" or "flower children," members of counterculture youth reached for drugs and engaged freely in sex. They turned away from the standards of a nation that had bestowed on them racial prejudices, the Vietnam War, and the U.S.-Soviet Cold War (with its threat of nuclear world destruction). The rebels rejected mainstream goods, goals, language, and dress. Men grew their hair long and both sexes wore simple garments: jeans and muslin shirts were standard. Some turned to cooperative living in communes, "checking out" from the larger society. Their behavior shocked other Americans, who saw it as a threat to their life styles and institutions.

The counterculture regarded songwriter **Bob Dylan** as a leading spokesman for the movement. His lyrics became a vehicle for social protest on three major issues of the era: civil rights, the antiwar movement, and the generation gap.

Dylan also attracted fans in the student movement of the 1960s. While the counterculture criticized the way things were, its members did not, as a rule, try to improve society. The student movement, on the other hand, asked individuals to participate more in their democracy. Leaders of the movement, such as Tom Hayden of the University of Michigan, helped organize students for political action. Hayden wrote a statement of beliefs (the Port Huron Statement) held by the group Students for a Democratic Society (SDS). The SDS condemned the machinelike nature of life in America, calling for a better system, and set out to improve society. Yet there was overlap between the counterculture and student movement, and in time the two grew closer together.

California became a leader in the student movement. In 1964 students at the University of California at Berkeley began a "free speech movement." School authorities refused to let them distribute protest material outside the main campus gate, but the students fought back with spirit. Joan Baez led them in singing "We Shall Overcome," and in the end, they won a victory. The university granted the students the same rights to free speech on campus as in outside society.

The movements of the era involved masses of people and a few well-known leaders. There were also lesser-known leaders who worked hard as organizers within the movements. A teacher at Stanford University in California, **Allard Lowenstein,** organized students to work for civil rights. Lowenstein, a champion of working within the system to create change, persuaded young people to become voters and go into the South to campaign for civil rights. Later he dedicated himself to getting the United States out of the Vietnam War.

Antiwar protests joined the civil rights demonstrations in the second half of the decade. The 1968 school year saw 221 campus demonstrations, many of them violent. Students protested against research done at their universities on deadly chemical weapons that were used in Vietnam, for example. Many were arrested or hurt. Still they protested, driven by the hope that they could effect change.

Their numbers growing, the young and discontented organized a concert at Woodstock in upstate New York in 1969, which attracted a crowd of more than 400,000. The concert proceeded peacefully, but a less organized one at Altamount, California, ended in a murder.

Violence continued in the new year. In 1970 Kent State University in Ohio called in the National Guard to control antiwar demonstrators, and four people were killed. Two more were shot to death at Jackson State University in Mississippi. Losing hope, young people in the 1970s began to give up on changing society and focus instead on their own personal lives. Yet the counterculture and student movements had lasting effects. Adults recognized the need for new civil rights laws and an end to U.S. involvement in Vietnam. They also admitted the need for warmer, more human relations in the modern world and became more willing to relax dress codes and other rules in mainstream American society.

Bob Dylan

1941-

Personal Background

Family life. Bob Dylan was born Robert Allen Zimmerman on May 24, 1941, in Duluth, Minnesota. He moved with his family to Hibbing, a dying iron-mining town in Minnesota's Mesabi Range, when he was six years old. Most of the inhabitants of Hibbing were recent Catholic immigrants. "The Zimmermans, however, were Jewish, and Bob therefore received an early taste of what it meant to be different, to be an outsider" (Nash, p. 304).

Dylan's father owned an appliance store, and his mother's parents managed a clothing store. He grew up in a conservative, loving, middle-class Jewish family. His family circumstances and the conformity of Hibbing's society left him feeling stifled. After he moved to New York's Greenwich Village to pursue a career as a folk singer, he invented a completely different upbringing for himself. He claimed to have been orphaned at an early age and to have run away from home no less than ten times between the ages of ten and eighteen. "In his reinvention of himself he had ridden the rails from sea to shining sea; met Woody Guthrie [an early idol] in California; jammed with [blues great] Big Bill Broonzy in striptease joints; and played piano for the pop singer Bobby Vee" (Moritz, p. 195). None of this invented background was true, but the process of reinventing himself proves that Dylan was a rebel, an outsider even in his youth.

▲ Bob Dylan

Event: Counterculture.

Role: Poet, singer, and songwriter Bob Dylan was the most influential force in the popular music of the 1960s. As a spokesman for the disenchanted citizens of that decade, he mounted a powerful attack on racism, injustice, and war. His best-known song, "Blowin' in the Wind," was the unofficial anthem of the civil rights movement.

Teenage ambitions. From childhood, Dylan loved music. He learned to play piano and guitar at an early age. A shy teenager (his friends remember him as a "quiet loner"), he expressed himself through his music, forming and leading several rock and roll bands while in high school and telling friends that his goal was to become a professional rock singer, more popular than even Elvis Presley. Like other teens of the 1950s, he imitated screen idols Marlon Brando and James Dean in his dress, speech, and attitude. "He wore a duck-tail haircut, rode a black Harley-Davidson motorcycle ... and hung out with 'greaser' kids" (Moritz, p. 195). He wrote in his high school yearbook that his ambition was to join the band of Little Richard.

Guthrie's influence. Dylan was an avid student of music. His study of the roots of rock music led him to the blues and American folk music. After graduating from high school, he enrolled at the University of Minnesota where he proved to be an indifferent student. He spent more time playing folk music in Dinkytown, the Beatnik section of Minneapolis, performing at The Ten O'Clock Scholar, a local coffeehouse. A friend gave him a copy of *Bound for Glory,* the autobiography of Woody Guthrie, the great folk singer and spokesman for the downtrodden during the Great Depression. "Dylan devoured the book, played Guthrie's records endlessly, and literally fused his identity with that of the hobo troubadour from Oklahoma" (Nash, p. 314). The discovery of Guthrie's work was a great turning point in Dylan's career. He became perhaps the finest interpreter of Guthrie's songs and expressed "sympathy with Guthrie's social consciousness, his concern for the helpless little people at the bottom of the pile, and his anger, in his words, at 'those who steal with their pens'" (Nash, p. 314). In the hands of Woody Guthrie, music was a social and political weapon. Bob Dylan's realization that music could be a vehicle for social protest led to his own development as the musical conscience of his generation.

Participation: Counterculture Movement

Dylan discovered. Dylan left the University of Minnesota after three semesters and migrated to Greenwich Village in New York City. He threw himself into the folk music scene there, singing regularly at clubs like Gerde's Folk City. At the same time, he met and became friends with his idol, Woody Guthrie, who was hospitalized in New Jersey, slowly dying from Huntington's Disease. Encouraged by Guthrie, Dylan began to write and perform his own songs, his most notable early effort being "Song to Woody," a tribute to the great folk artist. Dylan visited Guthrie often in the hospital, and the two men had long talks and played songs for each other.

> ## In Memory of Guthrie
> When Woody Guthrie died, Bob Dylan was the one who proposed a benefit concert to honor Guthrie's memory and to raise money to fight the disease that had taken his life. Two concerts resulted, one at Carnegie Hall in New York and a second at the Hollywood Bowl in Los Angeles. Both were huge critical and financial successes, due in large part to appearances by Dylan.

From Dylan recordings, it is obvious that he imitated Guthrie's style, "going so far as to adopt [his] fractured, Depression-era speech" (Moritz, p. 195). He also caught the attention of other folk singers, such as Pete Seeger, whose name was placed on an unofficial blacklist of musicians not to hire because of their politics. Seeger had refused to cooperate with Congress in its communist-hunting days of the 1950s and was greatly admired by Dylan for placing his principles above financial success. In return, Seeger came to regard Dylan as the finest writer of protest songs of his generation.

Dylan's performances in the folk clubs of Greenwich Village brought him to the attention of Robert Shelton, an influential New York columnist and music critic. He interviewed Dylan and wrote a glowing review in which he ranked the young midwesterner far above the other young folk singers of his time. A few weeks later, Dylan signed a recording contract with Columbia Records. He was signed by the legendary recording producer John Hammond (who had "discovered" jazz greats Billie Holiday and Count Basie and would later launch the careers of Aretha Franklin and Bruce Springsteen). Hammond "predicted musical greatness for the twenty-year-old performer with the abrasive voice, street-urchin charm, and Chaplinesque stage presence" (Moritz, p. 195).

Civil rights songs. It did not take Bob Dylan long to fulfill John Hammond's predictions of greatness. He did this by writing and recording a series of generation-defining protest songs. A number of these songs dealt with issues of race and civil rights. "The Ballad of Emmet Till" recounted the story of a young African American from Chicago who was beaten to death in Mississippi just for

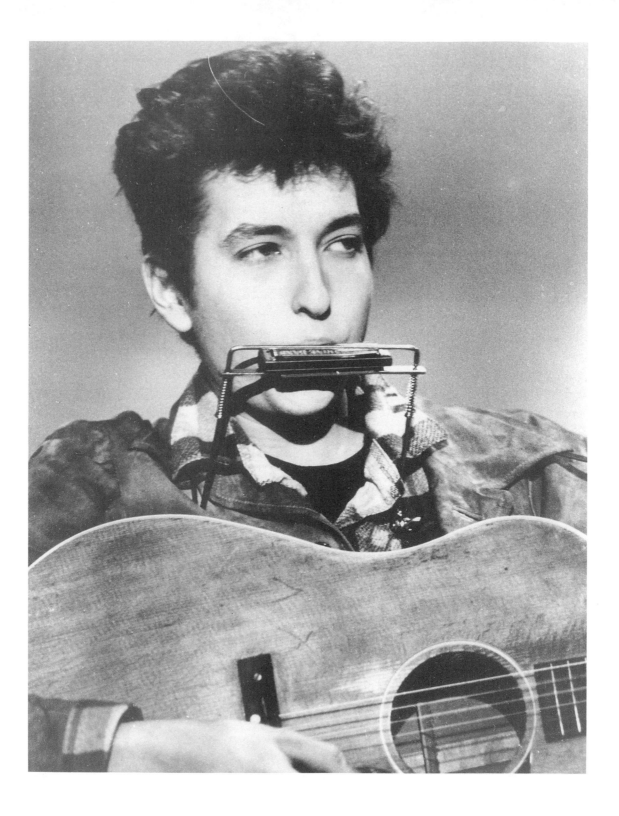

daring to speak to a white woman. "Oxford Town" was inspired by the violent outburst that greeted James Meredith's enrollment (the first black to do so) at the University of Mississippi. "Only a Pawn in Their Game" told of the murder of black civil rights leader Medgar Evers and helped keep alive the case until his murderer was finally convicted.

Dylan's support for the civil rights movement was at least partially inspired by his romance with a beautiful, intelligent young woman named Suze Rotolo (she appeared with him on the cover of his second album), who worked in the New York office of the Congress of Racial Equality (CORE). Perhaps Dylan's greatest protest song is the elegant, understated "Blowin' in the Wind," which poses a series of questions about racial justice ("How many years can some people exist/Before they're allowed to be free") and peace ("How many times must the cannon balls fly/Before

> ### "Only a Pawn in Their Game"—The Death of Medgar Evers
>
> The murder of black civil rights worker Medgar Evers in Mississippi in 1963 sent shock waves throughout the nation. Dylan reacted by writing "Only a Pawn in Their Game," a song first performed in Mississippi on the edge of a cotton patch for a mostly black audience of about 300 people.
>
> The killer, a white man named Byron de la Beckwith, stood trial twice before all-white juries in Jackson, Mississippi. Both trials ended with the juries unable to reach a verdict. In the years that followed, Beckwith boasted that he, in fact, had ambushed and murdered Evers. Thirty years later, in 1994, Beckwith was found guilty of murder by a mixed-race jury and sentenced (at the age of seventy-three) to life in prison. Dylan's song remains a tribute to Evers's life and death.

they're forever banned?"—Dylan, p. 97). It eventually became a spiritual anthem of both the civil rights and antiwar movements. "Blowin' in the Wind," a smash hit when recorded by the popular folk trio Peter, Paul, and Mary, was sung during the 1963 March on Washington, at the end of which Martin Luther King, Jr., delivered his famous "I Have a Dream" address.

War songs. Dylan produced an incredible outpouring of protest songs between 1962 and 1964. He would see an item in the newspapers or on television or simply overhear a conversation by friends and immediately write a song about it. "A Hard Rain's A-Gonna Fall," for example, reflects the tension of the Cuban Missile Crisis. Dylan used grotesque images in this song to convey his fear and anger about the dangers of nuclear holocaust. As with so many of his songs, he seemed to be expressing the feelings of many in his generation whose world and lives teetered on the brink of extinction. The anger of "Hard Rain" is expressed even more harshly in "Masters of War," a bitter attack against those who profit from war ("And I hope that you die/And your death will come soon"—Dylan, p.56).

A third antiwar song, "I Will Not Go Down Under the Ground" (also called "Let Me Die in My Footsteps"), was written when the sales of backyard bomb and fallout shelters (as protection from nuclear war) were still very brisk. Dylan rejects the fallout shelter mentality ("I will not go down under the ground/'Cause somebody tells me that death's coming round"—Dylan, p. 21). He chooses death above the ground over what he sees as a living death under the ground.

A matter of principles. Dylan proved very early in his career that he was an artist with integrity, unwilling to compromise his principles for money. He was booked to perform on television's highly rated program *The Ed Sullivan Show* on Sunday night, May 12, 1963. The CBS-TV censor decided at the last minute that Dylan could not be allowed to sing "Talking John Birch Paranoid Blues" (the John Birch Society was an extreme right-wing group that had accused President Dwight Eisenhower and Chief Justice of the Supreme Court Earl Warren of being agents of the communists). The censor feared that the TV station might be sued because the song compared members of the Birch Society to Adolf Hitler: "Now we (the Birch Society) all agree with Hitler's views/Although he killed six million Jews" (Dylan, p. 18).

This attempt to censor him enraged Dylan, who refused to substitute another song. "If I can't sing that song, I won't sing *any* song," he declared before stomping out of the studio (Dylan in Shelton, p. 166). Dylan emerged from this episode looking even more like a hero to his fans.

Dylan and Baez. Dylan's professional and romantic involvement with Joan Baez greatly widened his following. Before Dylan's arrival in New York, she was a star on the folk circuit, noted for her beautiful, pure soprano voice. Baez, who admired the political message songs by Dylan, invited him to go on a concert tour with her.

▲ Dylan performs with Joan Baez at the "Peace Sunday" nuclear disarmament rally at the Rose Bowl in Pasadena, California, June 6, 1980

Their appearance together at Rhode Island's Newport Folk Festival in July 1963 created a sensation. They performed "With God on Our Side," one of Dylan's most openly political works. The song attacks the patriotic myth that God approved of America's wars, instead arguing that "If God's on our side/He'll stop the next war" (Dylan, p. 93).

Dylan's appearance at Newport in 1963 marked the high point of his career as a singer/composer of protest songs. The songs he included in his third album, *The Times They Are A-Changin'* (also one of the tunes on the album), further established him as the spokesman for a new generation of rebellious, politically committed young people.

Baez accompanied Dylan on a concert tour of England, which marked the end of their romantic involvement; Baez was deeply hurt by Dylan's failure to invite her to perform with him before English audiences. Shortly after his English tour, Dylan married Sara Lowndes.

The new Dylan. Before going to England, Dylan had already begun to turn away from protest songs. His fourth album, *Another Side of Bob Dylan,* is composed entirely of inward-looking, deeply personal songs. The "new Dylan" brushed aside political causes. In his song "My Back Pages," he rejected songs that preach, explaining that in his early, protest period "I was so much older then,/I'm younger than that now" (Dylan, p. 139).

In 1965 Dylan proclaimed himself a rock and roll artist by "going electric." He stunned the audience at the 1965 Newport Folk Festival by appearing with an electric guitar and an amplified backup band. Folk purists tried to boo him off the stage. Other folk purists continued to boo Dylan at concerts following the Newport confrontation; they shouted out demands from the audience that he return to his earlier music. He refused to back down, asserting that he didn't want to be anyone's spokesman and that he only wanted to write from inside himself. This attitude reflected the "do your own thing" outlook that many young people began adopting in the sixties.

In 1965–66, Dylan produced three albums that expressed his new extremely personal style of song writing. *Bringing It All Back Home, Highway 61 Revisited,* and the double album *Blonde on Blonde* are generally regarded (along with the Beatles' *Sgt. Pepper's Lonely Hearts Club Band*) as "the finest recorded accomplishments in rock music in the decade of the 1960's" (Moritz, p. 196). By 1966, critic Joe Queenan argued, Bob Dylan had become the most important figure in rock history—more important than Elvis Presley, who did not write his own songs, and the Beatles, who were much influenced by Dylan's lyrics. Dylan's three albums greatly influenced the attitudes of Vietnam War protesters and the expanding drug culture of the decade ("Rainy Day Women #12 & 35," for example, contains the refrain "Everybody must get stoned"—Dylan, p. 221). Lyrics from Dylan's songs even found their way into college English courses, and a number of academics have argued that Dylan should be regarded as a major poet.

The accident. In 1966 Bob Dylan went on an exhausting world tour, backed by a group called the Hawks (they would later win fame as The Band). He had apparently been using drugs for several years and some of his friends feared for his health and safety. In July, vacationing with his new wife near Woodstock, New York, he suffered serious injuries as a result of a motorcycle accident.

> ## Generation Gap
>
> The Dylan song that best captured the mood of the 1960s was "The Times They Are A-Changin'." It was probably the first public expression of what was later called the generation gap, in which traditional attitudes were rejected by the young. In one section, the song addresses parents throughout the land, asking them not to criticize what they can't understand. It continues with the warning, "Your sons and daughters/Are beyond your command" (Dylan, p. 91). The song greatly influenced (and reflected) the defiant spirit of young people against those in authority.

Aftermath

Post–1960s popularity. Bob Dylan's accident may have saved his life. He apparently stopped using hard drugs and giving public performances and settled down near Woodstock, New York, as a devoted husband and father. Though still writing music, he stopped performing publicly. He released no more albums until 1968. His new work inspired the country rock movement (especially evident in his album *Nashville Skyline*). He accepted a role in and wrote the musical score for director Sam Peckinpah's film *Pat Garrett and Billy the Kid*. The peak of his post–1960s popularity was a 1974 cross-country tour with The Band. A year later, the album *Blood on the Tracks* (1975) was released. It is regarded by critics as a masterpiece equal to his greatest works of the sixties. Many of this album's songs reflect the pain Dylan experienced as his marriage fell apart. Dylan observed America's Bicentennial by embarking on the Rolling Thunder Revue tour. It was an unconventional tour with unannounced appearances at small clubs and on college

Some Dylan Songs on Issues of the Sixties	
Civil rights movement	"Only a Pawn in Their Game"
Antiwar movement	"Masters of War"
Generation Gap	"The Times They Are A-Changin'"

campuses. Among those who joined him on this tour were Joan Baez, Beat poet Allen Ginsberg, Arlo Guthrie (son of Woody), and playwright/actor Sam Shepard.

A religious experience. The decade of the 1980s brought with it the most controversial change in Dylan's life and work since the Newport Folk Festival of 1965. He converted to Christianity and recorded three consecutive albums made up of songs concerning his newfound Christian faith. *Slow Train Coming, Saved,* and *Shot of Love* are Dylan's musical legacies from this period.

This religious phase was short-lived. Dylan apparently returned to the Judaism of his youth and was spotted visiting Jerusalem in the mid-1980s. He toured with several groups in 1988 and that same year was inducted into the Rock and Roll Hall of Fame. In 1991 Dylan was given a Lifetime Achievement Award at the Grammy ceremonies, and in 1993 he performed at President Bill Clinton's inauguration.

Isolated causes. Since the mid-1960s, Dylan has refused to once again become a leading spokesman for social and political causes. Perhaps the most eloquent appeal came from Joan Baez. Her 1972 song "To Bobby" spoke of voices in the night crying for him.

Dylan has resisted this and all other requests to assume a position of leadership for any cause. He did, however, continue to write songs of protest after the decade of the sixties had ended. "George Jackson" was a passionate protest against the murder by prison guards of a black author and political activist. Dylan believed the authorities had staged a phony prison uprising to find a pretense for murdering Jackson. During the Rolling Thunder Revue, Dylan and his troupe played two benefit concerts for ex-boxer Rubin "Hurricane" Carter. In his song "Hurricane," Dylan argues that Carter was innocent of the murder charges against him and that he fell victim to a prejudiced American system of justice. In addition to such songs, Dylan has lent his name and talent to a number of fund-raisers for political causes. He has sung to protest against apartheid in

South Africa, to bring relief to the starving, homeless people of Bangladesh and Africa, and to raise money for Americans in danger of losing their farms. He is still, as he has always been, an artist with a strong social conscience.

For More Information

Dylan, Bob. *Lyrics, 1962–1985.* New York: Alfred A. Knopf, 1994 [1985].

Moritz, Charles, ed. *Current Biography Yearbook 1991.* New York: H.W. Wilson, 1991, pp. 194–99.

Nash, Roderick. *From These Beginnings: A Biographical Approach to American History.* Vol. 2. New York: Harper & Row, 1978.

Shelton, Robert. *No Direction Home: The Life and Music of Bob Dylan.* New York: Beachtree Books, 1986.

Williams, Paul. *Bob Dylan: Performing Artist.* 2 vols. Novato, California: Underwood Miller, 1990, 1992.

Andy Warhol

1928-1987

Personal Background

Andy Warhol was born Andy Warhola to a family of Ruthenian immigrants, probably on August 6, 1928. Ruthenia, a small country located near Poland and Czechoslovakia, was inhabited almost exclusively by farmers and shepherds. Like many people from Ruthenia, Andy's parents, Ondrej (Andrew) Warhola and Julia Zavacky, immigrated to America after the turn of the century in search of more job opportunities and a better life for their family. They settled in Soho, Pennsylvania, near Pittsburgh, where Andy was reportedly born at home. A small child with distinct facial features, the boy had deep-set eyes, a round nose, and strong cheekbones.

Industrial influence. In the first few years of Andy's life, he was subject to the typical Eastern European immigrant experience. He lived with his parents and two brothers in a tarpaper shack in Soho, where the pollution from the nearby Pittsburgh factories was so thick that streetlights had to be turned on at noon so that people could see through the haze of smog. Like other Depression-era immigrant children, Andy and his brothers had little to eat and wear, even though their father went to work in a nearby Pittsburgh factory every day. These conditions made the already fragile Andy sickly.

Childhood isolation. Andy was creative and mischievous, yet painfully shy. He excelled in school academically but did not

▲ **Andy Warhol**

Event: Counterculture.

Role: Andy Warhol was an artist who helped introduce the trend of pop art. His statements about modern society, expressed through his art, made him a leading spokesperson for the counterculture social movement of the 1960s and 1970s.

interact socially. In the third grade, he was stricken with St. Vitus's Dance—a nerve virus that gave him shaky limbs and blotchy skin. This condition made it nearly impossible for the already timid Andy to socialize with his classmates. He was removed from school and spent many months in bed at home, isolated from all children except his brothers. Andy's mother, worried about his well-being, brought him armfuls of childhood delights—comic and coloring books, paper dolls, chocolate bars, and autographed pictures from Hollywood stars. It was in this period of recovery that Andy created his first drawings.

When he was able to interact with people again, he remained very shy and physically weak. He had no interest in playing sports with other children his age and instead began drawing portraits of all his friends and relatives. His efforts brought him a great deal of praise. According to his family, the portraits were exceptional for a young boy.

Greatly influencing Andy were his weekly visits to Catholic Mass on Sundays with his mother. While his brothers wriggled around restlessly, Andy would spend the entire mass, which was at least seven hours long, silently staring at two-dimensional pictures of saints and other religious figures that hung from the wall in rows. For the rest of his life, Andy went to church on Sundays, always fixing his eyes on the colorful portraits. His later art shows that he was clearly influenced by these childhood images.

Raw talent. It seemed that whatever Andy produced was new and original. When he was about ten years old, one of his teachers recommended that he take extra drawing classes at the Carnegie Museum in Pittsburgh, next door to the Carnegie Institute of Technology. His teachers there were very impressed and recommended that he continue his artwork.

Inspired by the excitement surrounding his early work, Andy continued creating art. He worked as a window designer for an upscale department store during high school. Meanwhile, Andy took more classes than required per semester and graduated early so that he could attend the Carnegie Institute (now Carnegie-Mellon University).

Controversy and New York cockroaches. At the Carnegie

Institute, Andy majored in painting and design, worked as the art director on the campus literary magazine, and began creating controversial art. The first piece he submitted for an exhibition showed a man with his finger up his nose, entitled *The Broad Gave Me My Face, But I Can Pick My Own Nose.* The panel of judges, which included modern artist George Grosz, refused to include it in their show. Grosz urged the rest of the panel to reconsider, but Andy decided to hang it elsewhere, in the university's arts and crafts center. People practically ignored the contest exhibition and instead flocked to see Andy's shocking creation. It was 1948, and Andy was already emerging as a free-thinking trendsetter.

The following year, Andy graduated from college, moved to New York, dropped the final *a* from his last name, and became Andy Warhol. He lived in such shabby, insect-infested housing at the time that he later referred to this as his "cockroach period." One of his favorite stories to tell was when he went to *Harper's Bazaar* magazine seeking work as an illustrator and, upon opening his portfolio, a cockroach crawled out onto the editor's desk. She felt so sorry for him that she gave him an assignment.

His cockroach period did not last long, however. Soon his refreshing style of illustration was attracting attention from businesses throughout New York. Companies started hiring him to do commercial art (create product images for advertisements). Warhol's work began covering the pages of major magazines. In his early twenties at the time, he was already building a reputation as one of the finest working commercial artists in the nation.

Participation: Counterculture

The 1950s. While Warhol was succeeding in the commercial marketplace during the 1950s, America stepped deeper and deeper into a competition with the Soviet Union for world supremacy. Called the Cold War, this competition carried with it the threat of nuclear attack, which sent Americans rushing to invest in fallout shelters. Meanwhile, many of them worked hard to raise themselves into the middle class, an envied position in society. Standard to the middle-class life-style was a family with two parents, an average of two children, two cars, and one television set. With the

The Artistic Methods of Andy Warhol

In his 1950s commercial art, Warhol produced ink-on-paper images using a special process. He would draw on a glazed paper that did not absorb ink, then press his drawing to an unglazed sheet. The transfer produced a scratchy, blotted image. In his first pop art paintings, Warhol worked on stretched canvas. An opaque projector would project images on the canvas, which he then traced and painted. He next turned to a silk screen method and continued to use silk screens for years. Generally, Warhol's art lay in his selection and arrangement of images and colors. He also painted brush portrait backgrounds on his own, and in his later years, line drawings began appearing in his paintings.

spread of television came the rise of cultural idols such as Elvis Presley and Marilyn Monroe.

Although Warhol was a success in the commercial world of this period, he also struggled with it. He illustrated products and fashions for work; and for art's sake, he illustrated large comic strips. It was not a combination that contented him. In some ways, Warhol identified with the culture of 1950s America, but in most ways, he did not. Out of this unsettling position in society came a style of creative expression. Warhol helped invent and represent a new phenomenon: pop art.

Pop art. At the beginning of the 1960s, Warhol struggled to break out of the commercial world that had already brought him much success. He now lived in New York, where he owned a home of his own, which his mother also occupied. And his illustrations and department store window displays were better received than ever before. Warhol sensed, however, that even greater success was within his reach. He wondered how to achieve it.

After a long period of waiting for inspiration, Warhol decided to paint one of the items America loved best: money. The relationship between people and money, concluded Warhol, was a strange one—he knew this firsthand from enjoying a bit of financial success himself. In fact, Warhol once claimed that he did not understand anything but money, adding that "money is SUSPICIOUS, because people think you're not supposed to have it, even if you do have it" (Warhol, *The Philosophy,* p. 129). Apparently, images of money were intriguing to others, too, for Warhol's first paintings of one- and two-dollar bills enjoyed immense popularity. In creating these paintings, Warhol had taken his first steps toward becoming a pop artist.

He followed the money paintings with images that represented American culture: Coca-Cola bottles, stamps, baseballs, cars, movie

▲ Warhol's *Marilyn*, 1967, a portrait of actress Marilyn Monroe

stars and other celebrities, and, finally, Campbell's soup cans. The American art audience responded by declaring Warhol the king of pop art. Asked why he painted the soup cans, probably his most famous work, Warhol replied that he ate the soup every day as a child.

Pop art was simply the representation of American pop culture, which featured mass production, advertising, consumerism, fame, and fortune. By recognizing and showing the American people that these were their habits and values, Warhol became a spokesperson for the counterculture. Counterculture artists exposed and commented on society's customs and goals, reflecting a broader movement of protest and dissent in the nation at large.

Fame. In the 1960s, Warhol, as counterculture's representative, became one of the most celebrated American artists in history. Strangely, his new role bestowed upon him the very values his works exposed. He grew rich, famous, and idolized. Also his works became what they portrayed: they were mass-produced and - consumed.

Regarding fame, Warhol once commented wryly on how fleeting it was: "In the future everybody will be world famous for fifteen minutes" (Warhol in Colacello, p. 31). To capture these fleeting moments in print, he founded *Andy Warhol's Interview* magazine. Its interviews covered famous personalities from Hollywood movie stars to presidents.

Warhol would be surrounded by the rich and famous for the rest of his life. He chose during one period to go out every night to restaurants, clubs, and art openings. Wherever Andy went, in his ever-present silver wig, people followed him. He socialized with the most renowned personalities in American pop history, including Mick Jagger, Liza Minelli, Truman Capote, Jimmy Carter, John Lennon, and Jacqueline Kennedy Onassis. His art openings were among the most popular in the artistic world of the 1960s.

The Factory. Staying close to his industrial roots, Warhol created the Factory, which was his art and film studio as well as a meeting place. It was there that he employed workers to help produce his silk screens of Campbell's soup cans, Brillo soap pad

▲ *Campbell's Soup*, 1968, an example of Warhol's pop art.

boxes, and Coca-Cola bottles. There also he created a new style of image representation: repetition. A 1963 piece in this style, *Lavender Disaster,* shows fifteen separate images of the electric chair on a purple background. Other works showed repetitions of deadly car accidents, tuna cans, the *Mona Lisa,* and idols such as Marilyn Monroe and Elvis Presley, all on white or solid color backgrounds. Such pieces were produced by the dozens at the Factory, where Warhol spent many waking hours. In 1966, after creating one of his last pop art illustrations—a series of floating silver aluminum "pillows," called *Aluminum Clouds*—Warhol declared pop art dead and began using the Factory for the next phase of his artistic career: moviemaking.

The silver screen. Warhol's moviemaking phase started in 1963 and lasted into the early 1970s. Like his other creative pieces, his movies were an expression of the counterculture, but the film medium allowed Warhol more freedom than before. His movies reflected a more cultish, underground aspect of the counterculture than his paintings ever did. They starred a wide array of characters, including female impersonators, poets, and cult stars. Furthermore, the movies were practically unedited—Warhol did not believe in taking anything out.

The movie *Sleep,* for instance, is six hours long and shows a series of ten-minute shots of a man sleeping, the camera focusing on different parts of his body. According to Warhol, the film "started with someone sleeping and it just got longer and longer" (Warhol in Coplans, p. 156). With titles and subjects such as *Heat, Trash, Bad, Couch, Sleep, Eat, Kiss, Camp,* and *Gerard Has His Hair Removed with Nair,* Warhol's movies enjoyed a quieter following than his art.

Shot. Warhol was working on a film at the Factory on June 3, 1968, when a woman named Valerie Solanis, from the Society for Cutting Up Men (SCUM), approached him. Angry at Warhol for not producing her screenplay, she shot him point-blank in the chest and abdomen three times. She then shot a visiting curator, Mario Amaya, and ran away after the gun jammed. Warhol was rushed to the hospital and pronounced clinically dead at 4:51 P.M. As a last effort, doctors cut him open, massaged his heart into functioning, and operated on him for five hours. Miraculously, he survived. Solanis turned herself in and was sent to a mental institution and then released.

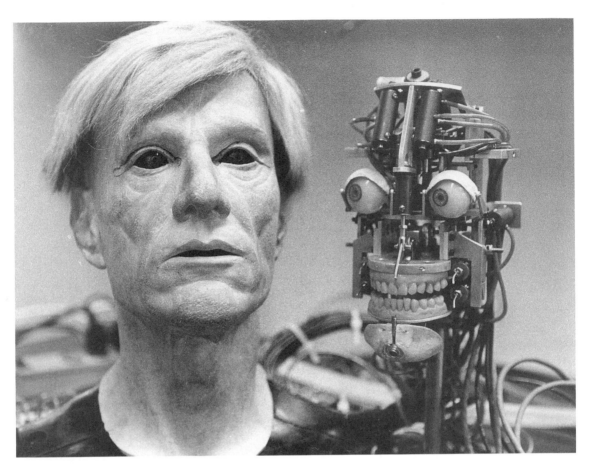

▲ A Factory project—crafting the head of a robot

About the experience, Warhol said, "Right when I was being shot and ever since, I knew that I was watching television. The channels switch, but it's all television" (Warhol, *The Philosophy,* p. 91). The story of his shooting *was* heavily covered on television but then quickly overshadowed by the shooting of Robert Kennedy just days later. For Warhol, the consequences were pain, difficult digestion, displaced muscles, and a chest full of scars. For Kennedy, the consequence was death.

Aftermath

Later work. Warhol was able to return to work after the shooting, although the effects of it, combined with relentless gall-

Sculpture

Warhol was greatly troubled by his inability to create sculpture that was as original as his paintings. His unsuccessful efforts included printing newspaper images on tin and then crumbling them. He talked also about designing a watch that measured twenty-four instead of twelve hours and started working at watch design in the months before he died.

bladder problems, slowed him down. Much of his work in the 1970s included film, retrospective shows on his past creations, and some portraits. Known for his early pop art, Warhol did not receive the same kind of attention for his later work.

The diaries. What kept Warhol busy during the last ten years of his life was creating *The Andy Warhol Diaries* with his friend Pat Hackett. Warhol and Hackett spoke on the phone every weekday morning for at least three hours. Hackett recorded every single conversation, eventually editing the lot of them down to about a third (over 800 pages) of their original size and publishing them. The project was very important to Warhol, who, figuring that he was going to be famous for longer than fifteen minutes, wanted to be understood.

The last days. The last time Warhol was seen in public was at a celebrity fashion show on February 17, 1987. He walked down the runway with Miles Davis, a musician whom Warhol greatly admired. Warhol offered to sketch a portrait for Davis for the payment of ten minutes of his jazz playing. They agreed on a date later in the week.

Unfortunately Warhol and Davis could never complete their deal. Warhol checked into "the place to have 'it' done," that is, checked into the hospital to have his gallbladder removed (Warhol, *The Andy Warhol Diaries,* p. 807). Hospitals frightened him. The day after the somewhat routine operation, Warhol died in his sleep. The public mourned the loss of an unconventional pop idol whose remarks were sometimes as curious as his art. Commenting on death, Warhol once said, "I don't believe in it, because you're not around to know that it's happened" (Warhol, *The Philosophy,* p. 123).

For More Information

Colacello, Bob. *Holy Terror: Andy Warhol Close Up.* New York: HarperCollins, 1990.

Coplans, John. *Andy Warhol.* New York: New York Graphic Society, 1990.

Warhol, Andy. *The Andy Warhol Diaries,* edited by Pat Hackett. New York: Warner Books, 1989.

Warhol, Andy. *The Philosophy of Andy Warhol: From A to B & Back Again.* New York and London: Harcourt Brace Jovanovich, 1975.

Allard Lowenstein

1929–1980

Personal Background

Parents. Gabriel Lowenstein was a teenage political activist in his native country, Lithuania. Arrested for helping to plan a general strike there, he was freed from jail on condition that he leave the country. He fled to the United States, where some of his relatives had already moved. After completing his education in New York at Columbia University, he began teaching at its College of Physicians and Surgeons.

Gabriel married Augusta Goldberg and the two started a family. They had a couple of sons, Bert and Larry, born four years apart. The burden of rearing a family on the $2,000 annual salary from the college weighed on Gabriel, and he abandoned his teaching to join relatives in the restaurant business. A third son, Allard Kenneth, was born on January 16, 1929. A year later Augusta Lowenstein died, leaving Gabriel to raise three young boys.

Within a year, Gabriel found a stepmother for his boys. Florence was a young Jewish woman who taught immigrants to speak and read English at a settlement house on the Lower East Side of New York. Gabriel married her, and the two set out to start a new life. They would later have a daughter named Dorothy.

Early life. Allard Lowenstein grew up in a troubled family. The two older boys refused to accept their stepmother. Also,

▲ Allard Lowenstein

Event: Student protests.

Role: An early anti-Vietnam War activist and still a believer in the American political system, Allard Lowenstein was convinced that "student power" could create necessary changes. In contrast to counterculture leaders, he succeeded in persuading thousands of young Americans of the 1960s to register to vote and to work within the political system for changes in the Vietnam War policy and in civil rights.

Gabriel had abandoned many of the Jewish traditions, in sharp contrast to Florence, who was a devoutly practicing Jew. If they were not fighting about religion, the two quarreled about money, which Gabriel began losing in his business ventures. Allard felt torn between his tender stepmother and his brilliant and opinionated father. He grew to love both, but to look to Florence for friendship and caring. She supported his interests, which ranged from politics to wrestling.

Since Gabriel had been a political activist, there was plenty of talk about politics in the Lowenstein home. Allard was drawn to the subject at an early age. When he was seven, he began passing out campaign fliers for Franklin D. Roosevelt. From that year on, he kept track of election returns and took stands on candidates for office. Young Allard, for example, opposed Fiorello La Guardia as mayor of New York, convinced that La Guardia had caused violent race riots in Harlem.

By age nine, Allard had taken an interest in the revolution in Spain, cheering for those who opposed the dictator Francisco Franco. This interest continued throughout his elementary school days. In his last year in elementary school, he organized a fund drive to help the Spanish resisters. The drive aimed to raise $5 for the cause, but Lowenstein's active leadership brought in $8.26.

College and politics. His father wanted Lowenstein to enroll in an Ivy League university—Harvard or Yale. Instead he chose to go to college at North Carolina University. It was a lucky decision, for at North Carolina Lowenstein met Frank Graham.

Graham was president of North Carolina University but would soon become a United States senator. After graduation in 1949, Lowenstein became a legislative assistant to Graham, and his political career began. For the next six years, he involved himself in Democratic politics.

Lowenstein also found time to earn a degree in law, which he received from Yale University in 1954. Before beginning to practice law, he decided to join the army. Lowenstein spent two years in the army, then returned home to begin law practice. But once more he was delayed. A friend asked him to travel to South Africa and report on the effects of apartheid, the policy of racial segregation there.

Lowenstein and two friends agreed to begin this investigation.

Brutal Mandate. Arriving in South Africa, the team witnessed firsthand the troubles caused by apartheid. South Africa, however, was not the part of Africa in which conditions for blacks were the worst. The three Americans heard stories about South West Africa, where blacks seemed to be treated even worse. That nation (now called Namibia) was so filled with racial hatred, mistreatment, and poverty that outsiders were barred from observing conditions there. Leaders of the black South West Africans secretly invited Lowenstein and his friends to visit them. The young Americans were smuggled in to speak with the black leaders and view the conditions. They were then smuggled out with papers describing what they had seen and heard. After some close brushes with arrest and even death there, the men returned to the United States. Lowenstein immediately began writing about their experiences. Called *Brutal Mandate,* his book called world attention to the terrible conditions under which blacks in South and South West Africa lived.

Lowenstein's Early Political Activities	
1950	Legislative assistant to Frank Graham
1950–1951	President, United States National Student Association
1952	National Chairman of Students for Stevenson
1956–1957	Educational consultant to the American Association for the United Nations (with Eleanor Roosevelt)
1958	Foreign policy assistant to Hubert Humphrey

Participation: Student Protests

Stanford. Lowenstein finally began to practice law in New York in 1960, but only for a year. He still found time for political action, serving as campaign chairman for congressional candidate William Ryan. Finding his law practice too confining, he left it in 1961 for a position as assistant dean and lecturer in political science at Stanford University in California. As the 1960s dawned, college campuses became centers of debate and demonstrations for civil rights and against American involvement in Vietnam. Much of this activity originated at the University of California at Berkeley. Nearby Stanford was drawn into the action.

Students at Berkeley demanded to have a voice in the way the school was governed. Seeking the same power, students at Stanford organized demonstrations. Lowenstein voiced his support for the students' ideas. On his way to becoming a Pied Piper of sorts, leading students to their glory, he started forming a group for civil rights actions. Lowenstein began his civil rights activism with a band of sixteen loyal Stanford students. Over the years, this group would grow to several thousand.

Plans were already being made to send students to Mississippi in a massive attempt to register black voters there. Independently, Lowenstein decided that the best chance for reform in America lay in organizing millions of students to work within the political system. A key to civil rights progress was mobilizing whites to participate in the struggle. With this in mind, Lowenstein began to call his friends to join in the southern civil rights demonstrations. He proved to be a capable organizer. (Lowenstein was later credited with encouraging as many as 25 million young Americans to become voters and hundreds to help in the demonstrations in Mississippi.)

University President J. Wallace Sterling, however, was not pleased with Lowenstein's aid to the rebel students at Stanford. As a result of his organizing activities, Lowenstein was fired.

The civil rights movement. For the next three years, Lowenstein lectured at North Carolina State University at Raleigh. From this position in the South, he was able to take an even more active role in the civil rights movement. He traveled to Mississippi to see conditions there firsthand. What he observed there struck him as worse than the beatings he had seen in South West Africa. Medgar Evers was a black organizer for the National Association for the Advancement of Colored People (NAACP). He had just been shot down in his own driveway by Mississippians opposed to civil rights (see **Bob Dylan**). Black and white civil rights leaders were outraged. "People were being beaten and arrested and terrorized, and nobody seemed to know or care," Lowenstein reported. "It was as if the Constitution of the United States had been repealed in Mississippi and didn't exist" (Lowenstein in Chafe, p. 180).

Something, he believed, must be done to bring pressure on Mississippi to accept black voters. Lowenstein remembered his days in South Africa, where a "day of mourning" was held on election day in protest of black oppression. Such action, he mused, suggested surrender to existing ways. What was needed was a positive day of demonstration. He decided to work with other civil rights groups to organize a dramatic demonstration.

The Student Nonviolent Coordinating Committee (SNCC) had been trying for some time to persuade blacks to register and vote, but their efforts had often resulted in beatings and imprisonment. Lowenstein thought it would call more attention to the problems in Mississippi to have a "day of voting." No one seems to know how this idea actually came about, but several of the civil rights leaders may have come up with it together. In any case, the idea was to hold a protest of Mississippi actions that kept blacks from registering and voting in the regular election. All the civil rights groups would organize an election for blacks. This would not be a legally binding vote but would be a newsworthy demonstration. Black leaders such as Charles Evers thought it was a good idea. They also thought the protest would be more dramatic if white students went to Mississippi to help with the registration and the balloting. In 1963 Lowenstein was given the task of raising money, recruiting workers, and publicizing the event.

Freedom Vote and Freedom Summer. Wherever Allard Lowenstein traveled, he made thousands of friends. His friendships were so lasting that he kept in touch with hundreds of college students and social activists by postcard and telephone most of his life. Now he called upon these friends to help organize, publicize, and raise funds for the first ever "Freedom Vote."

Black leaders called a black convention and nominated Aaron Henry, a black pharmacist, as candidate for governor of Mississippi and Ed King, a white minister, for lieutenant governor. Lowenstein returned to Stanford to meet with his old friends there and encourage them to get involved in the Mississippi action. One of them, Dennis Sweeney, wound up serving as an aide to Lowenstein throughout the affair. In the end, 55,000 black citizens of Mississippi voted at their local churches in the Freedom Vote. It raised considerable attention in Mississippi. White students gave the media plenty to write about and show on television. Many who came to help recruit voters and manage the voting were beaten or jailed.

Scare Tactics—The Deaths of Goodman, Schwerner, and Chaney

Two white volunteers, Andrew Goodman and Mickey Schwerner, arrived at the site of a church bombing in Mississippi with black civil rights worker James Chaney. After inspecting the church, the three left but were stopped and jailed for speeding. Later that night, they were released and then disappeared. Suspicions of foul play drew the Federal Bureau of Investigation (FBI) into the case. After five weeks of searching, on August 4, 1964, the bodies of the three civil rights workers were found buried in an earthen dam. Pursued in a wild car chase by the Ku Klux Klansmen, the three had been caught and murdered by members of the white racist group. Their purpose was to scare off civil rights volunteers, who, though frightened, refused to leave.

When jailed, they were threatened by police. Some just disappeared from the state—probably killed in panic by the local white citizens.

Lowenstein was himself harassed frequently. One evening he was arrested for failing to stop at a stop sign that didn't exist. Then he was arrested for loitering and threatened by the police with beatings. He came to his own rescue, identifying himself as a lawyer and demanding the right to one telephone call. In that one call, he talked to Franklin D. Roosevelt III, who he pretended was in direct contact with President John Kennedy. Lowenstein later told this story to his friends, explaining why the police treated him more gently after that arrest. Events such as these only served to build a stronger image of Lowenstein as a powerful leader of students.

One outcome of the Freedom Vote was a plan to carry out a "Freedom Summer" in 1964. Thousands of white students would be encouraged to work with black organizations to register blacks for the real elections. It is not clear who first developed the idea and even less clear who was in charge. Still, Lowenstein was an early leader in the event.

By this time, student movements throughout the nation were being influenced by radicals who called for violent action. The idea of no government at all or of government by collective agreement spread across the country. Some black groups, such as the NAACP, held to the cautious line of working within the system and with white advocates of civil rights. However, younger groups, such as the Student Nonviolent Coordinating Committee, began to disagree with these tactics. Black leaders in SNCC and other groups recognized their own abilities and distrusted white help.

The leaders of SNCC began to dominate the planning of Freedom Summer. Whether he fancied himself as the real leader or was impatient with SNCC, Lowenstein begin to withdraw from the project. His leaving was of little concern to young black leaders, since they were anyway beginning to think that improving conditions for blacks could best be handled with little involvement of whites.

As he withdrew from active direction of Freedom Summer, Lowenstein's personality seemed to change. His charm and energetic personality had persuaded many students to follow him into the civil rights movement. Now he seemed to feel that his followers should not question his decisions and his word should be law. As a result, some of his friends turned against him.

Though Lowenstein left the project, more than 1,000 whites descended on Mississippi to work with black civil rights volunteers that summer. Freedom Summer was, in the end, a limited success. It managed to get only 2,000 to 3,000 more blacks registered to vote. However, as a result of the project, black voters began to organize in the state. Also, the volunteers helped keep the public eye on racial abuses in Mississippi all summer long, and on actions that Americans could take to help stop them.

Getting America out of Vietnam. In 1966 Lowenstein married Jennifer Lyman, who would help him in his future campaigns against the war in Vietnam. The couple had three children: Frank Graham, Thomas Kennedy, and Katherine Eleanor. All were named for political friends of Lowenstein's.

The year following his marriage, Lowenstein began teaching at the City College of New York. It was here that he began his "dump Johnson campaign," an effort to get Lyndon Johnson out of the presidency. Johnson had been elected on a vow to end the Vietnam War. Instead, the war had dragged on, and more than 400,000 American soldiers had been committed to fighting it. Lyndon Johnson planned to run again for president in 1968. Lowenstein used his organizing ability to influence the Democratic nomination of a presidential candidate. He and his friends organized a Conference of Concerned Democrats to protest the war. Then Lowenstein set out to find another candidate for president instead of Lyndon Johnson. He called on his friend Robert Kennedy to enter the race at the convention. Kennedy, however, refused, so Lowenstein announced that he would support Eugene McCarthy for the office. Lowenstein held

▲ Lowenstein with a group of admirers outside one of his campaign head-quarters as he runs for reelection to the New York House of Representatives, October 23, 1970

firm in his support. When Robert Kennedy later did decide to enter the race, Lowenstein refused to help him. He had announced his commitment to McCarthy and would not go back on an agreement.

To eliminate Johnson, Lowenstein also became chairman of the Coalition for an Open Convention. This coalition hoped to replace some of the older, all-white delegations with people who were more sympathetic to civil rights and the antiwar movement. Support for Lowenstein's ideas grew so rapidly that Johnson decided not to run for reelection. The split among Democrats, however, cost them the election. Richard Nixon was elected president and claimed credit for withdrawing American forces from Vietnam.

Congress. Also in 1968, Lowenstein ran for Congress from the ninety-first district in New York. Elected, he served in the House of Representatives until 1971. In office he continued his vigorous opposition to the Vietnam War. He was one of the few in government to oppose the war on moral grounds, in contrast to others who came to oppose the war because it was becoming too expensive or too difficult to win. In a speech to the House, Lowenstein argued against Nixon's slow progress in withdrawing from the war:

> We cannot fight this war to keep governments in power that do not have popular support; governments that do not respond to the popular will. We have been in this particular orbit, this very bloody orbit, for many years now, and it is time to come home (Lowenstein in Stone and Lowenstein, p. 129).

Americans for Democratic Action. While Lowenstein served in Congress, politicians at home were redesigning the political districts. By the 1971 elections, his district had been redrawn in a way that gave Republicans the majority. He lost reelection to Congress but was not without a political base for very long. In 1971 Lowenstein became national chairman of the liberal (pro-change) organization Americans for Democratic Action (ADA). He taught at Yale and Harvard, continuing to oppose the Vietnam War through ADA. He also resumed his campaign to participate directly in government. In 1972 and again in 1974 he ran unsuccessfully for a seat in Congress.

With the power of ADA behind him, Lowenstein continued to speak out about political issues. So outspoken was his antiwar stance that he at one time was blacklisted by the White House. (Lowenstein was number seven on a list of President Nixon's enemies.) His 1970s activities included opposing the Nixon cover-up of the Watergate affair, in which presidential aides acted illegally by raiding the headquarters of the Democratic party. He also acted as adviser to California governor Jerry Brown in his bid for the presidency, called for investigations of the assassinations of John and Robert Kennedy, and served as U.S. representative to the United Nations Mission on Human Rights and as United Nations Ambassador for Special Political Affairs.

Aftermath

Divorce. Lowenstein's commitment to politics took him away from home frequently and interfered with his family life in other ways. In 1978 he and Jennifer divorced. Devoted for years to the family and her husband's quests, she set out to develop herself. "Maybe there was some sense," she explained, "that ... I want[ed] to do all the things that the women's movement started to talk about" (Chafe, p. 418).

The year after the divorce, Lowenstein went off again on one of his many trips. This time his purpose was to see what changes had occurred in Africa. On this final trip overseas, he took another look at apartheid in South Africa and studied the independent government of Zimbabwe.

The counterculture and the end. Since the early 1960s, young Americans had grown more and more restless. Some, such as Abbie Hoffman, had given up hope that working within the system could bring about change and had begun to talk of revolution. These champions of immediate action won over some of Lowenstein's early supporters. Several of his old Stanford associates became part of the movement to withdraw from society. A few joined communes, groups in which dissenters lived isolated from society. Some had chosen to drop out of society by using drugs. One of these was a former Stanford student and Lowenstein assistant, Dennis Sweeney. Sweeney had fallen out with Lowenstein and joined the SNCC in 1964. He and others had become even more out of step with Lowenstein when Lowenstein appeared to compromise with Democratic leaders in the bid to break up some of the older, all-white delegations by seating new delegates in the 1968 convention.

Lowenstein continued to work for civil rights and political reform long after the U.S. withdrawal from Vietnam. But repeated defeats at the polls made him wonder about his own choice to work within the system. Meanwhile, his old friend Sweeney had turned to using LSD ("acid") and had become increasingly tormented. Sweeney became more and more convinced that the world of politics was against him. Still, Lowenstein continued to communicate with and ask about his old friend, even though Sweeney seemed on the verge of madness.

On March 14, 1980, Sweeney called on Lowenstein in his law office. He was convinced that Lowenstein was responsible for major disasters—the death of the mayor of San Francisco, the crash of an airliner with 250 people aboard, and even the voices he seemed to hear in his madness. Lowenstein's loyalty to old friends made him accept Sweeney's call. As the two spoke in Lowenstein's law office, Sweeney drew out a revolver and fired seven shots, killing his long-time friend.

In tribute, Edward Kennedy summed up the accomplishments of Allard Lowenstein:

> There are black people in Mississippi who can vote because he was there in the civil rights movement.... There are American sons living out normal lives who did not die in Vietnam because he was there in New Hampshire in 1968.... There are political prisoners in the Soviet Union whose cause was heard ... because he was there in the United Nations. (Chafe, p. 463)

For More Information

Chafe, William Henry. *Never Stop Running: Allard Lowenstein and the Struggle to Save American Liberalism*. New York: Basic Books, 1993.

Stone, Gregory, and Douglas Lowenstein, eds. *Lowenstein: Acts of Courage and Belief*. New York: Harcourt Brace Jovanovich, 1983.

Viorst, Milton. *Fire In the Streets: America in the '60s*. New York: Simon and Schuster, 1979.

Immigration Reform and Experience

1924

National Origins Act of 1924 limits number of immigrants through quotas that favor European countries and Canada.

1954–1979

More than 98,000 Vietnamese refugees enter the United States under special refugee acts passed by Congress.

1953–1954

U.S. government conducts Operation Wetback to deport illegals and *braceros* who have remained in the country illegally.

1951

Mexican Americans form Hermandad Mexicana Nacional to protect migrant workers in San Diego, California.

1942

Congress reaches Migratory Labor Agreement with Mexico for importing *braceros,* or temporary workers.

1965

Under President Lyndon B. Johnson, Congress passes Immigration Act of 1965, which eliminates quota system.

1968

Bert Corona helps organize division of Hermandad for Mexican immigrants in Los Angeles.

1970

Le Ly Hayslip immigrates to the United States from Vietnam.

1986

Immigration Reform and Control Act offers to pardon illegals who entered the United States before 1982 and allows them to apply for citizenship.

1975

Vietnam War ends. More than a half million Vietnamese refugees begin to immigrate to the United States.

1973

U.S. troops leave Vietnam. Immigration laws give preference to Vietnam refugees.

1971

Dixon-Arnett Bill imposes fines on employers who knowingly hire "illegal aliens."

IMMIGRATION REFORM AND EXPERIENCE

Over the years, U.S. policy toward immigrants, or new-comers from other nations, has been shaped and reshaped. In the first half of the twentieth century, Asian immigrants were excluded from the United States, and most Latin Americans were accepted only on a temporary basis to fill the demand for workers. These policies changed greatly after 1965.

President Lyndon B. Johnson, inspired by his vision of a Great Society, was committed to far-reaching reform in immigration, just as he was in civil rights. Under Johnson, Congress passed the Immigration Act of 1965, which did away with a quota system that had been used for decades and that favored the nations of western Europe and Canada.

Under the pre-1965 quota system, U.S. immigration law had given each nation different limits. There were exceptions to the quotas; refugee acts had been passed at certain times to admit extra immigrants fleeing from persecution or war. In 1942, when there was a shortage of farm workers because of World War II, the United States and Mexico entered a special agreement. The Migratory Labor Agreement encouraged Mexicans to migrate at harvest time and pick crops for American farm owners. Hundreds of thousands migrated for temporary work. And after the war, a continued need for temporary workers led the United States to renew this labor agreement with Mexico.

Such agreements were rooted in the history of the Southwest, originally settled not by Americans but by Mexicans. In 1848, when the region changed hands, the 75,000 Mexicans there became U.S. citizens. Suddenly those crossing the Mexican border became "immigrants." A century later, they would be divided into legal and illegal immigrants.

About 61,000 Mexican immigrants were legally admitted to the United States from 1941 to 1950. At the same time, many illegal immigrants crossed the Mexican border without notifying the proper authorities. Added to these illegals were the temporary workers who stayed in the United States past their deadlines. Expected to return to Mexico at the end of their labor contracts, they instead stayed in America.

When American business slowed in the 1950s, the government cracked down on the illegal aliens. It conducted Operation Wetback, a campaign to deport, or send home, Mexican illegals as well as the *braceros* (temporary workers) who had remained in the country past their deadlines. Some 1.1 million were deported. In the process, many legal immigrants fell suspect, and some were mistakenly sent back to Mexico. Meanwhile, the crackdown did not seem to have a great effect. It served only to slow the entrance of Mexican migrants for a few months. Jobs in Mexico were scarce, and American business owners remained willing to hire illegals. They could be paid less because they did not enjoy the same minimum wage protection as U.S. citizens.

In the 1950s, Mexican Americans began objecting to the poor working conditions and pay, and started forming separate groups to improve their situation. Led by Phil and Albert Usquiano, Hermandad Mexicana Nacional, the Mexican National Brotherhood, for example, was organized in

1951 to protect the Mexican migrants who were working in San Diego, California. But new workers kept migrating to the United States—445,000 in 1956 alone. Most of these migrants applied first for work on farms. Farm owners, aware of the steady supply of new migrants to draw from, kept taking advantage of the workers. Salaries, food, and housing were poor.

Number of Legal Immigrants—1961–1990		
	Mexicans	**Vietnamese**
1981–1990	1,653,300	401,400
1971–1980	637,200	179,700
1961–1970	443,300	4,600

The new 1965 law changed the complexion of the legal immigrant population drastically, most immigrants to the United States now coming from Asia and Latin America instead of Canada and the nations of western Europe.

Many of the Asians, such as **Le Ly Hayslip,** were escaping the Vietnam War. As the war wound down, the number of refugees trying to enter the United States grew so large that the government had to set up camps in countries such as Thailand to hold and screen the applicants. The war ended in 1975, after which the United States accepted more than a half million refugees from Vietnam and neighboring countries. They had to make major cultural adjustments in the United States, yet it became a common goal among these immigrants to learn English and apply for full citizenship.

Mexico supplied the largest number of legal immigrants from Latin America, and many Mexicans continued to enter the country without legal documents, or papers. (These illegal migrants were in fact called "undocumented workers.") The government again conducted a crackdown in 1969, its agents taking suspects and illegals to the border and returning them to Mexico without a hearing or a trial. This time the workers had more help than before. A year earlier **Bert Corona** and some others had opened a Los Angeles, California, office of Hermandad to protect illegals there. Bringing a number of cases to court, Hermandad won some trials in which victims were improperly arrested. There had been no proof that they deserved to be deported. A leader in several Mexican American groups, Corona felt that immigrants

▲ A disabled Vietnamese war orphan is carried from a U.S. Air Force plane at Travis Air Force Base in California; the child is one of the first orphans evacuated from Vietnam, April 7, 1975

needed to be taught that they possessed certain rights even if they were not U.S. citizens. They could, for example, refuse to give the immigration office the information it needed to deport them. If they did not supply certain facts—what country they came from, when and how they came over, and through which port of entry—the immigration office would have to come up with this evidence on its own. Finding out the missing facts would take time, during which a lawyer could perhaps build a case for the migrant's staying in America. Or perhaps the whole issue would be dropped.

Corona believed that the illegals had a right to try to prove that they deserved to remain in the United States. To a certain degree, ruled the Supreme Court, the Constitution protected all people in the nation, citizen or not. Everyone enjoyed the right to a lawyer and reasonable bail.

In the 1970s, the government again tried to restrict traffic across the border. Laws were passed to force employers not to hire Mexican workers, and attempts were made by the Immigration and Naturalization Service (INS) to close the border between Mexico and the United States. By 1986 pressure from interested groups had persuaded Congress to enact a new law. Illegal Mexican residents were still denied the right to work in the United States, but those who had arrived "illegally" before 1982 were granted amnesty (that is, they could apply for U.S. citizenship without fear of being deported). Around 3 million came forward, turning to Hermandad and other organizations to help them learn English and complete the necessary papers for full citizenship.

Le Ly Hayslip

1949-

Personal Background

Ky La. Le Ly Hayslip was named Phung Thi Le Ly on her birthday, December 19, 1949. Born in Ky La, a small village located near Da Nang in central Vietnam, she was the youngest of six children and a small, sickly baby. Her mother raised her on water buffalo milk, nicknaming the child "she who is nourished by God." Le Ly's family was Buddhist, and her parents brought her up according to traditional Vietnamese values. Her father taught her to love and worship her ancestors and, setting an example for his children, placed great value on freedom. Her mother taught Le Ly to be humble, loyal, and highly moral and to fulfill one's duty to a husband.

During Le Ly's childhood, Ky La was continually attacked. The village suffered due to its location, which trapped the villagers in the war between the North Vietnamese and the South Vietnamese. The South Vietnamese supported President Ngo Dinh Diem, a Catholic with strong ties to the United States. The North Vietnamese, led by the Communist leader Ho Chi Minh, supported Vietnamese independence from Western domination. On the side of the North Vietnamese were the Viet Cong, guerrilla rebels in South Vietnam who opposed its government. The people of Ky La were torn between the two opposing sides, whose soldiers often entered the village and forced the people to help them. For example, the

▲ **Le Ly Hayslip**

Event: Vietnamese immigration to the United States.

Role: Le Ly Hayslip survived the Vietnam War and immigrated to the United States, eventually receiving her citizenship. She helped establish ties between Vietnam and the United States by founding a nonprofit relief agency for her home village in Vietnam and publishing her autobiography to share her experiences as a Vietnamese immigrant. The Oliver Stone film *Heaven and Earth* is her life story.

South Vietnamese dug trenches, hid weapons in the village, and tried to obtain information about the Viet Cong. When the South Vietnamese left, the Viet Cong would enter Ky La, steal the weapons, and use the villagers' houses as hideouts.

To avoid being killed, many villagers simply did what both the South Vietnamese and the Viet Cong demanded. Le Ly and her family, however, supported the Viet Cong and Ho Chi Minh for several reasons. South Vietnam had a Catholic leader, and Catholics often harmed the nation's Buddhists by burning their temples and fields. Also, Le Ly, along with the Viet Cong, believed that President Diem was under the control of the United States and that Vietnam, previously a French colony, had a right to its independence. Because they viewed the North as more independent than the South, many Vietnamese villagers supported the northern forces.

Viet Cong. Le Ly's closest brother, San Ban, left Ky La in 1954 and traveled to Hanoi to fight for the North. Le Ly herself joined the Viet Cong when she was approximately ten years old. She, however, was not sent away to fight. Along with other villagers, she prepared booby traps and decoys for the Viet Cong, and her main job was to inform them of enemy movements within the village. The Viet Cong took advantage of the fact that Le Ly was only a child, instructing her to make friends with the American soldiers and steal their supplies. Le Ly stole weapons such as grenades and basic items like toothpaste, soap, and bug repellent for the northern forces.

As a Viet Cong supporter, Le Ly was captured and beaten by the South Vietnamese on several occasions. Her mother's cousin, who had contacts with the government, rescued Le Ly the first time she was caught. The second time, the South Vietnamese took Le Ly to a place called My Thi, a prisoner camp famous for its cruelty. Many people died there, and those released often returned home insane. Le Ly was tortured at My Thi before her mother and cousin again came to her rescue. This time, however, the Viet Cong grew suspicious. Since few people were released from My Thi so quickly, the Viet Cong assumed Le Ly had switched sides and joined the South Vietnamese. When Le Ly returned to her village, the Viet Cong arrested her, held a people's court, and condemned her to death. Two Viet Cong soldiers took her into the jungle to shoot her, but raped her instead. According to Vietnamese beliefs, Le Ly was ruined for marriage and therefore condemned as an outcast for the rest of her life.

Saigon. Le Ly's life was in danger, and she could no longer live safely in Ky La. In 1965 she escaped with her mother to Saigon to look for her sister-in-law Hai. As they searched for Hai, Le Ly and her mother begged food and shelter from distant friends. In Le Ly's words, "Here we were less than the wind—vagabonds with only the clothes on our backs—ghosts who, unlike real people, had no place to sleep or even a way to keep ourselves fed" (Hayslip, *When Heaven and Earth Changed Places,* p. 115). When they located Hai, however, she could not help them. Hai worked as a servant and lived in her employer's house with no place for anyone else in her tiny room.

Luckily, Le Ly and her mother found jobs as servants in the house of a wealthy man named Anh. They lived in his house, and Le Ly became familiar with city conveniences such as indoor plumbing, which was not part of her country life. Le Ly lived there happily for three months until she fell in love with Anh. When Anh's wife realized Le Ly was pregnant, she threw both Le Ly and her mother out of the house. They could not return to Ky La, nor could they stay in Saigon. With nowhere else to go, they moved to Da Nang to join Le Ly's sister Lan.

Da Nang. Lan worked as a tea girl in Da Nang. Tea girls adopted American hairdos and clothes, befriended American soldiers, and often lived only on the presents of their boyfriends. While their mother stayed with a friend, Lan shared her small apartment with Le Ly until the baby was born. However, Lan viewed her younger sister as a burdensome country girl who interrupted all the partying that normally occurred. Le Ly, on the other hand, felt terrified of the American soldiers who frequented Lan's house and felt guilty about her dependence on her sister.

After Le Ly's first son, Hung, was born, she moved out of Lan's small apartment. Le Ly was fifteen years old at the time. She could not return to Ky La—not only because it was dangerous but also because her father was furious with her for becoming an unwed mother. Although he eventually forgave her and came to visit, Le Ly remained in Da Nang to support herself, her mother, and her new son. Other girls sold small items to the foreigners, who always seemed to have money, so Le Ly also went into the souvenir business. For several years, she sold items such as toothpaste, newspapers, and sunglasses to the American soldiers. She would buy these items in one place, then travel somewhere where these items were scarce and she could sell them for higher prices. Now that Le Ly maintained close contact with American soldiers, they no longer terrified her. She learned enough English to conduct business and became good friends with several Americans, despite her mother's disapproval.

Culture clash. Le Ly witnessed many social changes in Vietnam that deeply affected her. Traditional Vietnamese values were replaced by foreign ones as a result of the war. The influx of American money produced a new, wealthy class of people who valued American ways of life. The elderly, who were formerly treated with the utmost respect, now begged for food from the wealthy to keep from starving to death. Once Le Ly returned to Ky La only to find that the Americans had leveled half the village in order to gain a better fighting zone. Village children ate garbage, and the surrounding jungle was transformed into a bombed-out desert. For Le Ly, however, the worst part was the destruction of the Buddhist shrines:

> Houses could be rebuilt and damaged dikes repaired—but the loss of our temples and shrines meant the death of our culture itself. It meant that a generation of children would grow up without fathers to teach them about ancestors or the rituals of worship. Families would lose records of their lineage and with them the umbilicals [cords] to the very root of our society—not just old buildings and books, but *people* who once lived and loved.... Our ties to our past were being severed, setting us adrift on a sea of borrowed Western materialism [preoccupation with possessions], disrespect for the elderly, and selfishness. (Hayslip, *When Heaven and Earth Changed Places,* p. 195)

The rapid changes convinced Le Ly that she should not raise her son, Hung, in Vietnam. When her father, driven desperate by the war, committed suicide, Le Ly decided that Vietnam was only a country of death and that when the opportunity arose, she would immigrate to America.

While in Da Nang, Le Ly held many jobs, living hand to mouth to support herself, Hung, and her mother. She worked as a hospital nurse and as a waitress in a casino. Once, she was desperate enough that she sold herself to two American soldiers for $400—enough money to support herself, her mother, and her son for an entire year. Although she was not interested in boyfriends, she eventually met an American named Ed who offered to marry her and take her back with him to San Diego. Ed was twice her age and Le Ly was not in love with him, but she cared for him and agreed to become his wife. They married secretly in Da Nang, because Le Ly's mother would have forbidden her daughter's marriage to an American.

On February 11, 1970, Le Ly gave birth to her second son, Tommy. She prepared to leave Vietnam with her family, meanwhile experiencing poor treatment from her community because she had married an American. She was shunned and often cheated in her business dealings. There was difficulty too with the government, which obstructed emigration. Officials required enormous amounts of paperwork, and Le Ly spent most of her life savings paying officers who required bribes in exchange for the required documents. Finally, on May 27, 1970, Le Ly and her two sons immigrated to the United States via Hawaii to begin their new life.

Participation: Vietnamese Immigration

The first year. Le Ly found adjusting to her new life in San Diego difficult for several reasons. Refrigerators and supermarkets, for example, were new to her. The first time she went grocery shopping, Le Ly filled a whole cart with one food item because she was accustomed to stocking extra food in case of shortages. She was shocked to discover that Americans did not bargain for the price of items as in Vietnam. Also, Le Ly encountered some American customs that terrified her, such as Halloween. Many Vietnamese people believe in ghosts, so the costumed children who knocked on her door on Halloween night shocked Le Ly. She spent the rest of the night in bed shaking with terror.

Problems also arose due to differences between American and Vietnamese values. The traditional Vietnamese value humble behavior and group harmony. Americans value independence and often consider humble behavior as passive or weak. Given these differences, Ed's family viewed Le Ly as a fragile woman who could not take care of herself or her husband. Le Ly, meanwhile, felt lonely and isolated because nobody knew Vietnamese or understood her previous experiences and the ordeals she endured. Her new family preferred Ed's son, Tommy, to her first son, Hung (who was now called Jimmy), and sometimes commented unkindly about her as if she were not there. Her husband's friends laughed at her mannerisms, such as the way she bowed when pouring tea. Furthermore, money was a continual problem because Ed, a construction engineer, had trouble finding a permanent job. One year after Le Ly immigrated to the United States, Ed was transferred back to Vietnam, and Le Ly happily returned with him.

Return to Vietnam. Le Ly and her family returned to Vietnam for over a year, living mainly in An Khe and Saigon. When Le Ly had first left for the States, she was too ashamed to tell her mother she had married an American and instead instructed a maid to simply tell her mother that she was gone. Upon returning, Le Ly apologized to her mother, who refused to believe that she had emigrated. In the spring of 1972, American troops began to withdraw from Vietnam, and the communists stepped up the fighting with small local skirmishes. Once, during a stay in An Khe, the town was attacked. Dishes fell off the shelves, lights went out, and Le Ly hid with her family underneath the table.

After more than a year in Vietnam, Ed's job ended. Saigon had not yet fallen to communist forces but had grown increasingly dangerous after the American withdrawal. It was very unsafe because there were many prostitutes, drug dealers, and thieves. As rents and other prices soared, Le Ly tried to convince her family, especially her sister Lan, to return with her to the United States. Everybody refused, and Lan reminded her of the letters of misery she had written during her one year abroad. So it was with a heavy heart that Le Ly returned to the United States on July 17, 1972.

Back to the United States. Upon her return, Le Ly continued to experience difficulties. She was unhappy in her marriage because she was not in love with Ed, and they disagreed about many things, such as the way to raise their children. Furthermore, problems with Ed's relatives continued; they regarded her as a woman who had married solely for money. Some time later, when Ed grew sick and began to cough uncontrollably, Le Ly took him to a doctor. The doctor diagnosed him with chronic emphysema, and Ed died in the hospital shortly thereafter. Le Ly's culture taught her that the family, especially the husband, stood at the center of everything that was important, and Ed's death left her with feelings of guilt for not loving and serving him enough. She could only ease her conscience through her faith—by constructing a shrine to Ed according to her Buddhist beliefs and offering food and flowers to his soul.

Like most Vietnamese, Le Ly believed in working. Ed had forbidden her to work outside the home, but after his death, Le Ly experienced severe financial difficulties and so took her first job in the States. She found work as a housekeeper, and later as a nurse for $2.50 an hour, which was the most money she had ever earned. Slowly Le Ly grew more Americanized. She learned to drive and eventually saved enough money to buy her own car, yet she continued to experience misunderstanding and prejudice because of her background. For example, it is common in Vietnam for elder children to care for their younger siblings for short periods of time. Once, when Jimmy was seven, she left him to baby-sit Tommy while she went grocery shopping, and because she did not hire a sitter, her neighbor reported her to the police for child neglect.

The fall of Saigon. In early 1975, President Gerald Ford began to evacuate the few U.S. troops still in Vietnam. The end of the war was approaching, and clearly North Vietnam was going to be the victor.

Back in the United States, Le Ly worried about her family members in Vietnam, many of whom were in danger from the northern forces. The North Vietnamese would consider her sister Lan, whose sons both had American fathers, a traitor. Furthermore, Le Ly's immigration to America drew suspicion to the family. When Lan's telegram for help arrived on April 19, 1975, Le Ly realized that unless she rescued her sister and nephews, they would die. But thousands of Vietnamese people were trying to leave the country at this time. All official channels were clogged; even Lan's American boyfriend could do nothing to help them.

Through her Asian friends, Le Ly had met a U.S. army soldier named Dennis Hayslip who had fallen deeply in love with her. Dennis had asked Le Ly to marry him, but she had refused. When Dennis discovered that Le Ly needed help, he offered to go to Vietnam and rescue her sister if Le Ly agreed to marry him. Vietnamese beliefs hold that individuals are free to think about love but are often fated to marry someone else. This perhaps helped change Le Ly's mind. In any case, when Dennis proposed another time, Le Ly consented to the bargain.

True to his word, Dennis flew to Vietnam and rescued Lan only two days before Saigon fell to the North Vietnamese forces. Most refugees had no time to plan their emigration, escaping any way possible, by military aircraft, by boat, or by foot. Many people were killed or robbed during their attempts to escape; others simply starved to death.

Saigon, South Vietnam's capital city, fell to the communists on April 30, 1975. Tens of thousands of Vietnamese afterward fled the country and tried to immigrate to the United States. During the first immigration wave, which occurred in 1975, approximately 132,000 Vietnamese arrived in the United States. These immigrants were somewhat wealthier and better educated than their later counterparts, and Americans viewed them with sympathy, as people who needed help and to whom America had a moral obligation. Le Ly's sister would fall into this first wave of immigrants.

While Dennis was gone, Le Ly spent three weeks anxiously watching the fall of Saigon on television. Dennis, however, returned safely with Lan and her sons, although Lan had been robbed of most of her life savings and barely escaped with her life. Le Ly kept her part of the bargain, and on July 21, 1975, she married Dennis Hayslip.

The United States was legally unprepared for the large numbers of Vietnamese immigrants. The 1952 Immigration and Nationality Act set limits on immigration and provided for the entrance of only a couple of thousand Vietnamese. Congress, therefore, passed several resettlement acts between 1975 and 1980 to deal specifically with refugees from Vietnam and its neighboring countries. In 1980 the Refugee Act was passed, granting asylum to persons fleeing a country for persecution based on race, religion, nationality, or affiliation with a particular group. Approximately 900,000 refugees escaped to the United States between 1975 and 1989.

Continued troubles. Le Ly Hayslip's final son, Alan, was born on December 19, 1975. Despite this blessing, however, her new marriage did not go well. Her husband, Dennis, was a deeply religious Baptist and disagreed with her Buddhist beliefs and her independent nature. Protective and jealous, he drank heavily, and often threatened her or sabotaged her projects. For example, when Hayslip opened her home to Vietnamese children who had no place to live, her husband grew furious with jealousy. When she opened a delicatessen, he stole her car and her money until the business failed and Le Ly suffered a nervous breakdown. Things progressed from bad to worse, and when divorce became likely, her husband kidnapped Alan. Alan was eventually returned safely to Hayslip, and shortly thereafter the police found her husband suffocated in his van. Shocked by his death, Hayslip continued to deal with tragedy by turning to her faith as she had in the past:

> More than the lightness of a lifted burden, it was the same quiet, transcending joy I eventually felt after my father's death, when he began to visit me in dreams. Then I learned that I would never be alone in life, that only by letting go would I have the capacity to reach for more. Now, having lost two soulmates, I felt ready for my next stage of growth. (Hayslip, *Child of War,* p. 183)

Aftermath

Independence. After her husband's death, Hayslip studied to obtain U.S. citizenship. She took business classes and successfully invested the insurance money she received from Dennis's death. She opened an extremely successful Vietnamese restaurant called Hollylinh and, with Jimmy's help, started writing her autobiogra-

---

A Second Wave

A second wave of approximately 127,000 Vietnamese entered the United States in 1977. While the American people had welcomed the first wave, their reception for the second wave was cooler. These later immigrants, often called "boat people," were generally poorer and less educated than previous refugees. Seen as fortune seekers or people fleeing economic depression, they were often resented by Americans and accused of communism.

phy. By 1985 they had completed almost 300 pages, despite her third-grade education. She also maintained her Buddhist beliefs by frequenting a Buddhist temple and obtaining spiritual advice from the monks. Although her sons tried to convert her to Christianity, Hayslip held steadfastly to her Buddhist faith.

Confronting the past. Despite her financial success, Hayslip remained unhappy. She wished to return to Vietnam to pay her respects to her ancestors and visit her mother once more before her death. In the late 1980s, however, the United States had no formal relations with Vietnam. Visas were difficult to obtain and the government was suspicious of anyone wishing to travel there, especially a Vietnamese returning home.

Yet Hayslip persisted until she succeeded, returning once again to Vietnam in 1986, after sixteen years in the United States. She had many reasons to fear returning to Vietnam. As a youth, the Viet Cong had listed her name on their death list, and she was known as a black marketeer. She visited Jimmy's father, Anh, and showed him pictures of his other children, whom he had sent to live in the United States. Next she sought out her relatives in Da Nang and Ky La, only to discover that in some ways the war had not yet ended. Her relatives greeted her with a mixture of fear and joy; they feared for their safety because of her visit. Despite the tensions, however, Hayslip was able to visit with her mother.

During her stay in Vietnam, Hayslip witnessed the agonizing poverty brought about by the war and communist rule. After leaving, she realized she could not ignore what she had seen and confessed to a friend:

> I'm always thinking about Vietnam—what I can and should do to help. In Da Nang and Saigon, outside restaurants like this, cripples and beggars line up for food all day long. The scraps we throw away daily could feed those people for a week. It just isn't right.... Here, I work like crazy and all I get for my troubles are more bills and more worries and headaches. Am I really so much better off with two houses instead of one, or three houses instead of two? Where does it all end? (Hayslip, *Child of War,* p. 256)

Hayslip, who by this time was a millionaire, decided to use her wealth to help her people in Vietnam. She founded a relief agency called Dong Tay Hoi Ngo, or East Meets West, and also involved herself in Youth Ambassadors of America, an organization dedicated to improving relations with Vietnam. In 1989 her autobiography, *When Heaven and Earth Changed Places,* was published. Hayslip regarded this as a great accomplishment because she saw the autobiography as a way to help America understand the sufferings and trials of the Vietnamese people as well as a lesser-known side of its own history. Her story reached an even larger audience when the filmmaker Oliver Stone made the autobiography into a major motion picture, *Heaven and Earth.*

Phung Thi Le Ly Hayslip currently lives with her sons in southern California. Her foundation, East Meets West, has worked to improve conditions in Vietnam by building structures such as schools and clinics near her home village of Ky La and by providing relief in other areas.

For More Information

Hayslip, Le Ly. *Child of War, Woman of Peace.* New York: Doubleday, 1993.

Hayslip, Le Ly. *When Heaven and Earth Changed Places.* New York: Doubleday, 1989.

Rutledge, Paul James. *The Vietnamese Experience in America.* Bloomington: Indiana University Press, 1992.

Bert Corona

1918-

Personal Background

Child of the revolution. Bert Corona was born into a revolutionary family. At the age of thirteen, his father, Noe, began to fight in the Mexican Revolution to overthrow the long and corrupt rule of Porfirio Díaz. Noe joined the forces of Pancho Villa, one of the most powerful rebels.

About 1911 Noe Corona was assigned to seal off Chihuahua City, which threatened to send out federal troops against Villa's forces. There he met Margarita Escápite Salayandía. Margarita and her mother, Ynez Salayandía y Escápite, were rebels in their own right. Both had decided to ignore the general feeling in Mexico that women should stay home, bear children, and restrict themselves to tending the household. Ynez became one of the few female doctors in Mexico, and Margarita became director of a teacher's college. Also, they were Protestants in a mostly Catholic country.

After fighting in the Battle of Juárez, which resulted in Díaz's fleeing the country, Noe returned to woo Margarita. The two married twice, in the Mexican city of Juárez and in El Paso, Texas. They settled in El Paso, and their first two children were born there. Bert was the second child and first son, born May 29, 1918.

Early life. Corona attended primary schools in El Paso. It was in these schools that he first experienced racism. Although he was

▲ **Bert Corona**

Event: Defending the rights of Mexican immigrants.

Role: As a builder of the Hermandad Mexicana in Los Angeles and organizer of the brotherhood throughout the United States, and as one of the founders of Centros de Acción Social Autónomo, Bert Corona has defended the rights of Mexican Americans who entered the United States without official documentation.

spared because he already spoke English, other students were spanked and forced to wash their mouths with soap for speaking their own language, Spanish. Margarita objected to these actions so strongly that she took Bert out of the El Paso schools and sent him to a boarding school in Albuquerque, New Mexico. He attended Harvard Boys School for the fourth and fifth grades. One of Corona's early protest experiences occurred in the fifth grade.

The Mexican students at Harvard often objected to the ideas of history presented by their Anglo teachers. For talking back to the teachers, some students were sent to the physical education teacher to be spanked. When the students protested, school administrators threatened to throw some of them out of school. The students organized a strike, refusing to attend class until their demands were met. It was successful in keeping the students from being expelled, forcing the physical education teacher to apologize, and putting a stop to spankings for just questioning a teacher. In his oral biography, Corona proudly remembers that "This was my first strike!" (Corona in García, p. 46). It would not be his last.

Athletic scholarship. Corona returned to El Paso and attended El Paso High School. There he played basketball on the varsity team, despite his young age—he had advanced through school so rapidly that he graduated high school at age sixteen. Corona was very young, so he played two years on El Paso community teams before accepting an athletic scholarship to the University of Southern California.

In 1936 a full athletic scholarship was very different from the scholarships of later years. Corona found that his scholarship was really a recommendation to a company that was willing to hire him. An athletic scholarship meant that a student could work full- or part-time while playing university sports and studying. Corona began taking a full course of studies in commercial law while working nearly full-time at his "scholarship" job. Because he had worked for a medical drug company in El Paso, he found a job at the Brunswick Pharmaceutical Company. It was there that he got his first taste of labor organizing.

The Longshoremen's Union. Brunswick hired nearly 2,000 employees who were not yet organized by the labor unions. When the Longshoremen's Union decided to organize farm workers in

Orange County, south of Los Angeles, Brunswick seemed to the union officers to be a good place to find help. The union asked Brunswick employees to help organize the farm workers. Corona accepted the invitation. He was always ready to support any cause he thought would help Mexican Americans, and many of the farm workers were Mexican immigrants.

Corona helped recruit union members and led them in strikes for better wages and better treatment by the farmers. In 1936, for example, he led 2,500 Mexican workers in a strike that stopped work on the region's $20-million orange crop.

Soon after he agreed to help the Longshoremen's Union with farm workers, the union also decided to organize warehouse workers, starting with the Brunswick company. At that time, medical warehouse workers were receiving half the pay of warehouse workers in the food industries. Corona agreed to help organize a union for Brunswick workers and was fired for his efforts. By this time, he had decided that helping unions was more important than his studies at the university. When Harry Bridges of the Congress of Industrial Organizations (CIO) offered him another job as a union organizer, Corona decided to temporarily abandon his college education. For nearly a decade, he served the CIO as an organizer for the canning and packing industries and for Allied Workers of America. Working with more seasoned organizers such as César Chávez, he learned to be an excellent organizer and his fame grew.

Politics. By 1948 Corona had grown concerned about the mistreatment of "wetbacks" (people who came from Mexico without the permission of the United States government). Two years

> ## Some of the Political Activities of Bert Corona
>
> | | |
> |---|---|
> | 1959 | With Eduardo Quevada, organized the Mexican American Political Association (MAPA). |
> | 1960 | Encouraged Mexican Americans to vote for John Kennedy (Viva Kennedy). |
> | 1962 | Campaigned for Pat Brown for California governor (Viva Pat Brown). |
> | 1964 | Was chairman of the Mexican American campaign to elect Lyndon Johnson for U.S. president (Viva Johnson). |
> | 1967 | Served on the United States Civil Rights Commission. (Corona felt the Civil Rights Commission was too compromising and racist to be effective and soon publicly resigned this appointment.) |
> | 1968 | Participated as a delegate in the Democratic National Convention. Campaigned for Robert Kennedy for president (Viva Bobby Kennedy). |
> | 1973 | Supported Tom Bradley for mayor of Los Angeles. |

▲ **The interior of a migrant labor shack**

later, he became regional organizer for the National Association of Mexican Americans. He gained a reputation for being able to influence Mexican American citizens. Becoming a member of the Northern California Democratic Campaign Committee, Corona actively supported Democratic candidates for the next two decades.

Undocumented workers. Corona also served as a consultant to the U.S. Department of Labor and stepped up his efforts for those he called undocumented workers (and which the Immigration and Naturalization Service [INS] called illegal aliens). Corona spent more and more energy on behalf of the workers who had entered the United States without proper authorization.

After World War II, the INS stepped up its efforts to cancel work visas of Mexicans living in the San Diego area. As early as 1951, union leaders Phil and Albert Usquiano organized La Hermandad Mexicana Nacional (The Mexican National Brotherhood). Its purpose was to struggle against the INS in the San Diego area. In

1968 Corona brought this organization to Los Angeles and began to spread it across the nation. The Hermandad offered advice to undocumented workers about their rights under the United States Constitution. Corona and the other organizers of Hermandad believed that, once in the United States, the workers were entitled to the same protection under the Constitution as United States citizens.

The Hermandad also showed Mexicans in the United States how to organize to achieve better working conditions and better housing. Corona's Hermandad proved that undocumented workers could unite and win victories in the courts and in the fields. It offered support to those who had previously accepted terrible living and work conditions out of fear that the INS would deport them if they caused trouble. Soon the Hermandad was so busy with political action and recruiting that Corona found a need for a new social service organization.

CASA. The idea was that social services (rent control or assistance, medical aid, legal advice, and even some labor organization) would be better obtained by forming local groups. People within a given area would be served from an office in their own community. Each office could sometimes operate independently to serve special needs of the local community. Corona and his friends established CASA (Centros de Acción Social Autónomo, or Centers for Autonomous [Independent] Social Actions). But the word *casa,* which in Spanish means "home," was significant for another reason, too. It pointed up the community-based plan behind the organization. CASA began to serve Mexican communities in the United States much like earlier mutual assistance groups had served towns in Mexico. From time to time, CASA organized other groups for special purposes. The Coalition for Fair Immigration Laws and Practices began in 1978. The Casa Carnalismo was organized to fight drug dealing in Mexican communities. Sin Fronteras became an organization that stood for open borders, taking a stand in the controversy over illegal immigration. Women as well as men were active in organizing CASA and its offshoot organizations. Outstanding among them were Soledad "Chole" Alatorre and Blanche Taff.

"Chole" Alatorre. Alatorre was born in San Luis Potosí, Mexico, where her father served as an officer in the Railroad Workers' Union. From him, she learned the value of organizing large groups of people to fight for a single cause. Alatorre married in Mexico, and she and her husband moved to Los Angeles, where many Mexican nationals were working for low pay in the garment industries.

Alatorre easily found work making swimsuits in the Rosemary Reid Company. Soon the company made her a section supervisor, but because she was beautiful, its managers found they could save money by also using her as an advertising model. The freedom of the two jobs allowed Alatorre to inspect the whole plant, which led to her deciding that the garment workers needed to organize. But before she could organize enough workers, the plant moved.

Alatorre changed jobs and became a union steward and contract negotiator. In one company, she organized a strike that won better wages and work conditions. The unhappy owner then called the INS. Immigration agents found thirty-three undocumented workers in the company and threatened to take them back to Mexico. Alatorre sought help and found it in the Hermandad, which was led by Corona. She joined Hermandad and eventually became its national coordinator. Meanwhile, she joined Bert Corona in organizing CASA.

Blanche Taff. The daughter of Polish Jewish immigrants, Blanche Taff was active in the Democratic Youth Federation. It was at one of the federation's fund-raising parties that she met Bert Corona. Taff dated Corona and began to support him on the picket lines of various strikes. Eventually the two eloped to Yuma, Arizona.

Blanche Corona faced a difficult situation. She supported Corona's efforts and wanted to join him in some of his activities. At first, however, Corona held to the old-fashioned notion about marriage that "the woman works at home." He had to yield to Blanche, though, when his own activities failed to bring in enough money to support a growing family. Thereafter, Blanche Corona became an active supporter of Corona's efforts and influenced the change of his view of women's roles. The couple formed a lasting bond and raised a family of three children: Margo, David, and Frank.

The fall of CASA. The Hermandad continued its efforts to recruit and support Mexicans everywhere in the United States. Corona believed that every organization required good and steady workers and recruited Hermandad members from the working-class Mexicans. By contrast, the home-based CASA was an organization in which college students, young businesspeople, and emerging politicians were the strongest workers. Eventually, these younger people took over CASA. They also took over Sin Fronteras in San Antonio and moved it to Los Angeles in 1975. The young people proved less patient than the older organizers and seemed unwilling to learn how to enlist others to work with them. In 1977 the director of Sin Fronteras objected to their tactics and resigned. CASA began to fade. Eventually, Corona withdrew from the organization. He still worked in Hermandad, however, and turned his attention to immigration laws.

Participation:
Fighting for Fair Immigration Laws

The immigration laws. Throughout most of its history, the United States has had laws aimed at controlling the influx of immigrants to the country. The 1798 Alien and Sedition Act authorized the president to throw out any citizens believed to be a threat to the nation. Economic conditions in the 1800s encouraged importing low-wage workers to help with such activities as railroad building. Once here, however, the immigrants were viewed as threats. New laws banned immigration from some countries and limited them from others. In 1882 Chinese immigrants, at first welcomed as needed laborers, were refused admittance to the United States. In 1907 President Theodore Roosevelt threatened even stronger laws and persuaded the Japanese government to refuse to allow Japanese laborers to sail for America.

World War I upset Europe and resulted in large emigrations from that continent. The result was a wave of laws that set quotas, or limits, on immigrants to the United States. By 1929 the flow of new citizens to the United States had been reduced to 142,000 each year. Movement to the United States was further slowed by laws that demanded that immigrants be able to read and write English and show proof of the ability to support themselves. Not until 1965 were the quotas removed. Even then, newcomers to America were allowed to stay only if (1) they had close relatives in the country, (2) they had a profession, (3) they had job skills needed in the United States, or (4) they were refugees from their native countries.

Mexican immigrants. Mexico had once owned a large part of the southwestern United States, and many Mexicans thought they had claims to the land. Furthermore, Mexican workers had been encouraged to cross the border over the years to provide labor in industries such as agriculture and clothing manufacture. Also, many Mexican leaders in the United States believed that the border was an artificial one—that geography really made the Southwest and Mexico a single country. The thousand-mile-long border between the two countries had never been very well controlled, and for years Mexicans and U.S. citizens moved freely both ways across the line. Thus, Mexican workers had difficulty seeing why immigration authorities began to view Mexican workers who remained in the United States as "illegals." Over the years, the authorities placed stricter and stricter limits on immigration from Mexico. By the 1970s, as few as 20,000 Mexicans were allowed to enter the United States legally.

Corona and Hermandad began to oppose the INS in the late 1960s and early 1970s. He prepared information packages that told Mexican workers how they were protected under the U.S. Constitution. They did not have to incriminate themselves by giving information to the INS. Nor did they have to allow INS investigators into their homes without warrants. Agents of the INS often raided homes, farms, and businesses looking for illegal aliens. As the government stepped up such activity, some U.S. citizens were caught in raids and deported just because they looked Mexican. Corona's organization, Hermandad, began to take the INS to court. He helped find birth certificates and other legal documents that saved many people from being sent out of the country.

New immigration laws were proposed to help the INS. These new laws tried to stop Mexicans from entering the United States for work by discouraging the employer from hiring them. Under the proposed laws, an employer would be guilty of a crime if the employer hired an "illegal."

Corona and his aides objected to such proposals. For example, Corona opposed the proposed Dixon Arnett Bill, which would have made employers liable for penalties if they hired "illegal aliens." This state bill was soon made a national issue by a proposal in Congress called the Rodino Bill. Corona also opposed this bill and succeeded in preventing its passage for several years. He argued that such a bill illegally turned employers into agents of the government. The idea would also be a burden on Mexicans who were working in the United States legally and even U.S. citizens who were of Mexican descent, who would become subject to suspicion because of their looks. To prevent this mistreatment of Mexican Americans, Father Theodore Hesburgh and his commission had proposed that Mexican immigrants be required to carry a national identification card. Corona argued that this would be an insult to Mexicans everywhere and would not solve the problem. Despite Corona's efforts, public pressure and prejudice against job competition from Mexicans finally led to the passage of a 1982 law that imposed penalties for hiring Mexican "illegals."

The public pressure stemmed from controversy over the illegal population, and debate continued after the 1982 law was passed. Like Corona, some Americans rose up to defend the rights of illegal immigrants. Others pointed to their effects on the larger population, arguing that they used up badly needed social services, which belonged to U.S. citizens.

The Immigration Act of 1986. In 1986 Congress passed a new immigration law. Although it stopped short of requiring Mexican immigrants to carry identification cards, it did hold employers responsible if they hired undocumented workers (workers without visas or work permits, called green cards). By this time, several million Mexican workers had settled in the United States. Many of them had not tried to become U.S. citizens for fear that the INS would deport them. The 1986 act attempted to remedy this situation by providing amnesty—Mexicans in the United States without documents could apply for citizenship without interference by the INS or other government agencies. The act appeared to be a step forward for Mexican Americans, and some accepted the invitation to become citizens.

Corona and Hermandad began to advise these potential citizens so they could benefit from the 1986 law. At the same time, Corona spoke out against it. In his view there were many flaws in the new law. The most serious problem was that it ignored millions of Mexican immigrants. The new law provided amnesty only for those who had come to the United States without documents before 1982. Strictly applied, even students and workers who had entered on visas before 1982 and stayed when the visas expired could not apply for citizenship under the new law.

The law also required proof that those applying for citizenship would not be a financial burden to the United States. While at times many American workers of all ethnic backgrounds request short-term welfare help, Mexicans could not apply for citizenship if they were on welfare during the amnesty period.

Corona also opposed the act because it required applicants for citizenship to prove that they were learning the English language. This seemed to him to be an attempt to take away from the immigrants their Mexican culture and heritage, leaving Mexican Americans without roots to their past. He continued to speak out about these "flaws" in the 1986 Immigration Act even as he helped workers with their applications and need for instruction.

In spite of these "flaws," Corona's Hermandad encouraged Mexicans in the United States to take advantage of the opportunity to gain citizenship. Hermandad organized offices to help with the paperwork involved and classes to help with the English-language requirement. Altogether, Corona and Hermandad helped more than 160,000 Mexican Americans gain citizenship under the new act.

Aftermath

The struggle continues. In his lifetime, Bert Corona has been a union organizer, a champion of Mexican Americans, and a university teacher (Stanford University and California State University at Los Angeles). He has participated in many of the organizations that are considered to be politically left, even far left. (Left describes groups that sometimes advocate extreme measures to achieve equality and freedom for citizens.) While never joining the Communist Party, Corona earnestly studied communism and socialism to find the good in these political movements. He has not been afraid to join any movement to defend the rights of workers and organize them for action, particularly workers of Mexican descent. Moreover, Corona himself has created major organizations to help Mexican Americans.

Because of Corona's work and that of others like him, great

strides have been made toward helping Mexican Americans improve their position in the United States. Although Corona, now in his seventies, has backed off from some of his leadership roles, he continues to be active in Hermandad. In his words:

> Will I ever retire? No. I want to be able to do more things and see more things. I think we're entering into a very exciting epoch.... A lot of things will be happening that I'd like to be around to participate in and to see. (Corona in García, p. 340)

For More Information

García, Mario T. *Memories of Chicano History.* Berkeley: University of California Press, 1994.

García, Mario T. *Mexican Americans: Leadership, Ideology, and Identity, 1930–1960.* New Haven, Connecticut: Yale University Press, 1989.

Gutierrez, David G. *CASA in the Chicano Movement.* Working Paper Series, no. 5. Palo Alto: Stanford Center for Chicano Research, 1984.

Portes, Alejandro, and Rubén G. Rumbaut. *Immigrant America: A Portrait.* Berkeley: University of California Press, 1990.

Chicano Rights

1939
Luisa Moreno organizes group (El Congreso) to fight for rights of all Spanish-speaking peoples in the United States.

1943
Zoot Suit riots break out in Los Angeles, California.

1952
César Chávez begins working for the Community Service Organization.

1962
Chávez starts the National Farm Workers Association.

1965
Luis Valdez begins theater company, El Teatro Campesino, to aid farm workers in their struggle.

1965–1970
Farm workers mount nationwide strike against grape industry.

1966
Chicano leaders are invited to the White House to meet with President Lyndon B. Johnson.

1967
Valdez takes El Teatro on cross-country tour.

1968
Chicano high-school students conduct walkouts in Los Angeles. Race for U.S. president involves Mexican Americans.

1969
Corky Gonzáles sponsors first National Chicano Youth Liberation Conference.

1970
National Chicano Anti-War Moratorium ends in death for newsman Rubén Salazar.

1975
Agricultural Labor Relations Act guarantees the right to collective bargaining for California farm workers.

CHICANO RIGHTS

Mexican American men and women, also called *mexicanos* or *chicanos,* or *mexicanas* or *chicanas,* respectively, waged a struggle for basic rights that blossomed in the 1960s. It began, however, several decades earlier, with the founding of Mexican American interest groups, such as El Congreso Nacional del Pueblo de Habla Española (El Congreso) and the National Farm Workers' Association (NFWA). The idea for El Congreso came from Luisa Moreno, a community organizer in New York. Though the Spanish-speaking population had settled in groups—Puerto Ricans in New York, Cubans in Florida, and Chicanos in the Southwest—Moreno argued that they formed a national, not just a regional, minority.

News reporters called attention to Chicanos, the largest of the groups. Riots broke out against them in 1943, sailors and soldiers attacking young Mexicans dressed in zoot suits (pegged-bottom pants, a long jacket, and a porkpie hat). Feelings had risen to a boiling point due to a 1942 murder case blamed on seventeen Chicano youths. Some newspapers had condemned all Mexican Americans as criminals, helping to stir up emotions that finally erupted into the riots. Members of El Congreso organized a defense committee for the young Mexicans who were arrested during these riots.

Several years later, in 1949, the Community Service

Year Founded and Purpose

1939 El Congreso Nacional del Pueblo de Habla Española (El Congreso, a national congress of Spanish-speaking peoples)—to win basic rights for all Spanish-speaking groups in the United States.

1947 Community Service Organization (CSO)—to address community issues; to register voters and get Mexicans politically involved.

1949 Asociación Nacional México-Americana (ANMA)—to achieve full rights and better conditions for Spanish-speaking workers.

1960 Mexican American Political Association (MAPA)—to get Mexicans to participate in politics and become U.S. citizens.

1962 National Farm Workers' Association (NFWA)—to win better wages and working conditions for Chicano farm workers; a union.

1969 La Raza Unida—to promote Mexican American candidates for elected office; a third political party.

Organization (CSO) helped elect Edward Roybal to the Los Angeles City Council. He was the first Chicano elected to the council in more than fifty years, and his election was part of an intentional effort to involve Chicanos in politics.

Chicanos began to organize on their own behalf in other fields too. A CSO leader, Saul Alinsky, taught them to picket and demonstrate against people who mistreated a minority group. The idea was to embarrass society and force it to deal with the mistreated. Alinsky hired young organizers such as **César Chávez** and Bert Corona to work for the CSO.

Ten years later, Chávez founded the National Farm Workers Association (NFWA), a union dedicated to improving the lives of Chicano workers. In 1965, with NFWA membership at 1,700, Chávez joined a strike by Filipino farm workers against San Joaquin Valley growers. Attracting widespread attention, the strike for the first time thrust the rights of Spanish-speaking Americans into the national spotlight. Coupled with the strike, the NFWA began a nationwide boycott of California table grapes. Publicity for the strike and boycott was spread by a theater company formed by **Luis Valdez,** El Teatro Campesino, which dramatized the plight of farm workers. Valdez helped make the strike a national issue, taking his troupe on tour. By 1970, 17 million Americans had stopped buying table grapes, and Chavez's Chicano union had joined with the Filipinos' union to form the United Farm Workers (UFW). In 1975 California passed a law requiring growers to recognize the UFW as the official bargaining agent for farm workers. Instrumental in these victories were Helen Chávez and Dolores Huerta.

▲ **Migrant farm workers picking cabbages**

Like Martin Luther King, Jr., César Chávez attracted outside sympathy for his cause by using nonviolent tactics—fasting, picketing, and boycotting. Chávez gained support from national politicians such as Senator Robert Kennedy. Traveling to Delano, California, Kennedy held hearings so that farm workers could testify to their mistreatment.

Efforts to register Mexican Americans to vote paid off. Their needs became a national concern for the first time in the 1968 election for U.S. president. Outside California, other actions on behalf of Mexican Americans helped broaden the movement too. In New Mexico, an ex-preacher, Reies López Tijerina, argued that the U.S. government had in the past seized lands from Chicanos unfairly to promote the mining, ranching, and timber industries. His movement, the Alianza, clashed violently with local officials and took over some national parks before Tijerina himself was arrested.

There was, in addition to the land-grant movement, a student movement. In 1968, 10,000 Chicano students walked out of high schools in Los Angeles to demand more teachers and courses connected with their Spanish heritage. The action inspired more walkouts in California, spreading also to Texas and Colorado. A couple of years earlier, in Denver, Colorado, Rodolfo "Corky" Gonzáles founded the Crusade for Justice, stirring Chicano youths to political action. Gonzáles, a former boxer and powerful organizer, inspired young people. His group sponsored the first National Chicano Youth Liberation Conference in Denver in 1969, at which a plan was presented for a Chicano homeland. Called Aztlán after the Aztec's first mythic homeland, it was to be located in the Southwest. Chicanos, the plan went, would recapture the region and set up their own separate nation-state there.

Another student group, the Brown Berets, organized a committee to stage anti–Vietnam War demonstrations. A 1970 demonstration in Los Angeles, the National Chicano Anti-War Moratorium, ended in disaster. Many of the 20,000 to 30,000 who participated suffered police beatings, and Rubén Salazar, a newsman critical of police brutality, was killed. Whether or not his death was accidental remains unclear.

Not satisfied that the Democratic Party was serious about meeting their demands for better housing, education, and job opportunities, Chicanos formed a third political party, La Raza Unida. It held one national convention in El

Paso, Texas, in 1972, then became a minor force in American politics. In 1974 the Supreme Court ruled that schools must meet the needs of children with limited English skills, which meant federal funds for bilingual education, and efforts were mounted in the 1970s and 1980s on behalf of illegal immigrants. But generally there was little improvement for Chicanos, and the struggle slowed. Though some progress has been made in uniting all the Spanish-speaking people of the United States, this is a goal still to be reached.

César Chávez

1927-1993

Personal Background

Born on March 31, 1927, outside Yuma, Arizona, César Estrada Chávez grew up on a farm, working in the fields and among the farm hands he would later organize. The second of Juana and Librado Chávez's five children, César lived on his parents' farm until the age of ten, when the Great Depression forced the family to move.

California dreaming. Falling behind on his mortgage payments, César's father lost his 160-acre farm in 1937 and, like so many other Americans, moved his family to California's Northern Central Valley in search of work. But dreams of a better life in California soon evaporated. There were few if any steady jobs for farm workers in the San Joaquin Valley, and the Chávez family was forced to take to the road with each changing season in order to keep working. Traveling from farm to farm, César and all the members of his family worked in fields from Fresno to Bakersfield, picking grapes, lettuce, peas, or whatever crop was ready for harvest. The Chávez family became one of thousands of migrant working families who moved through California's agricultural belt during the 1930s, living in migrant camps and finding work whenever and wherever they could.

Migrant life. Life was hard for the Chávez family, not only because of the constant traveling but also because working condi-

▲ César Chávez

Event: Chicano rights movement.

Role: A Chicano (Mexican American) farm worker raised in the heart of California's agricultural belt, César Chávez founded the first successful farm workers union in the United States. Using peaceful means such as strikes, boycotts, and fasting, Chávez succeeded in attracting national and worldwide attention to the plight of United States farm workers and in helping them win rights.

tions were so poor and wages so low. The average annual income for a migrant farmworker in the late 1930s was just $1,378, less than half the national poverty level of $3,100. Furthermore, work was only available an average of 137 days a year, and harvest time usually coincided with the hottest days of summer. Temperatures would rise above one hundred degrees Fahrenheit in the arid San Joaquin Valley during this part of the year. César and his family, who often worked as grape pickers, were forced to stoop in the blazing sun to harvest crops. Not only did they endure physical pain and exhaustion for very low wages, but they were also routinely exposed to harmful pesticides that were commonly sprayed on the crops.

Education. From the age of seven, César both worked and went to school, attending more than thirty-five different schools through the seventh grade. He never officially graduated from high school but got a solid education from working in the fields. From his daily experiences, he learned firsthand about the poverty and injustice suffered by migrant workers. Because the farm workers had no union, farm owners could hire and fire them at will. Lack of a union also allowed the owners to pay subpoverty wages without providing any health care or vacations and to expose workers to harmful pesticides without adequate protection. Also, because farm owners employed many illegal immigrants, they "blackmailed" their employees, threatening to deport them if they ever went on strike or slowed down their work pace. In short, the migrant workers, as César learned, were powerless in contrast to the growers for whom they worked.

Barrio life. All of César's young life was spent living in extreme poverty in the worst of migrant slums. César often had to walk barefoot to school through the mud because his family—though always working—was too poor to buy him shoes. He fished in local streams and scrounged the countryside for greens to eat, later recalling that "otherwise we would have starved" (Chávez in Dunne, p. 5). The Chávezes made their home in anything from cardboard shacks to cars to houses without heat or electricity, as did most migrant workers.

Growing up amid such hardship had a profound effect on young César. The images of his youth were scenes of mistreatment—workers being threatened with deportation for asserting their rights and children put to work in the fields for as little as ten cents per hour in violation of child labor laws. He saw workers being forced to pay transportation fees to and from the growers' fields and being charged inflated, or jacked-up, prices for goods at grower-owned stores located in migrant camps. Many owners did not allow Chicano workers into their restaurants and called them "wetbacks." Used loosely for Mexicans, it was an offensive term that branded them as illegals who had sneaked across the Rio Grande River into the United States. The dirty shacks that filled the barrios, as well as the racist remarks and behavior from white farm owners to their Chicano workers, burned into César's brain and never left him.

A glimpse of hope. In 1939, when César turned twelve, the Chávez family moved to San Jose, and César got his first glimpse of hope for bettering the life of his *campesinos,* or fellow farm workers. César's father and uncle went to work for a dried fruit factory and joined the Congress of Industrial Organizations (CIO), which was beginning to organize some farm workers. César's father became very active in the union and held many meetings in his home, which César overheard. He listened to his father and other CIO members planning strikes and watched them making picket signs. Though they usually lost their strikes because union membership was so small, their efforts made a deep and lasting impression on César. From his father's efforts, César realized that unionization was possible. He learned how to conduct a strike. And, most important, he understood why his father's efforts failed and reasoned that if agricultural workers ever built a strong enough union, they might win a strike and better their lives.

Participation: Chicano Rights Movement

Unions and the CSO. At the age of nineteen, after serving in the navy during World War II, Chávez returned to California and the life of a farm worker. He lived first in Delano, where he met and married his wife, Helen; eventually the couple settled in San Jose and began their family of eight children. The Chávezes moved into a very poor barrio in San Jose called Sal Si Puedes, which means "get out if you can," and went to work in the surrounding apricot orchards.

During this time, Chávez was recruited by the Community Service Organization (CSO). By chance, a local CSO organizer named Fred Ross went to Chávez's home in 1952 to discuss the CSO's activities and to enlist help with their voter drive project. The CSO was helping migrant workers gain U.S. citizenship and registering Mexican Americans to vote. As Ross discussed the CSO project with Chávez, it soon became apparent that Chávez would be a great asset to the organization. Ross listened to the small, reserved Chávez talk so movingly about the plight of the migrant worker and then, realizing Chávez's tremendous potential as a community leader, offered him a job. Feeling he might be able to do some good for his community, Chávez accepted.

Development of a leader. Chávez became chairman of the CSO's voter registration drive and began canvassing small farming communities throughout northern California. At first very shy and unsure of himself, Chávez would call meetings and then sit in the back until the crowd began milling around, wondering where the leader was. Finally, Chávez would emerge from the back and, overcoming his fear, speak to those in attendance and urge them to register and vote.

Determined to become a more confident speaker and leader, Chávez taped his CSO meetings and at night tutored himself to read, write, and speak better. After improving himself in these areas, he developed what he called his "schemes" or "tricks" to win over the community and prod people into action. He said, "I found out that if you work hard enough, you can usually shake people into working too, those who are concerned. You work harder, and they work harder still" (Chávez in Dunne, p.70). Chávez learned that the most effective leaders guide their followers by example and so worked harder than anyone, never appearing to be anything other than a fellow farm worker dedicated to helping his community. He took a vow of poverty, continuing to wear the same clothes and live in the same old house and working continually from early morning until late into the night.

Chávez was determined to win over everyone he met—even the most doubtful—and soon discovered that the harder a guy is to convince, the better leader or member he becomes. When you exert yourself to convince him, you have his confidence and he has good motivation (Chávez in Dunne, p. 70). With Chávez providing the example and exerting himself completely, the CSO voter drive proved highly successful. Within a year, Chávez registered more than 4,000 Mexican Americans to vote, and in the next eight years he helped more than 30,000 Hispanic immigrants acquire U.S. citizenship and work permits (green cards).

From CSO to NFWA. During his ten years with the CSO, Chávez helped the Chicano community in all areas, from registering voters to helping workers get driver's licenses and legal representation to enrolling the neediest in welfare programs. In 1958 Chávez was so successful he was promoted to general director of the national arm of the CSO. But even as he was rising through the ranks of the CSO, he was growing increasingly discontented with the group. He wanted the CSO to back his call for unionization of farm workers but soon found that they would not do so. When his farm union proposal was rejected at a CSO convention in 1962, Chávez resigned. He promptly started his own organization, the National Farm Workers' Association (NFWA), dedicated to helping agricultural workers form a major union.

Delano. Refusing any major contributions to his new organization to avoid subjecting it to any outside influence, Chávez began the NFWA with his life savings of $1,200. He and his family, who established their home and NFWA headquarters in Delano, took a grassroots, or local, approach to starting the NFWA. Doing most of the work themselves, they went out into the fields "planting an idea" among the farm workers of starting a union (Dunne, p. 72). Distributing leaflets, traveling to farms and vineyards to speak to workers directly, and holding nightly meetings in his house, Chávez slowly began to publicize his cause and build membership in the NFWA. By 1965 he had 1,700 members and could begin thinking about staging a strike for better wages and working conditions.

Helen. While Chávez concentrated on the membership drive

A Hero's Heroes

César Chávez established NFWA headquarters at Forty Acres ranch in Delano and set up, among other things, a makeshift medical clinic for workers, a union meeting hall, the NFWA credit union, a cooperative market, headquarters of the union newspaper, *El Malcriado*, and the union's administrative offices. His simple office was decorated with images of his heroes: Robert F. Kennedy, Martin Luther King, Jr., Mahatma Gandhi, the Virgin of Guadalupe (patron saint of the worker), Dorothy Day (a Catholic relief worker in New York), and Catholic priests Daniel and Philip Berrigan (arrested for protesting the Vietnam War).

and strike tactics, Helen ran the NFWA credit union, started by the Chávezes to help union members establish credit. Helen taught herself bookkeeping and became a major force in the community by assisting her fellow farm workers in managing their money. At the time, few major banks would extend any credit to Chicano farm workers, and the NFWA credit union helped attract many union members. In addition to her roles as credit union manager and mother of eight children, Helen worked in the fields. Her labor here contributed to the family's income, which during the early years of the NFWA was very low.

La huelga—the strike. In the fall of 1965, the NFWA staged its first major strike. Though Chávez did not believe the union was strong enough yet, a sister union, made up mostly of Filipino grape pickers (members of the Agricultural Workers' Organizing Committee [AWOC]) staged a walkout in the Coachella Valley, and the NFWA joined it. AWOC members were asking for a wage increase, from $1.10 per hour to $1.40 per hour. Within days, the Coachella ranchers gave in to union demands, but farther north, in the San Joaquin Valley, owners continued to pay only the lower wages.

Chávez determined that the NFWA should take up where the AWOC left off. The time had come to stage a major strike against all vineyard owners throughout the San Joaquin Valley for better wages. Chávez addressed his union members on September 16, 1965, and called for a strike vote. Comparing the U.S. farm workers' plight to the struggle of Mexican peasants for independence in Mexico 155 years earlier, Chávez rallied the crowd:

> We Mexicans here in the United States, as well as all other farm workers, are engaged in another struggle for the freedom and dignity which poverty denies us. But it must not be a violent struggle, even if violence is used against us. Violence can only hurt us and our cause. The law is for us as well as the ranchers. The strike was begun by the Filipinos, but it is not exclusively for them. Tonight

▲ Chávez and other leaders of the farm workers

we must decide if we are to join our fellow workers. (Chávez in Dunne, pp. 79–80)

The vote to strike was unanimous, and the following Monday, NFWA members walked off the job and filled picket lines throughout the valley.

Chávez goes national. What began as a small strike against San Joaquin Valley ranchers soon escalated into a national economic boycott of all California table grapes and related products. Three months into the strike, ranchers refused to recognize the NFWA or meet any demands. So, Chávez decided to change tactics. He knew that the pickers' strike was having little economic impact on the growers because they made the bulk of their income from food processing and distribution. Therefore, he decided to stage a boycott of all of the farmers' products on a national level in hopes that the negative publicity would force the owners to give in to NFWA demands.

Chávez specifically targeted two companies, the DiGiorgio Corporation (owners of S & W and TreeSweet) and Schenley Industries. Between them, the two multimillion-dollar corporations controlled nearly 10,000 acres in Delano and relied heavily on national canned goods sales for the bulk of their revenue. Chávez set up boycott centers in thirteen major cities and recruited more than 10,000 volunteers to distribute leaflets, make phone calls, raise money, and picket grocery stores.

Widespread support. As the strike and boycott gained momentum, Chávez received backing from other unions, such as the AFL-CIO, the Teamsters, and the International Longshoremen's and Warehousemen's Union (ILWU), whose members refused to move Schenley and DiGiorgio products. College students also rallied to the cause. Already politically active in civil rights and anti–Vietnam War demonstrations, they now supported the farm workers by joining picket lines and staging campus protests.

Recognizing Chávez as an emerging, important civil rights leader, politicians, clergy, and other civil rights leaders soon flocked to California to show their support. Robert and Ethel Kennedy and Coretta Scott King visited Chávez in Delano several times. Kennedy, along with Senator Harrison Williams, called for congressional hearings on the strike and proposed an amendment to the National Labor Relations (Wagner) Act to protect agricultural workers' rights under existing labor laws. Chávez also enlisted the help of the Catholic church and received support from California's seven bishops, who appealed to Congress to pass the Williams amendment.

Only want equality. By March 1966, the half-year NFWA/AWOC grape pickers strike had become the longest-running farm workers' strike in the history of California. The U.S. Senate Labor Relations Subcommittee on Migratory Labor held hearings in Delano on March 16 to help settle the strike. The growers, on one side, insisted the strike was ineffective and that the majority of farmworkers did not support the NFWA. On the other side, Chávez claimed the opposite was true and asked that workers be given the opportunity to vote on the question of unionization. Chávez also appealed to the senators to pass the Williams amendment:

> All we want from the government is the machinery—some rules of the game. All we need is the recognition of our right to full and equal coverage under every law which protects every other working man and woman in this country. (Chávez in Matthiessen, p. 126)

Pilgrimage. True to his philosophy to lead by example, Chávez thrust himself into the forefront of the boycott movement. After the Senate hearings, he led a 250-mile, twenty-five-day pilgrimage, from Delano to Sacramento, California's capital. Aware of the emotional impact of Martin Luther King's earlier civil rights march in Selma, Alabama, Chávez used the pilgrimage to increase public support for the boycott and to pressure Governor Pat Brown to enter the dispute on NFWA's behalf. Chávez led hundreds of NFWA supporters, from Catholic clergy to barefoot children, as they wound their way through the San Joaquin Valley carrying banners of the Virgin of Guadalupe and the Aztec eagle flag of the NFWA. El Teatro Campesino (the farm workers' theater) performed in rallies at night, portraying the mistreatment of the farm workers in skits, and typically wound up each evening by singing the spiritual "We Shall Overcome" (see **Luis Valdez**). Reporters flocked to cover the march. Rallies to raise money for the NFWA were held throughout the country, and by the end of the twenty-five-day journey, Schenley Industries announced it would accept all of Chávez's demands (which included increasing wages and allowing the NFWA to organize farm workers and bargain on their behalf).

The fight goes on. Though Schenley proved to be a major victory, the boycott and strike continued against DiGiorgio and spread to many other companies, including Dow Chemical. Fasting for a month at a time, leading long marches throughout the Southwest, and holding regular union meetings at his NFWA headquarters in Delano, Chávez continued to press for change for the next decade.

From 1968 to 1975, Chávez won major victories for the Chicano community. By 1970 NFWA membership had increased to 70,000—including DiGiorgio's Sierra Vista grape pickers—and 17 million Americans had stopped buying table grapes because of

Chávez's boycott. In 1975 the state Agricultural Labor Relations Act was passed, establishing collective bargaining power for farm workers in California for the first time in U.S. history. Chávez hoped the success of farm workers would translate into success for all Mexican Americans. "The awareness of the people has been magnified a thousand times over," Chávez said in 1970. "It seems to me that, once union members are taken care of in terms of better wages and working conditions, the union must involve itself in major issues of the times. The scope of the worker's interest must motivate him to reach out and help others" (Chávez in Day, pp. 9–10).

Aftermath

Final Years. The NFWA later joined with the Filipino farm workers and changed its name to the United Farm Workers of America (UFW). Though the high point of its activity was in the 1970s, Chávez continued to press his cause until his death in 1993. He focused mainly on farm workers' rights but also protested war and violence and encouraged the Chicano community to engage in a "cultural revolution" by celebrating Mexican history and incorporating Mexican customs, art, and music into American life.

On April 23, 1993, at the age of sixty-six, Chávez, weak from fasting, died in his sleep while on union business in San Luis, Arizona. More than 30,000 turned out for his funeral.

The next generation. Dissent has weakened the UFWA, whose membership has dropped to 10,000. The grape boycott continues, attracting little attention or support in the 1990s. But UFWA members such as Chávez's son-in-law, Arturo Rodriguez, who succeeded Chávez as union president, remain dedicated and committed to seeing Chávez's dreams come true.

For More Information

Day, Mark. *Forty Acres.* New York: Praeger, 1971.

Dunne, John Gregory. *Delano: The Story of the California Grape Strike.* New York: Farrar, Straus & Giroux, 1967.

Matthiessen, Peter. *Sal Si Puedes: César Chávez and the New American Revolution.* New York: Random House, 1969.

Luis Valdez

1940-

Personal Background

Luis Miguel Valdez was born in Delano, California, on June 26, 1940. The second of Armida and Francisco Valdez's ten children, Luis grew up as a migrant farmworker, laboring in the vineyards and on the ranches that fill the fertile San Joaquin Valley.

Education. Beginning at the age of six, Luis both worked in the fields and went to school. Though his family moved continually, traveling throughout the San Joaquin and Santa Clara valleys to harvest whatever crops were in season, Luis managed to attend school regularly and do well in his classes. His parents usually arranged for the family to be in Delano each fall so that the children could keep attending the same school. However, the year that Luis was ready for first grade, the Valdez family could not return to Delano in time and he was sent to a school in Stratford.

Theater inspiration. Attending the first grade in a new town turned out to have a tremendous impact on seven-year-old Luis. The Stratford school was staging a Christmas play and Luis was cast as a monkey. He was given a mask and a costume that, he said, "impressed me more than my own clothes because they were in better shape" (Valdez in Mills, p. 3). Luis was very excited about performing in the school play, but just before it was staged, his family moved again. Recalling how crushed he felt, Luis describes the

▲ Luis Valdez

Event: Chicano rights movement, 1965–present.

Role: Because of his pioneering work as a playwright, actor, and director, Luis Valdez is known as the "father of Chicano theater." He founded El Teatro Campesino, the farm workers' theater, which is dedicated to promoting Chicano rights and inspiring social activism. He also created the play form called the *acto*, a type of political skit that depicts social injustice in Mexican American life and encourages audience members to take action against oppression.

effect on him: "I tried to fill the gap—it was an unbridgeable gap, I know that—but what a way to find a direction in life. It created a consuming hunger to continue to perform" (Valdez in Mills, p. 3).

Not being in the play left Luis with a burning desire to perform on stage. But rather than mope or feel angry that he was denied the opportunity, he decided that he had the power to remedy the situation. When he returned to Delano, he organized the kids in his neighborhood into their own theater group. Writing, directing, and performing original plays, Luis discovered not only his love and talent for the theater but also that people have the power within themselves to change upsetting conditions. "If you feel short-changed," he remarked, "fill the gap yourself," and that is what he began to do (Valdez in Mills, p. 3).

Environmental impact. Luis was educated by his environment as much as by his teachers. All his life, he lived in poor migrant camps and did the backbreaking work of a field hand for as little as ten cents per hour. He experienced racist treatment by many farm and business owners in Delano, who would not allow Chicano farm workers into their restaurants or retail stores. Growing up, he witnessed owners take advantage of farm workers on a daily basis, an experience that eventually prompted him into political action.

College and beyond. Luis graduated from high school and was accepted to San Jose State College in 1960. Majoring in English, he concentrated most of his effort on writing plays and developing his knowledge of theater production. He won a regional playwriting contest in 1961 with *The Theft,* and two years later the college drama department staged his production of *The Shrunken Head of Pancho Villa*. With this second play, Luis began to develop political themes that would recur throughout his work in the future. Using a "black comedy" style, he raised the issues of oppression of Chicanos and loss of Chicano culture in America—subjects he knew well from growing up as a migrant farm worker in California. In the next few years, Luis Valdez would expand on these themes and create his own form of expressing them.

San Francisco theater. After Valdez graduated from college in 1964, he went to work with the San Francisco Mime Troupe. This experimental theater company was working with a form of theater called agitprop. A combination of agitation and propaganda, the agitprop plays dealt with political issues of the time, such as the Vietnam War, and promoted political activism. Working with the group, Luis learned new staging and production techniques as well as how political messages could be conveyed through art. The skills Luis acquired in his year with the Mime Troupe proved to be of tremendous value in his next project, founding El Teatro Campesino—the first grassroots theater for Chicano farm workers.

Participation: Chicano Rights Movement

César Chávez and El Teatro Campesino. In 1965 César Chávez was beginning a five-year strike by farm workers against San Joaquin Valley ranchers (see **César Chávez**). Valdez left the Mime Troupe that year and returned to Delano. He got a job working with Chávez's National Farm Workers Association (NFWA, now known as the United Farm Workers of America) and founded El Teatro Campesino to help raise money for the strike and spread news of its causes to the public.

Combining his knowledge of Chicano history, satire, theater production, and farm worker hardships, Valdez created a type of play called the *acto* to dramatize the plight of the farm worker and inspire audience members to take action against injustice. Because the actos dealt specifically with the Chicano community, the type or "genre" of theater Valdez created became known as *teatro chicano* (Chicano theater). Valdez believed that theater should "affect and modify and change and give direction to society" (Valdez in Mills, p. 3). He specifically wanted his work to "inspire the audience to social action. Illuminate specific points about social problems. Satirize the opposition. Show or hint at solution. Express what people are feeling" (Kanellos, p. 283).

Called the DiGiorgio acto, the most successful acto produced by El Teatro Campesino shows how Valdez accomplished these goals. The play portrays a strike scene between farm workers and growers from the DiGiorgio Corporation, a major table grape producer in Delano whose products Chávez had targeted to boycott. Using the black comedy style, the acto begins with the DiGiorgio character bullying workers, threatening to have them fired and deported for striking and leading a boycott of DiGiorgio products. The workers hold a rally and the governor of California appears. At first, the governor supports DiGiorgio, but as the workers increase their chants of "Viva la huelga" (long live the strike), he changes his position and joins in with the workers, shouting "Huelga! huelga!"

El Teatro Campesino usually performed at NFWA rallies for the Chicano community, with Valdez serving as the writer and director but seldom acting. Valdez firmly believed that the theater "must never get away from la Raza [the Chicano community].... If la Raza cannot come to the theater, then the theater must go to la Raza" (Valdez in Kanellos, p. 284). Therefore, he took El Teatro Campesino on the road, performing in union halls, at outdoor rallies, and in 1966 on Chávez's famous 250-mile pilgrimage through the San Joaquin Valley to the state capitol in Sacramento.

Though opponents accused Valdez and his theater company of being too radical and even communist, the Chicano community heartily embraced them and became inspired by their message. Valdez described the actos as "hammer blows" to his audience, designed to wake them up and jar them into action. "They had a startling effect on our audience ... because finally somebody was stating what was so obvious" (Valdez in Mills, p. 3).

Cultural celebration. Valdez hoped not only to inspire political action with his plays but also to promote and celebrate Chicano culture. He believed that the United States was not open enough to human variety and that the country was in desperate need of influence from other cultures. "Our campesinos find it difficult to participate in this alien North-American country," he said, insisting that schools taught only European history and culture and alienated peoples of non-European backgrounds (Valdez in Matthiessen, p. 129). Valdez began writing plays that incorporated Aztec and Mexican folklore and history into modern-day themes, creating a truly "grassroots" theater that "idealized and romanticized the language and culture of the mexicano in the United States" (Valdez in Mills, p. 3).

Expansion. In 1967, after great success with the NFWA in Delano, Valdez took El Teatro Campesino across the country. Estab-

▲ A scene from *Zoot Suit,* Valdez's best-known play

lishing their Centro Campesino Cultural in Del Rey, California, El Teatro Campesino toured the nation, performing to great critical acclaim off-Broadway and in Los Angeles. In 1968 they were awarded the off-Broadway Obie Award, and in 1969 and 1971 received the Los Angeles Drama Critics Circle Award. During these years, as the theater company flourished, Valdez began broadening his message and exploring new themes. He looked at the issues of Chicanos in the Vietnam War, the conquest of Aztec/Mexican culture in America, and the "miseducation" of minorities who are not taught their culture in public schools (Kanellos, p. 285). His plays had tremendous impact on the nation, as Chicano communities, for the first time, turned out in droves to support his work.

   Theater to film. In 1976 Valdez had his first play produced on television, and in 1977 he toured Europe with El Teatro Campesino, performing the lead in the acto *La Carpa* himself. In 1978 Valdez produced his most successful play to date, *Zoot Suit,* which ran eleven months in Los Angeles. Based on a true story about Chicanos wrongly accused of murder, *Zoot Suit* was made into a movie in 1981 and won several awards for Valdez, including a Golden Globe Award in 1982. Showing how strongly people were influenced by Valdez's work, *Zoot Suit* inspired a "*pachuco* craze," in which Chicano kids throughout southern California began wearing zoot suits and mimicking the behavior of the *pachuco,* a poor farm worker.

Sexism/criticism. Though widely praised as the founder of Chicano theater, Valdez has received criticism for his treatment of women in his work. Some critics accuse him of promoting sexist stereotypes—of always portraying his female characters as either virgins or loose women—and not placing women characters in lead roles. Critic Katherine Diaz wrote that Valdez's play *Caminos* (1984) promoted "the usual stereotypical images of my [Chicana] community" and insisted further that Valdez was encouraging the misperception that all Mexican men are "drunks and lechers" and that Mexican women should be kept in their place (Kanellos, p. 289).

Yet, whatever criticism might be waged against Valdez, he is still widely credited for starting the Chicano theater movement in the United States. Critic Jorge Huerta notes that "no other individual has made as important an impact on Chicano theater as Luis Valdez. Indeed, it is impossible to discuss Chicano theater without talking about Valdez, for he initiated this vital movement" (Lomelí and Shirley, p. 291).

Aftermath

Changing subject matter. In 1987 Valdez had his greatest box office success with *La Bamba,* the story of ill-fated Chicano rock star Ritchie Valens. Though not his most critical success, the film provided a breakthrough for Valdez into mainstream theater and has led to several other major film projects.

Though no longer concentrating solely on political issues, Valdez still believes he is making significant strides for the Chicano community. "If we had done the same thing for nineteen years we would have died," he said recently of the development of El Teatro Campesino. "I'm no less political than anyone who was working on civil rights in the 1960s and is doing something else now. We must continue to change in order to survive politically, economically, artistically" (Valdez in Mills, p. 3).

For More Information

Harper, Hillard. "The Evolution of Valdez and El Teatro Campesino." *Los Angeles Times,* 15 October 1984, sec. 6, p. 1.

Kanellos, Nicolás. "Luis Miguel Valdez." In *Dictionary of Literary Biography.* Vol. 122. Detroit, Michigan: Gale Research, 1992.

Matthiessen, Peter. *Sal Si Puedes: César Chávez and the New American Revolution.* New York: Random House, 1969.

Mills, Kay. "A Matter of Changing Perspectives." *Los Angeles Times,* 3 June 1984, sec. 4, p. 3.

Women's Rights

1963
Betty **Friedan** publishes *The Feminine Mystique.*

1963
Led by Eleanor Roosevelt, committee issues U.S. report on the American woman. Congress passes Equal Pay Act.

1968
Some women split from NOW, form Women's Equity Action League (WEAL). Other women begin their own small groups.

1967
Executive order bans sex discrimination in federal employment.

1966
Friedan helps found the National Organization for Women (NOW).

1964
Civil Rights Act becomes law; Title VII of the act bans discrimination on the basis of sex.

1970
WEAL sues to end discrimination on college campuses. Friedan organizes Women's Strike for Equality.

1971
Friedan, Bella Abzug, **Gloria Steinem,** and Shirley Chisholm form Women's Political Caucus.

1972
Congress passes the Equal Rights Amendment to the U.S. Constitution, sends it the states for ratification.

1972
Steinem publishes first full issue of Ms. magazine.

1973
Roe v. *Wade* legalizes abortion.

1986
150,000 participate in pro-choice "Marches for Women's Lives" in Washington D.C., and Los Angeles, California.

1982
Deadline for states to ratify the Equal Rights Amendment expires without enough states approving it. Amendment dies.

1981
Sandra Day O'Connor becomes first woman Supreme Court justice.

1977
Abzug chairs first National Women's Conference. Phyllis Schlafly chairs opposing, pro-family conference.

WOMEN'S RIGHTS

The women's rights movement was revived in America in the 1960s, following decades of little activity. After women gained the vote in 1920, the movement grew quiet. The number of women working outside the home increased slowly as the decades passed. Then came World War II, which swept more women into the work force than ever before. Employers suddenly hired women as machine welders and into other, "male" positions. But when the war ended, society pushed women back into the home, and many willingly returned there. Magazines, motion pictures, and other sources spread the image of America's ideal woman. She served as a wife, mother, and hostess who helped advance her husband's career.

Circumstances forced some females to continue working after the war despite this ideal. They mostly returned to jobs viewed as proper for women, serving as secretaries, clerks, nurses, telephone operators, or schoolteachers. But a few women kept working in the new, less traditional jobs, and more females enrolled in college than ever before.

One of these college-goers, **Betty Friedan,** conducted a survey of women, sharing the results in her 1963 book *The Feminine Mystique.* Focusing on middle-class women, Friedan raised doubts about whether serving as mother and

▲ **Women demonstrate for peace and equality in New York City, August 26, 1970**

housewife was as satisfying as society claimed. Her book helped spark a revolution among women, who began rising up to demand their fair share of rights in the United States.

Movements of the time contributed to the revolution. Women played secondary roles in the civil rights groups. Female civil rights workers mostly took notes and performed clerical tasks while the male workers made the decisions. Aware of playing an inferior role, the women objected. Meanwhile, members of another movement, the counterculture, rejected standard American values and experimented with roles and behaviors. These actions helped infect the larger society with a questioning spirit about the course of their lives.

The government also began asking questions. Under President John F. Kennedy, a commission investigated the position of women in America. In 1963 it issued a report confirming that American women suffered from discrimination in the workplace and elsewhere. Laws were passed to help correct the inequalities. The Equal Pay Act of 1963 made it unlawful to pay less to any employee on the basis of sex, and a 1967 executive order banned discrimination on the basis of sex in the U.S. government or companies with which it made contracts. Between these two measures came the Civil Rights Act of 1964. It would be applied often on behalf of women and protected them in relation to getting hired, fired, or paid.

Civil Rights Act of 1964, Title VII

It shall be ... unlawful ... to fail or refuse to hire or to discharge any individual, or otherwise to discriminate against any individual with respect to his compensation [pay] ... because of such individual's race, color, religion, sex, or national origin.

As in the civil rights movement, however, unequal treatment persisted despite the new laws. Also, as in the civil rights movement, citizens organized to make sure the new laws were enforced. In 1966 Friedan, with 300 women and men, formed the National Organization for Women (NOW), which would become the leading women's organization and the largest since the 1920s.

Other groups would splinter off from NOW. Abortion, the operation performed to end a pregnancy, was illegal at the time, and this concerned members of NOW. However, some lawyer-members preferred to focus not on abortion but on job issues and inequality on college campuses. In 1968 they split off to form the Women's Equity Action League (WEAL). Both groups wrote letters to senators, drafted petitions, lobbied, and testified before government committees to achieve change.

Purpose of NOW

"To take action to bring women into full participation in the mainstream of American society NOW ... in truly equal partnership with men." (Judith Papachristou, *Women Together* [New York: Alfred A. Knopf, 1976], p. 220)

A set of other, smaller groups also appeared in the late 1960s. Known as radicals, their members ran the small groups differently from NOW or WEAL. Instead of writing letters and sending around petitions, for example, they staged

Some felt that life was even more limited for women than it was for blacks. In 1971 Fannie Lou Hamer, long active in the civil rights movement, announced that she suffered more discrimination from being a woman than she did from being black.

demonstrations to call public attention to women's issues. Also, the small groups encouraged discussion of personal experiences, which helped their members become aware of exactly how they had been deprived of their rights.

As the women's movement grew in the 1970s, the small and large groups moved closer together. There was agreement on some issues and disagreement over others, even within NOW. Four of its members, however, agreed on the importance of organizing a political arm. In 1971 Friedan, along with Bella Abzug, **Gloria Steinem,** and Shirley Chisholm, formed the Women's Political Caucus, a pressure group for women in the Republican and the Democratic political parties.

By 1972 Steinem had replaced Friedan as the main leader of the women's movement. A writer herself, Steinem was disturbed by the movement's middle-class image, largely created, she felt, by *The Feminine Mystique.* Steinem worked to broaden the movement, beginning *Ms.* magazine, which dealt with issues such as women's jobs and abortion.

Some minority women, feeling that NOW did not in fact serve their needs, began their own separate groups. The National Conference of Puerto Rican Women was formed in 1973, as was Black Women Organized for Action.

Women's groups in general scored a major victory in 1973. In *Roe* v. *Wade,* the Supreme Court ruled that abortion was legal in the first three months of pregnancy. Other sex-related issues surfaced over the years. There was controversy, for instance, over whether it would hurt the movement to admit that some members were lesbians.

In 1977 different women's groups participated in the International Women's Year Conference in Houston, Texas. Its purpose was to identify and find ways to eliminate barriers that still kept women from fully participating in American life. The Equal Rights Amendment (ERA), not yet ratified, remained a major issue. Phyllis Schlafly, women's rights opponent, was working to defeat the amendment. She formed her own women's organization, held her own conference in Houston, and published a monthly newsletter, mounting a Stop-ERA campaign. The ERA, she warned, would lead to women's being drafted into the military. Schlafly discouraged its passage in other ways too, mounting an effective campaign. When the 1982 deadline arrived, only thirty-five states had ratified it. This was three short of the number needed, and the amendment died.

> ## Equal Rights Amendment
>
> Equality of rights under the law shall not be denied or abridged by the United States or by any state on account of sex.

Even without the ERA, women had made gains. Salaries improved, and companies adopted quotas to make sure enough women were being hired. In 1981 Sandra Day O'Connor became the first woman Supreme Court justice. Yet controversy has continued, particularly over keeping abortion legal. Pro-life advocates oppose it. Pro-choice champions support it, defending, as their name suggests, a woman's right to choose this option. In general since the 1960s, American women have gained a greater range of choices. Yet some regard the struggle for equality with men as having barely begun.

Betty Friedan

1921-

Personal Background

Betty Naomi Goldstein was born in Peoria, Illinois, on February 4, 1921, one year after women won the right to vote. The daughter of a Russian Jewish immigrant jeweler and a former newspaperwoman, Harry and Miriam Horowitz Goldstein, Betty was taught by her parents to strive for excellence in all that she did. She grew up a very self-confident, bright young woman with dreams of going to college and having a family.

Writing influence. Encouraged by her mother to enter the journalism profession, Betty began writing for her school newspaper in junior high. She continued to write in high school, where she revealed her enterprising nature when she started a new campus magazine with a male classmate. The magazine venture educated her in more than just the publishing field. When her co-editor told her that he would like to be her best friend if only she were a boy, Betty began to realize the limits society placed on men and women in the 1930s. It struck her as sad that society would accept her as the boy's love interest but not as his best friend. She wanted to be both! Though Betty did not realize it yet, she would dedicate much of her adult life to changing the limited roles of the sexes.

College. Betty graduated from high school at age seventeen and was accepted to Smith College in Massachusetts. At Smith, a

▲ Betty Friedan

Event: Women's rights movement.

Role: Betty Friedan largely began the late-twentieth-century women's rights movement in the United States. As author of *The Feminine Mystique* (1963), she identified the problem with confining women to limited roles in American society. Among her many accomplishments, Friedan founded the National Organization for Women in 1966 and continues to work for human rights and equality of the sexes.

very fine women's college, Betty's sense of self and pride in being a woman grew. During her four years there, she developed her writing ability as well as an interest in psychology, which she chose as her major. She excelled in her studies and graduated with honors in 1942, earning a degree in psychology. She moved west in 1943 to attend the University of California at Berkeley. After completing one year of graduate study, she was offered a scholarship to get her Ph.D. degree. But, as was common at this time, she feared that she might become a spinster if she accepted the scholarship and spent the next four years studying. She therefore turned it down and moved to New York City in 1944 to work as a reporter on a workers' newspaper.

New York. The year that Betty arrived in New York, America had just entered World War II, and with men off at war, there were ample job opportunities in the city for women. Though not well paid, Betty gained valuable experience reporting for the workers' press in New York. Covering strikes and labor disputes, Betty learned about discrimination in the workplace—not only by employers against male workers but also by employers and unions against women. Women were paid a fraction of what men earned to do the same job, and when men returned from the war, women were fired without warning or compensation. Even worse, women who belonged to labor unions were not taken seriously by labor leaders. Their complaints were rarely heard and the unions seldom did anything to help them gain fair pay or get their jobs back.

While Betty reported for the workers' press, she became very politically active in New York. She attended rallies to end the war and helped arrange illegal abortions for women she met in college and at work. In 1947 she met Carl Friedan, an actor returning from the Soldier Show Company in Europe. He was planning to start a summer theater in New Jersey. The two fell in love, married, and had their first son, Daniel, shortly thereafter.

Friedan continued to report for the workers' press until 1949, when she became pregnant with her second son, Jonathan. When she asked for a second maternity leave (temporary absence from work for new mothers), the small newspaper fired her. Back then, employers routinely fired women when they became pregnant. Men could have careers and families, but it was nearly impossible for women to have both. Again, as with her high school magazine editing experience, Friedan was faced with an either/or choice. She responded by leaving her career to become a full-time wife and mother. The family soon moved to the suburbs, where a third child, Emily, was born.

Living the lie. Her life as a homemaker led Friedan to develop a theory on women. It concerned the dangers of what she saw as a myth—the idea that women should be completely satisfied with their roles as wives and mothers and that somehow it was abnormal to want a career or an identity separate from the family. Friedan developed her idea in 1956 from information she received in a questionnaire she sent out to her other Smith College graduates. After spending nearly a decade living the home life that society promised would satisfy every woman, Friedan felt incomplete. Something was missing from her life, and she asked the other women if they felt the same. To her astonishment, Friedan found she was not alone in her dissatisfaction. Most of her classmates, who had also given up their careers to become full-time wives and mothers, responded that they too felt incomplete, some even deeply depressed. Told that they should be wholly satisfied living their lives for their husbands and children, Friedan and her classmates felt guilty for wanting more out of life. It was not that they wished to give up their families; they simply wanted to use their well-developed minds for more than just deciding which laundry detergent gets clothes the cleanest. They wanted careers as well as families, but few women were willing to admit that out loud in 1956.

When Friedan read the responses to her questionnaire, she felt both panicked and relieved. It was comforting to know that she was not alone in her views but, at the same time, greatly disturbing to learn that so many women were so unhappy. Friedan knew that she must write about what she had learned because, she reasoned, the Smith women might just be examples of a wider problem. Perhaps this feeling of being dissatisfied was a national epidemic.

Article rejected. Friedan organized her data into an article and submitted it to several national women's magazines. One by one, the male editors who controlled *The Ladies' Home Journal, McCall's,* and other leading publications rejected the article, saying only "sick" women could possibly feel dissatisfied being full-time wives and mothers. But Friedan knew otherwise and set out to turn her article into a book.

Participation: Women's Rights Movement

The Feminine Mystique. Friedan worked on her book while her children were at school, slowly developing her main idea over the next five years. Using her well-developed research skills, she conducted interviews with women across the nation and gathered information on everything from the history of women's struggle for voting rights in America to the rate at which college graduates had children during the 1940s and 1950s. Just as she suspected, Friedan found that the Smith graduates were not alone in their feelings, and by 1963 she came up with a label for the silent suffering that millions of women were experiencing. She called it "the feminine mystique" (Friedan in Reynolds, p. 135).

Controversy. However, many were not ready to hear what Friedan had to say. First, her agent refused to handle the book, and when she found a publisher on her own, the company would only issue a few thousand copies. Many were not willing to admit that a feminine mystique existed, and Friedan's agent and publishers thought most men and women would feel threatened by the book's main idea. Once the book was released, however, support for it was far greater than expected. By 1966 more than 3 million copies were sold.

It seemed that the "strange stirring ... sense of dissatisfaction" that Friedan and her college friends felt was common (Friedan, *The Feminine Mystique,* p. 15). The feminine mystique, which told women they should be completely content sacrificing their own dreams for their families, appeared to be taking its toll on millions of American women. In her book, Friedan showed that suburban housewives from California to Maine were suffering from a sense of emptiness. Though many were living the female American Dream by going to college and raising a family, they felt incomplete and even obsolete, or used up, once their children were grown.

Friedan maintained that women's unhappiness stemmed from society, which "does not permit women to accept or gratify their basic need to grow and fulfill their potentialities as human beings" (Friedan in Reynolds, p. 137). She advocated a "new life plan" that would allow women to have both families and careers and would give them the respect and compensation they deserved for being full-time wives and mothers (Reynolds, p. 138).

Reluctant leader. Though she had not planned to start a revolution, Friedan, in fact, began the modern women's liberation movement—the movement to gain equal rights for women—with the writing of *The Feminine Mystique*. Friedan was immediately cast as the leader of it. Letters of support from women throughout the nation began pouring in to her, with most saying that the book drastically changed their lives.

Friedan took her new leadership role very seriously. She began lecturing throughout the country, explaining her ideas for change and dispelling the myth that women should be totally satisfied being wives and mothers. Friedan wanted more than to just criticize the current climate in which women lived; she wanted to offer real solutions that could be applied quickly and relatively easily. She advocated professional training and shared jobs, where two women share the same position and split the hours of work. This would accommodate the millions of mothers who wanted to work and spend time with their children. She called for day care centers to be set up at or near offices and maternity-like leave for men as well as women so that both parents could share in early childhood experiences without having to sacrifice their careers. Friedan was a pioneer in her efforts to reinvent America's institutions. Also, she became one of the first of her era to call for ratifying the Equal Rights Amendment to the Constitution, which would outlaw sex discrimination.

NOW. As Friedan toured the country advocating her ideas, she began to realize that women needed a national organization to promote their interests. Inspired by the civil rights movement, which had just succeeded in getting the Civil Rights Act of 1964 passed, she met with women in Washington, D.C., to discuss starting "an NAACP for women" (Friedan, *It Changed My Life,* p. 61). At the Washington Hilton Hotel in June 1966, Friedan and several others, including Kay Clarenbach of the Women's Bureau, Dorothy Haener of the United Auto Workers union, and Muriel Fox, a top public relations expert, wrote out on a napkin the first major structure of the women's movement. They set out to take the actions needed to bring women into the mainstream of American society "now" and to obtain full equality for women, in fully equal partnership with men (Friedan, *It Changed My Life,* p. 83). That brief purpose became the cornerstone of the National Organization for Women (NOW), which was officially launched a few months later on October 29, 1966.

Friedan became NOW's first president, a post she held through 1970. Clarenbach was named chairman of the board, and Richard Graham, head of the Equal Employment Opportunity Commission, was named vice president. NOW did not have an official office but was run through various members' homes and workplaces. Mailings were sent out of the United Auto Workers building in Detroit, public relations was handled through Fox's office, and NOW headquarters were located at Friedan's apartment on West 72nd Street in New York City.

Title VII. Under Friedan's presidency, NOW concentrated on enacting Title VII of the Civil Rights Act of 1964, which outlawed discrimination on the basis of race or sex. This provision, though passed in 1964, was never enforced by the Justice and Labor Departments and was scoffed at by employers, who continued to advertise "men only" job opportunities. Friedan made it NOW's mission to see Title VII enforced and to get women equal pay for equal work, since they were paid sixty cents for every dollar men earned. She also directed activities for legalizing abortion and making birth control widely available. In 1970 Friedan led a march of 20,000 women through Washington, D.C., to promote these reforms.

By the 1970s, NOW was making significant strides in its campaign for equality. Title VII was beginning to be enforced throughout the country, women were being admitted to more and more professional schools formerly restricted to men only, and rapid changes were occurring in the workplace (which began to adopt shared jobs and to guarantee maternity leave). Friedan had come a long way from the day when she was fired for being pregnant, act-

▲ Friedan is flanked by activist and comedian Dick Gregory and Representative Barbara Mikulski (D-Md.) at a march for the ratification of the Equal Rights Amendment (ERA), July 10, 1978

ing to make American society a land of equal opportunity for all its citizens, male and female, whether they chose professional careers, domestic careers, or both.

Equal Pay for Equal Work

Betty Friedan was one of the first to advocate that women be paid and respected for all of the domestic and volunteer work they do in their roles as wives and mothers. She noted how, though women's liberation has been largely successful, women still do the bulk of traditional so-called woman's work, such as cooking and cleaning, and that this work remains underpaid because women are the ones who do it. Friedan has suggested that in order to remedy this, we change the concept of "equal pay for equal work" to "equal pay for work of comparable value" (Friedan in Gilbert, p. 331).

Family life. When Friedan moved to New York in 1966, her marriage had long been in trouble. She and Carl finally divorced in 1969, and she kept custody of Emily, then fourteen. Jonathan and Daniel were already in college, studying to be an engineer and physicist. Emily would go on to become a physician.

Aftermath

Friedan reaches out. From 1970 to 1973, as the women's movement reached its peak, Friedan turned her attention to the women who were not yet fully on board. She, unlike others in the movement, wanted to include even the doubtful homemakers in the struggle for equality, which she considered the reason for all human revolution and for American democracy. Calling it a *human* rights movement, Friedan reached out to men and to women through her column in *McCall's* magazine entitled "Friedan's Notebook." In the monthly report, she explained that the women's movement was not a threat to motherhood and that men and women both profited from female equality:

> Some worry that we'll lose our femininity and our men if we get equality. Since femininity is being a woman and feeling good about it, clearly the better you feel about being yourself as a person, the better you feel about being a woman. And, it seems to me, the better you are able to love a man. (Friedan, *It Changed My Life,* p. 192)

Friedan's columns reached 8 million readers and had a profound impact on mainstream society.

Leaves NOW. In 1970 Friedan resigned the presidency of NOW to concentrate on political reform (promoting the Equal Rights Amendment), teaching, and writing. She was finding herself increasingly at odds with some other women's "lib" (liberation) leaders who, she felt, were promoting "female chauvinism" (the opposite of male chauvinism), in which women consider men second-class citizens. She saw these leaders as endangering the progress of the women's movement. Friedan felt women's liberation should be about choices and equality of opportunity and should include all who believed in those ideals.

She defined feminism as a woman's right to "move in society with all the privileges and opportunities and responsibilities that are their human and American right. This does not mean class warfare against men, nor does it mean the elimination of children" (Friedan, *It Changed My Life,* p. 245). Friedan thought that some leaders were seen as anti-motherhood and antiman, and she feared that if the women's movement were defined in those terms it would surely fail.

In 1975 Betty Friedan was named Humanist of the Year. Through the 1970s, 1980s, and into the 1990s, she taught in various universities and campaigned vigorously for passage of the Equal Rights Amendment, which has been repeatedly defeated. She continues to write, lecture, and teach. In 1981, thinking about the movement she had done so much to create, Friedan wrote:

> There is no question today that women feel differently now about themselves than they did twenty years ago.... It has been great for women to take themselves seriously as people, to feel some self-respect as people, to feel that they do have some equality even though we know it has not been completely achieved.... We're only beginning to know what we're capable of. (Friedan, *It Changed My Life,* pp. 330-31)

For More Information

Friedan, Betty. *The Feminine Mystique.* New York: W.W. Norton, 1963.

Friedan, Betty. *It Changed My Life.* New York: Random House, 1976.

Gilbert, Lynn, and Gaylen Moore. *Particular Passions.* New York: Clarkson N. Potter, 1981.

Reynolds, Moira Davison. *Women Champions of Human Rights.* Jefferson, North Carolina: McFarland, 1991.

Gloria Steinem

1934-

Personal Background

Born on March 25, 1934, in Toledo, Ohio, Gloria Marie Steinem had an unusual childhood. Her mother, Ruth Nuneviller Steinem, suffered from psychological illness and her father, Leo Steinem, worked as a traveling antiques dealer and small-time resort operator. Though well-intentioned parents, they were unable to provide a stable home life for Gloria and her older sister, Susan.

On the road. The Steinems spent the summers at their resort in Clark Lake, Michigan, and traveled the country in a dome-topped trailer the remainder of the year as Leo bought and sold antiques from Florida to California. Ruth spent most of her time in bed and often experienced fits of depression that produced hallucinations and occasionally violent and self-destructive behavior. Though a college-educated and intelligent woman, Ruth was a "nonperson" to Gloria, who did not really get to know her mother until well after high school (Steinem, p. 132).

Early education. Because the Steinems traveled so often, Gloria did not attend school regularly until age ten. Instead, her mother, who had a teaching certificate, tutored Gloria while they were on the road and instilled in her a deep respect for books and a love of reading. Still, Gloria missed out on the companionship that daily elementary school provides. Her favorite childhood memories were of sum-

▲ **Gloria Steinem**

Event: Women's liberation movement.

Role: As a writer and an activist, Gloria Steinem has been a leader in the late-twentieth-century women's rights movement. She has worked to make abortion legal, pass the Equal Rights Amendment, and promote equality of the sexes among all races and social classes. Steinem's achievements include founding *Ms.* magazine—the first national women's magazine run by women.

mers spent at the resort, where she played with her friends and learned to tap dance. But this last and only trace of a carefree childhood ended when the family split up in 1944. Mr. Steinem moved to California to work, Susan went off to Smith College in Massachusetts, and Gloria and her mother moved to Toledo, Ohio.

Toledo turmoil. Life drastically changed for Gloria in Toledo. She and her mother were truly on their own, and, in short, their roles reversed. Ruth became very ill and was unable to care for herself, let alone for her daughter. So, at age ten, Gloria took on the role of mother. In addition to attending school, she did the shopping, cooking, and housekeeping. Gloria and her mother lived in a worn-out house with no heat and slept in the same bed to keep warm. They rented out the lower half of the house to help meet expenses, and Gloria performed in local tap dance productions to earn extra money. During these years, Gloria's only escape was through movies and books. She read nearly three books a night and visited the movie theaters every weekend that she could afford it. She especially liked books by Louisa May Alcott, who wrote *Little Women,* about a mother and her daughters who took care of themselves while the husband, father, and brothers were off at war. Gloria's favorite movies were Shirley Temple orphan stories, in which Shirley was always adopted by ideal parents. Gloria liked to pretend that she too had been adopted and that, like Shirley Temple, some wonderful family was going to come and rescue her.

Though life was trying in Toledo, Gloria did well in school. She had both boy and girl friends through high school and stayed active in tap dancing and in the local Eagles Club. Like her father, Gloria had show business dreams. Though she planned to go to college, she assumed she would eventually become a Rockette, dancing at the famous Radio City Music Hall in New York City.

In her senior year of high school, Gloria's life changed. Her sister, realizing how ill their mother was, arranged for Gloria to move to Washington, D.C., with her while their father agreed to take care of Ruth for the year. With the pressure of caring for her mother lifted, Gloria flourished. She was elected vice president of her graduating class and did so well in her studies that she was accepted to Smith College, where Susan had gone.

Smith. Entering in 1952, Gloria was deeply affected by her time at Smith College. She was not only impressed by the beauty of the wooded, stately campus but also inspired and challenged by the intellectual activity going on there. A highly reputable women's college, Smith provided Gloria with the safe and stable environment she had never known as a child. The availability of books was "heaven" for her, and the diversity of students was educational (Henry, p. 24). The more privileged students taught Gloria the fine arts and helped improve her French grammar, while Gloria, in turn, provided practical knowledge about daily living and won over her classmates with her independence. Once ashamed of her family and upbringing, Gloria learned at Smith that her background was an advantage. The experience led her to advise others: "Don't worry about your background; whether it's odd or ordinary, use it, build on it" (Steinem in Henry, p. 23). This is exactly what she began to do in college.

Political roots. Her self-confidence growing, Gloria majored in government and became politically active on campus. She volunteered for Adlai Stevenson's presidential campaign and wrote a student newsletter about her experiences, also studying abroad for a year in Geneva, Switzerland, and writing for the Smith student newspaper. During these years, Gloria learned not only about politics but also about the history of writing and activism in her own family.

When they saw each other on the weekends and during vacations, Susan and Gloria discussed their family history and visited their mother, who now lived in a rest home and was in much better health. Gloria learned that her mother's mother had been a suffragette who helped win for women the right to vote and that her mother had worked as a reporter. Suddenly Ruth Steinem was an actual person in Gloria's life. In effect, Gloria was meeting her mother for the very first time, and she had a powerful revelation upon learning the causes of her mother's breakdown. Ruth had been a very successful columnist and editor for the local Toledo newspaper but was forced to give up her career when she married Leo Steinem. By the customs of the day, she was not allowed both a career and a family and consequently suffered from depression. For Gloria, this demonstrated the extreme dangers of restricting women. Clearly there was a pressing need for change.

Furthermore, Gloria realized that her mother's illness was never taken seriously precisely because she was a woman and "her functioning was not necessary to the world" (Steinem, p. 133). Gloria became determined to make women's functioning necessary to the world and to address their concerns. Just as her mother was emerging as a separate person, Gloria Steinem was emerging as an activist for women's rights.

With a degree in government, Gloria graduated from Smith with the high honor of Phi Beta Kappa in 1956 and accepted the Chester Bowles Asian Fellowship to study in India for two years. En route, she stopped in England for the summer. However, the stopover turned into more than just a brief vacation. Events in Great Britain forever changed Gloria Steinem's life.

Abortion. Engaged to her college boyfriend, Steinem became pregnant. Before she realized her condition, however, she broke the engagement in order to pursue her education. Upon learning she was pregnant, she faced an agonizing decision. She could return to the United States, marry, and have the baby—essentially giving up her career and education as her mother had done. Or she could have an abortion—and operation to end the pregnancy—and fulfill the dreams her mother had been unable to realize. Steinem desperately wanted a career and strongly felt she was not ready for marriage or parenthood. But because abortion was illegal in the United States and England, she did not think she could have a safe one. Then, through a friend, Steinem discovered that in England a doctor could deem the pregnancy "a health risk" and perform the operation. Steinem decided that she must have the abortion and found a doctor who would do it. Without telling a soul, she had the operation and left for India. Because of the tremendous pain, guilt, and shame she felt, she did not discuss the abortion again for fifteen years.

Participation: Women's Rights Movement

After nearly two years of study and activism in India, Steinem returned to the United States anxious to write about her experiences. During her stay in the poverty-stricken country, she learned about oppression firsthand and also discovered the power of peaceful demonstration. She wrote a guidebook about India, *A Thousand*

Indias, and hoped publishers in New York would be anxious to put her writing talents and political insights to use. However, when she landed in New York, she learned that few women were hired as reporters, and she could not find a job. One *Life* magazine editor went so far as to say, "We don't want a pretty girl, we want a writer," assuming that an attractive young woman was not capable of working as a professional journalist (Steinem, p. 15).

The freelancer. Disappointed but not completely discouraged, Steinem continued to look for work in her field. After two years, she landed a job with *Help!* magazine as an editorial assistant. It was not as well respected or as serious a publication as she would have liked, but she was happy to have the job and made the most of it. Through her job, Steinem was soon meeting the movers and shakers of New York City, one of whom was Bob Benton, editor of *Esquire* magazine. He encouraged her to try her hand at freelance writing and published her first signed article in September 1962. A major breakthrough for Steinem, the article led to other assignments and soon she was a regular contributor to *Esquire, Glamour,* and other magazines. By 1963 she was earning enough to embark on a full-time freelance career.

Hitting the glass ceiling. Though Steinem's career was on the rise, she still was not getting serious political assignments. Although she wanted to report on presidential candidates and important issues of the day, her male magazine editors assigned her celebrity interviews and suggested she go undercover as a *Playboy* bunny waitress. With little choice in the matter, Steinem accepted the bunny mission, hoping to report on the discrimination and sexual harassment that occurred at New York's Playboy Club. She intended it as a strong piece of investigative reporting. However, when the article was published in June 1963, few regarded her effort as a serious journalistic endeavor. Rather than focusing on her work to expose the injustice she found at the club, editors only saw that she had worked as a bunny and refused to take her seriously as a writer. Thus, the article that she hoped would be a stepping-stone to better assignments turned out to further limit her career for the short term.

Finally a breakthrough. For the next five years, Steinem freelanced and continued to push for political assignments. She also wrote for the television show *That Was the Week That Was.* As a successful freelancer and one of a handful of women television writers, she was becoming something of a celebrity in New York. By 1968, through her "celebrity" status, Steinem was finally able to land an important political assignment. She covered Senator George McGovern's presidential campaign, and that, in turn, led to a position at *New York* magazine. As a founding editor, Steinem had story selection power, which meant that she could choose the articles she would write. For the first time, she said, "my work and my interests began to combine" (Steinem, p. 16). Her career as a political writer and activist had begun.

Writer and activist. In her new role as contributing editor and political columnist for *New York* magazine, Steinem covered everything from the assassination of Martin Luther King, Jr., to United Farm Workers demonstrations led by César Chávez. She not only reported the events but also joined many of the efforts, marching, speaking, and helping to raise money for the causes she backed. Her work and political activity taught Steinem to organize effectively. At first she was not sure why she felt so strongly about working for the oppressed, but then, while attending abortion hearings in 1969, it became clear. "I finally understood why I identify with 'out' groups. I belong to one too" (Steinem in Henry, p. 69).

Steinem suddenly realized that women were oppressed as a class and a sex and that she shared much in common with millions of other women who had also had abortions. This was a shocking revelation and a major turning point in Steinem's life. She had not before realized that such a majority of women felt oppressed by society and that so many had suffered as a result of restrictive government policies on abortion and other issues. Now well versed in political activity and organization, she turned her attention to promoting women's interests.

New wave of feminism. Steinem's entire literary focus shifted to exploring the current women's liberation movement and explaining the theories of "new feminism" to a wide audience. She traced the roots of the early women's rights movement to Sarah and Angelina Grimké. Sisters, they began as abolitionists and found that working for civil rights for women was necessary too:

The sex and race caste systems are very intertwined and the revolutions have always come together, whether it was the suffragist and abolitionist movements or whether it's the feminist and civil rights movements. They must come together because one can't succeed without the other. (Steinem in Gilbert, p. 164)

Her article that expanded on this idea, "After Black Power, Women's Liberation," won the Penney-Missouri Journalism Award for being one of the first to explain the new wave of feminism of the 1970s.

Through her research, Steinem also discovered something about the women's liberation movement, started by Betty Friedan in 1963 (see **Betty Friedan**). It seemed to be geared only toward older white women. Steinem felt that "despite the many early reformist virtues of *The Feminine Mystique,* it managed to appear ... with almost no reference to black women or other women of color" (Steinem, p. 5). Steinem believed that she could serve as a "bridge" between the generations and could unite other women of color to help broaden the appeal of the feminist cause.

Toward that end, she marched with thousands of women—young and old, black and white—in the New York City Women's Strike For Equality and struck a friendship with Dorothy Pitman Hughes, an African American who founded one of the first community day care centers for working mothers in New York. Hughes greatly influenced Steinem's development as a feminist leader. She urged Steinem to speak publicly to promote women's equality, and together the two set out on a speaking tour of the nation. Calling for legalized abortion, equal pay for equal work, and passage of the Equal Rights Amendment, which would outlaw sex discrimination, Steinem and Hughes made a tremendous impact on society. Crossing racial and class barriers, they were able to attract support from women and men throughout the nation. The two formed the Women's Action Alliance to develop women's educational programs and in 1971 planned to publish their own magazine. Run by women for women, it was to be a forum for feminist issues. They named it *Ms.* and put out the first issue in January 1972.

Willing to testify. Believing that women have "gotten where we are today ... mainly through individual women telling the truth," Steinem decided she must add her personal story to the national abortion debate (Gilbert, p. 163). In 1972, with the country locked

▲ Steinem with Pat Carbine, editor-in-chief of *Ms.,* January 29, 1980

in heated debate over whether or not abortion should be legal, Steinem announced publicly that she was one of millions who had an illegal abortion, and she called on the Supreme Court and federal government to make the choice legal. In addition, she coined the phrase "reproductive freedom" to signify that what women were asking for was *choice,* or "the right to decide whether or not to have a baby" (Henry, p. 76). Because of Steinem's strong personal stand and that of others like her, public sentiment shifted to "pro-choice." In 1973 the Supreme Court case *Roe* v. *Wade* legalized abortion.

Feminism defined. Though Steinem was popular among most feminists, she received a lot of criticism:

> I've been attacked viciously on a personal level for my ideas. It makes you want to go home and cry and never do anything again ... what's harder for all of us [feminists] to take is attacks by other women who appear to believe the same things we do.... It's self-hatred. (Steinem in Gilbert, p. 165)

Steinem truly hoped that her efforts would help promote a "sisterhood" among all women, regardless of political party, race, religion, or economic status. She defined feminism as simply "the belief that women are full human beings" (Steinem in Gilbert, p. 167). In Steinem's view, feminism was asking a basic question: Why do people have to assume that one group has to dominate the other? Why not assume there will be cooperation instead of domination?

Aftermath

Woman of the Year. For her accomplishments, Steinem was named Woman of the Year in 1972 by *McCall's* magazine. Since then, Steinem has continued to write, speak, and contribute to *Ms.* magazine. She has been a founder of several organizations, including the *Ms.* Foundation for Women, the National Women's Political Caucus (a nonpartisan organization that promotes pro–equality women candidates), and the Coalition of Labor Union Women. In the fall of 1993, Steinem—who describes her greatest accomplishments as "making a difference" and giving birth to ideas (Steinem, p. 11)—was inducted into the National Women's Hall of Fame in Seneca Falls, New York.

For More Information

Daffron, Carolyn. *Gloria Steinem.* New York: Chelsea House, 1988.

Gilbert, Lynn, and Gaylen Moore. *Particular Passions.* New York: Clarkson N. Potter, 1981.

Henry, Sondra, and Emily Taitz. *One Woman's Power.* Minneapolis, Minnesota: Dillon Press, 1987.

Steinem, Gloria. *Outrageous Acts and Everyday Rebellions.* New York: Holt, Rinehart and Winston, 1983.

Native American Rights

1924
American Indians are awarded full U.S. citizenship.

1960s
U.S. policy changes to self-determination (self-rule).

1956
Wilma Mankiller relocates from Oklahoma to San Francisco, California.

1953-1958
U.S. government switches to termination (ending reservations) policy, wants Indians to relocate into cities.

1934
Indian Reorganization Act reverses U.S Indian policy, encourages Indians to perpetuate tribal customs.

1968
Ben Nighthorse Campbell begins the search for his ancestry.

1969
Mankiller and other Indians seize Alcatraz Island under law that gives Indians rights to abandoned U.S. property.

1972
Members of the American Indian Movement seize the Bureau of Indian Affairs.

1973
200 Indians occupy the town of Wounded Knee, South Dakota, and are evicted by U.S. troops.

1975
Congress passes Indian Self-Determination and Education Assistance Act.

1993
Campbell is elected to the U.S. Senate.

1990
Congress passes Native American Grave Protection and Repatriation Act.

1987
Campbell is elected to the U.S. Congress.

1985
Ross Swimmer, Cherokee chief, takes charge of the Bureau of Indian Affairs. Mankiller becomes head Cherokee chief.

1978
Congress passes American Indian Religious Freedom Act.

NATIVE AMERICAN RIGHTS

The 1960s saw a surge of ethnic pride on the part of different minority groups, including Native Americans. Individuals such as **Ben Nighthorse Campbell** began searching out their tribal roots. Tribes meanwhile pressed for the right to join in the decision-making about federal programs and monies for the roughly 500 tribal groups.

The tribes pushed for a new policy, self-determination, the right of Indians themselves to help determine and control the benefits they would receive. Adopted as official U.S. policy in 1970, self-determination aimed to help Indians become independent of federal control without cutting off badly needed support. Today's Indians suffer more from poverty and disease than any other group and depend largely on U.S. benefits for survival. As one tribesman observed, the government has become the Indian's new buffalo.

Three spheres of government have continued to exist within the United States—the federal government, the state governments, and the tribal governments. In the struggle to coexist, the tribal governments have been subjected to a changing set of policies by the federal government.

Federal policy switched from almost fifty years of trying to destroy the tribal unit to trying to restore tribal independence and help preserve Indian cultures. Begun by John Collier and known as the Indian New Deal, this new policy lasted another fifty years until the U.S. government did another about-face. In the 1950s it moved to terminate, or end, the reservations and its involvement with Indian affairs. Congress began transferring to state governments the responsibility for law and order among tribes in their areas and offered to pay a sum to Indians if they would relocate from reservations to cities. Of those who participated—for example, future Cherokee chief **Wilma Mankiller**—one third eventually returned to their reservations.

Soon this policy too was abandoned. Tribes that had been terminated and crossed off federal lists pushed for the government to reverse the decision so they could again ben-

efit from its programs. Ada Deer led her tribe, the Menominee, in a successful drive to win back recognition.

Observing the civil rights and anti-war movements of the 1960s, other Indians became more active on their own behalf. They started bringing cases to court, in which they sued the government for violating treaties. In 1967 the courts ruled that the Seminole Indians had been forced to give up their land for too low a price in 1823. The government had to pay the tribe more money, even though 144 years had elapsed.

Indians also began a Red Power movement. In 1969 individuals from a number of tribes (Sioux, Navajo, Cherokee, Mohawk, Puyallup, Yakima, Hoopa, and Omaha) seized Alcatraz Island off San Francisco, California. The rebels, including Mankiller, held the island property for the

▲ **Indians protesting discrimination in hiring at the Bureau of Indian Affairs office in Denver, Colorado, 1970.**

next nineteen months before federal officials removed them. The Alcatraz incident launched a number of similar incidents in the early 1970s. In 1972 protesters came to Washington, D.C., traveling, as they described, across a "Trail of Broken Treaties," meaning treaties in history. For six days, they occupied the Bureau of Indian Affairs, and violence resulted.

More violence and one death occurred in 1973, when Indians seized the village of Wounded Knee, South Dakota, for ten weeks. As the decade wore on, the violent incidents subsided. Congress passed a landmark law, the Indian Self-Determination and Education Assistance Act of 1975. Trans-

DECLARATION OF THE RETURN OF INDIAN LAND
HOW DID WE LOSE OUR LAND?
WARS - MASSACRES - FRAUD - OCCUPATION - EXPROPRIATION -
FORCED SALES - DIVISION OF TRIBAL LANDS - DEPRIVATION OF WATER - FLOODING.
WHO TOOK IT?
GOVERNMENT - RAILROAD - OIL - MINING - TIMBER COMPANIES - SETTLERS.
HOMESTEADERS - ROBBERS.
WHEN ENGLAND RULED OUR RIGHT TO OUR LAND WAS RECOGNIZED
BY THE BRITISH CROWN. AFTER THE REVOLUTION, INDIAN TITLE WAS RECOGNIZED
BY THE UNITED STATES IN PROCLAMATIONS BY PRESIDENTS, IN TREATIES & IN STATUTES.
VAST AREAS OF THE UNITED STATES WERE CEDED BY INDIAN TRIBES TO THE GOVERNMENT.
COULD ANYONE BELIEVE THAT ANY INDIAN TRIBE WOULD VOLUNTARILY CEDE THEIR
ANCESTRAL LAND, MORE PRECIOUS TO THEM THAN LIFE ITSELF, AND THE SOLE SOURCE
OF SATISFACTION FOR THEIR SPIRITUAL, RELIGIOUS AND MATERIAL NEEDS? ALMOST BEFORE
THESE TREATIES WERE SIGNED THEY WERE BROKEN - IN ORDER TO TAKE STILL MORE LAND.
FINALLY, WITHIN THE PAST TWO OR THREE DECADES THE GOVERNMENT HAS
CONFESSED THE WRONGS DONE TO THE INDIAN PEOPLE. STATUTES HAVE BEEN PASSED
CONCEDING ILLEGALITY, UNCONSTITUTIONALITY AND UNCONSCIONABLE BEHAVIOR AND THE
COURTS AND THE INDIAN CLAIMS COMMISSION HAVE BEEN AUTHORIZED TO FIND SPECIFICALLY
THE TIMES, PLACES AND VICTIMS OF THESE WRONGS.
HOW DOES THE GOVERNMENT PROPOSE TO RIGHT THESE WRONGS?
IN PLACE OF THEIR LAND THE GOVERNMENT OFFERS TO THE INDIAN TRIBES, AND
THE INDIAN PEOPLE. MONEY. HOW MUCH MONEY? FOR CALIFORNIA THEY OFFER
47¢ CENTS AN ACRE FOR LAND WHICH, IN SOME AREAS, IS WORTH 5 MILLION TIMES THAT.
FOR THE HUNDREDS OF BILLIONS TAKEN FROM OR EARNED BY INDIAN LAND - NOTHING.
FOR MORE THAN ONE HUNDRED YEARS THAT INDIANS HAVE BEEN WITHOUT THEIR LAND - NOTHING.
WILL INDIANS ACCEPT MONEY FOR THEIR LAND?
TO THE GOVERNMENT OF THE UNITED STATES THE INDIAN PEOPLE SAY:
YOU CANNOT BE RELIEVED FROM YOUR LEGAL AND MORAL OBLIGATIONS,
YOUR CONSCIENCE CANNOT BE ASSUAGED, THE HISTORICAL, SPIRITUAL AND MATERIAL NEEDS
OF THE INDIAN PEOPLE CANNOT BE SATISFIED - EXCEPT BY WHAT WE
AND BY THIS DECLARATION AFFIRM

Alcatraz Island declaration by Indians of All Tribes

ferring control from the U.S. government to the tribes, the act permitted them to contract with the government, at its expense, to perform services formerly provided by federal workers.

By the late 1970s, activity centered more squarely on Congress and the courts. Congress, for example, passed the American Indian Religious Freedom Act of 1978, guaranteeing the right of Indians to practice their native religions.

Brought to the courts were cases about the rights of tribes to offer gambling, levy taxes, and control the water in rivers and streams on their reservations. Early in the century the Supreme Court had declared that a treaty was not a grant of rights *to* Indians but rather a grant *from* them to non-Indian society. The Indians, reasoned the Court, reserved the rights to what they had not granted. Using this reserved-rights doctrine, judges made some decisions in favor of Indians in the 1970s and 1980s.

In 1990 Congress passed another act in recognition of Indian rights. For years the U.S. government had collected Indian skeletal remains and artifacts in museums. The new law (Native American Grave Protection and Repatriation Act) declared that U.S. museums and other government-funded places must return to tribes their ancestors' remains and artifacts.

Besides passing such acts, the U.S. government has employed Indians in high office. In 1985 Cherokee chief Ross Swimmer was appointed head of the Bureau of Indian Affairs. The appointment was in keeping with the policy of self-determination. For the first time in decades, an Indian assumed the top Indian affairs post in the U.S. government. Also, Congress received into its ranks a member of Indian descent who was elected by the voters of Colorado. Ben Nighthorse Campbell won election to both houses, becoming the first Native American to serve in the Senate in sixty years.

Indian Organizations

The Red Power movement was born as early as 1944, when Indians formed the National Congress of American Indians. In 1961 young radicals founded the National Indian Youth Council. In 1968 George Mitchell and Dennis Banks organized the American Indian Movement (AIM), the spokesgroup for Indians who lived in the cities. These groups brought together Indians from scattered tribes, helping to build a collective, pan-Indian movement.

Wilma Mankiller

1945-

Personal Background

The Cherokee. Much that has happened in the life of Wilma Mankiller is a reminder of the larger Cherokee history. Once the Cherokee lived in Tennessee and across the South. By the early 1800s white settlers were pushing them out of their native lands. Some left willingly and established new bases in Arkansas, only to be moved later to Indian Territory (Oklahoma). Some refused to leave and hid out in the forests of the South, later forming an Eastern Cherokee nation. Two-thirds of the Cherokee were finally rounded up and forced to travel, mostly by foot or boat, across what became known as the Trail of Tears to a reservation in Oklahoma. Once there, they were again neglected or mistreated by the government and by white settlers. In Oklahoma, as in Tennessee, there were Cherokees who tried to adopt white ways. The result was a mix of some Indians who kept to Cherokee customs and others who joined economically and socially with whites. The confusion that resulted would greatly affect Wilma Mankiller's early life.

Parents. In the late 1800s, the United States government tried to break tribal bonds by changing the way in which the various Native American groups owned land. Most Native American groups held land in common. The government, granting plots to individual Indians, encouraged them to try the white way of personal landownership. Wilma Mankiller's grandfather was granted 160 acres of

▲ **Wilma Mankiller**

Event: Rebuilding the Cherokee Nation.

Role: Wilma Mankiller was inspired to active participation in Indian Affairs after Indian tribes claimed Alcatraz Island, near San Francisco, California. She helped create a model community for Cherokee Indians in Bell, Oklahoma, and then became the first woman to serve as head chief of the Cherokee Nation.

land in eastern Oklahoma, at a place called Mankiller Flats. Eventually this land became the homestead of Charley Mankiller, who eked out a living as a subsistence farmer. When he was twenty-one years old, Charley met and married a fifteen-year-old Dutch-Irish woman, Clara Irene Sutton. Charley and Irene, as she was called, raised eleven children and remained devoted to each other until Charley's death. Wilma Pearl Mankiller, born November 18, 1945, was their sixth child.

Early life. The Mankiller family was poor but happy. They rented a small house in town, then lived in a frame house built by Charley at Mankiller Flats. Beyond the small farm plot lay a woodland of oak and sycamore. Fox and deer roamed the woods. It was pleasant land, though not a rich holding. Made entirely of wood except for the tin roof, the house had only four rooms in which to cram the growing family. There were no utilities. Wilma and some of the other children carried home all the water that the family used from a spring a quarter of a mile away. Coal oil lamps lit the small rooms at night. Meals were cooked in a wood-burning stove, which also heated the house. It had no bathroom, so the family used an outhouse.

Charley and the boys raised some crops for sale and some for the family table. To supplement the food they raised, the family purchased large sacks of flour. Irene would save the sacks, turning the material into underclothes, dresses, and shirts for the children. In time, Charley and the oldest boy, Donald, began traveling to Colorado each year, where they were hired to harvest broomcorn (used to make brooms and brushes). They brought home badly needed money to the growing family.

Separated from nearby neighbors, the Mankillers lived happily in this poverty-level setting. Evenings were spent listening to Charley tell stories of Cherokee history. During the day, everyone had chores to do, and the children attended the local Rocky Mountain Elementary School. Wilma remained in this school until the fifth grade. It was here that she first grew wary of white people; one of her earliest memories concerns their making fun of her because of her flour-sack underpants. Generally, though, life was pleasant on Mankiller Flats. But this would change in the early 1950s.

San Francisco. In 1950 Dillon S. Myer became commissioner of the Bureau of Indian Affairs. Myer had pushed for removing Japanese Americans from their homes in the West as a precaution against spying during World War II. He was in charge of moving them into hastily constructed, guarded communities, or concentration camps. Now, in 1950, he proposed a plan for dealing with the American Indians. It would be better for them and for the United States, Myer believed, if the Indians were scattered throughout the general population instead of being concentrated in Oklahoma. They would be forced, he argued, to adopt white ways. By 1953 Myer had moved on, but his successor, Glenn Emmons, pressed this idea until Congress passed a law providing aid for those American Indians agreeing to follow this plan of action.

Conditions in Oklahoma were becoming increasingly difficult, and some Indians agreed to move. A two-year drought finally convinced Charley and Irene Mankiller to leave their land. In 1956 they agreed to go to San Francisco on the promise that the Bureau of Indian Affairs (BIA) would help them find jobs and a place to live. The whole family was saddened to leave Oklahoma, and even more unhappy when, on arriving in San Francisco, they discovered that their new living quarters, selected by the BIA, were upstairs in a broken-down hotel. Wilma later likened the move to the earlier march of Cherokees along the Trail of Tears.

For eleven-year-old Wilma, the move was a great shock. Leaving a home without even running water, she arrived suddenly in a place that had television, inside plumbing, and elevators. In San Francisco, the children entered public schools in which others made fun of their speech and looked down on their poor clothing. The BIA helped Wilma's father get a job in a rope factory at $45 a week, not enough to support a family that included nine children and would soon include ten. Don, the oldest son, also took a job in the rope factory, but the family still barely made ends meet.

Soon the BIA found them an apartment in the Potrero Hills section of San Francisco, and later Charley and Don squeezed out enough money to make a down payment on a small house in Daly City. The whole family began to spend hours at the San Francisco Indian Center. Banding together, the Mankiller sisters started reading to each other to lose their accents. But Wilma hated the new city. She found one escape.

Runaway. Wilma's Grandmother Sitton had moved to Riverbank, California, which was sixty miles away. Taking a bus to her grandmother's place, Wilma ran off from home again and again. Grandmother Sitton would always call Wilma's parents to come fetch her. Finally, when Wilma was in the eighth grade, her parents agreed to leave her with her grandmother for a year.

While she was away, her older brother Don married. Without his financial help, Charley and Irene could not keep the house in Daly City. In 1960 they moved to a smaller place in the Hunter's Point area near the navy shipyards. Wilma joined them there when she returned from her grandmother's.

The family's frequent moves brought Wilma into contact with people of different ethnic backgrounds. In Daly City, the neighbors had been mostly Mexican American. At Hunter's Point they were mostly Samoan and African American. Wilma witnessed constant battles between the Samoans and the blacks. She also observed that the backbone of these poor neighborhoods was their womenfolk:

> The women [of ghetto communities] are particularly strong. Each day, they face daunting problems as they struggle just to survive. They are mothers not only of their own children but of the entire community. (Mankiller, p. 110)

While at Hunter's Point, Wilma's father quit his job at the rope factory to become a longshoreman. Soon he became a union organizer, a social activist, and a model for Wilma to follow in her future life.

Independence and marriage. Although the Indian Center grew more and more important to Wilma, she remained unhappy. As soon as she graduated from high school, she decided to strike out on her own. Her older sister Frances had already found her own apartment, and Wilma moved in with her. She took a job as a clerk in a financial office. The job bored her; she had to call people who owed money and ask them for payment. At least she was earning a salary and meeting new people, though. Among her new acquaintances was the son of an Ecuadorian doctor, Hector Hugo Olaya di Bardi, who had come to San Francisco to attend college. Hugo fell in love with Wilma, bringing fun into her life and taking her places she had never been before. He convinced her that they should wed, and the two got married at Reno, Nevada, on November 13, 1963.

Hugo's father gave the newlyweds a wedding gift of $1,000 to spend on their honeymoon—a bus trip to Chicago and back. Once more, Wilma would see a different part of American society.

Back in San Francisco, she fell ill with severe back pain and nausea. The back pain, said the doctor, was caused by a kidney infection, which could be treated with medicine. Turning to the cause of her nausea, the doctor shocked Wilma by informing her that she was pregnant. Wilma gave birth to a girl, Felicia, in 1964 and then to a second daughter, Gina, in 1966.

Despite these additions to their family, Wilma and her husband were growing in different directions. Hugo was quite conservative, while Wilma was fascinated by the civil rights and antiwar movements that were swirling around San Francisco. She wanted to become active in real-world issues. First, however, she felt a need for more education. After a brief stay at Skyline Junior College, Wilma enrolled in a sociology program at San Francisco State College.

Alcatraz. By the late 1960s, San Francisco had become a hotbed of protest in America. Students at the University of California and at Stanford University had organized to demand more rights in the government of their schools. Black activists had formed groups to organize demonstrations for civil rights. Students in all the colleges were calling on the government to withdraw from the Vietnam War. In 1969 some Native Americans decided to demand fair treatment for the hundreds of treaties broken by white governments. The place to act had already been suggested.

In the 1950s, the United States abandoned its federal prison on Alcatraz Island. A few representatives of Indian tribes used the 1868 Treaty of Fort Laramie to claim the property. The treaty held that if land acquired from the Indians was not in use, its ownership reverted, or went back, to them. Alcatraz had been abandoned, so a few Indians occupied it in 1964. Their claim was denied, and they were removed.

In 1969 a group of fourteen Indians tried to claim the island again. They came prepared in case the government demanded payment for the land (the U.S. government had already considered selling Alcatraz Island for a bid of $2 million). Out of their total, which amounted to less than $100, the Indians bought $24 worth of beads and cloth, the price that whites had paid to Indians for Manhattan Island in earlier times. Alcatraz, reasoned the Indians who went there, was certainly no more valuable than Manhattan.

The fourteen Indians were removed from Alcatraz. Eleven days later, they returned. Now eighty-nine in number, the Indians brought with them food, water, and sleeping bags. Prepared to stay, they remained on the island for eighteen months. Wilma's brothers and sisters joined in the capture of Alcatraz, whereas Wilma, who had young children at home, only visited the island occasionally. Her role, she felt, was to stay on the mainland and raise money for the supplies needed by those who stayed on the island.

Mankiller felt that she contributed valuable aid during the Alcatraz incident. After Alcatraz, she became increasingly active in movements for Native American rights and women's rights. She stepped into the position of director of the Native American Youth Center in Oakland. There she worked with Native Americans who had dropped out of school and with students in an after-school program. Her enthusiasm at the center helped raise funds and attracted volunteers to lend their assistance in various programs. Though not a large woman (Mankiller was short and stout), she appeared to be both fearless and imaginative. When a program needed volunteers, Mankiller would gather them from nearby bars in which some Native American men spent their idle time.

Pit River tribe. For many years, the supercorporation Pacific Gas and Electric Company had claimed large areas of land in northern California. An earlier treaty granted some of this land to the Pit River Indians. In the early 1970s, this tribe decided to challenge the powerful utilities company in court. Mankiller volunteered to help and worked for five years in a San Francisco law office to establish a fund to cover the costs of the huge court battle. Visits to the Pit River Tribe took her and her daughters around northern California and gave them a view of other Native American groups and their

▲ Native Americans laying claim to Alcatraz Island celebrate a Thanksgiving feast in the former prison's exercise yard; the food was sent by boat from sympathetic restaurants, November 28, 1969

histories. Everything she saw reminded her of the experiences of her own people, the Cherokee.

In 1976 she divorced Hugo and took her two daughters home to Oklahoma. Her first plans were to construct a house on the old Mankiller land and build a more simple life for her two daughters. Back in Oklahoma, Mankiller needed a job. After many applica-

263

tions, she was hired by the Cherokee Nation to write proposals for grants to improve Cherokee life.

Once her simple house was built, she grew restless again and began graduate studies at the University of Arkansas. It was while traveling to Tahlequah, Oklahoma, the Cherokee headquarters, that she was involved in a tragedy. In 1979 the car she was driving crashed head-on into another car that was trying to pass slow traffic on a stretch where visibility was poor. Mankiller suffered broken bones and other injuries. Seventeen surgeries were required to repair the damage, but the emotional hurt was as difficult to heal: a very dear friend of Mankiller's, the driver of the other car, was killed in the crash.

Participation: Rebuilding the Cherokee Nation

Bell, Oklahoma. When she recovered from the auto accident, Mankiller returned to her job with the Cherokee Nation. In 1981 she developed a proposal to help the small community of Bell, Oklahoma. It was to be a model that other communities could follow in rebuilding Cherokee settlements. Mankiller had become convinced that Native Americans should become independent and self-reliant. Bell would be the first of the communities to be redeveloped.

Mankiller secured the money to rebuild or repair several of the houses in the small community and to supply these houses with a reliable water source. She directed the rebuilding and the construction of pipeline to bring in water. The nearest steady source of water was sixteen miles away. Completing this task in 1981, Mankiller gained a reputation for effectiveness among the Cherokee. Chief Ross Swimmer, the elected head of the Cherokee Nation, was impressed by her work.

Deputy chief and chief. In 1983 Ross Swimmer faced a new election and needed a strong running mate. Mankiller was persuaded to run for the position of deputy chief. The Cherokee constitution called for the deputy chief to take over if the elected chief left office. Mankiller did not anticipate that happening. Her aim was to continue urging the Cherokee people to do things for themselves in order to raise their self-esteem. Swimmer was reelected chief with Mankiller as deputy chief of the Cherokee Nation of Oklahoma.

Two years later, President Ronald Reagan nominated Swimmer to become assistant to the secretary of the interior. The government needed him to take charge of the Bureau of Indian Affairs. It was a challenge too great to pass up, so Swimmer resigned as Cherokee chief. Mankiller took his place, becoming the first female to serve as head chief of the Cherokee Nation. *People* magazine chose her as Woman of the Year. When questioned by the magazine, former chief Swimmer responded that he had no concerns about Mankiller's becoming head chief. "She knows her strengths and her weaknesses and she is one sharp business woman" (Swimmer in *People,* December 2, 1985, p. 91).

Remarriage. During the Bell community redevelopment project, Mankiller had worked with a quiet but powerful Cherokee named Charlie Soap. The two found that they had many common interests, forming a friendship that grew. In 1986 they married. Charlie Soap became a major adviser and supporter of Chief Mankiller.

As chief. Mankiller followed the path taken by the two previous chiefs in their efforts to improve life for the Cherokee, and she planned immediately to involve the Cherokee people in their own community improvements. Her efforts were recognized when, in 1987, the Cherokee people elected her to be chief for another four years.

To improve the economy of the Cherokee Nation, Swimmer and then Mankiller began to develop industries. The Cherokee chief served as head of a corporation that included a motel, an electronics manufacturing plant, and a bank. Because of these efforts and her work in women's organizations, Mankiller became nationally known, her picture appearing on the cover of *Ms.* magazine (1988).

Reuniting the Cherokee. Perhaps one of Mankiller's greatest achievements was a step she took toward reuniting all the Cherokee people. During the period leading to their great migration westward, the Cherokee had broken into three major groups.

Some had negotiated with the U.S. government and moved to Arkansas before the great migration. Two-thirds had resisted until they were rounded up in prisons and then forced to march westward. A few, making up the third group, had rebelled against removal, hiding out in the Tennessee woodlands and eventually settling on a Tennessee reservation. They became known as the Eastern Cherokee. In the mid-1800s, the first two groups resolved their differences and reunited. But the Cherokee remained divided as Eastern and Western tribes. In 1987 Mankiller called and presided over a conference of all Cherokee, taking a first step toward reuniting the whole Cherokee Nation.

Aftermath

More misfortune. Mankiller was two years into her elected term when misfortune struck and then struck again. In 1989 she grew so weak that she was driven to a Tulsa, Oklahoma, hospital. There she discovered that she suffered from a form of muscular dystrophy. Treatment required another surgery to remove her thymus gland. She also discovered that the kidney ailment that had killed her father and grandfather had now become a serious threat to her own life. Only a kidney transplant would save her from death. Many people, among them her brothers and sisters who had returned to Oklahoma, volunteered to be tested as possible donors. Finally, her older brother Don, who still lived in California, proved to be a good prospect and agreed to give his sister a healthy kidney. Both the thymus treatment and the 1990 kidney transplant proved successful.

Reelection. Mankiller had hardly missed a step in her work for the Cherokee and for women. In 1991 the Cherokee people reelected her as head chief of the Cherokee Nation. She has continued, in this position, to work for the welfare of her people and to raise Cherokee self-esteem. There are now schools for Cherokee children that teach the Cherokee language and customs, knowledge that Mankiller believes builds pride among the people.

Chicago Tribune reporter John Hughes once asked Mankiller how she would like to be remembered. In reply, she simply said, "I want to be remembered as the person who helped us restore faith in ourselves" (Mankiller in *Chicago Tribune,* January 20, 1988, p. 1).

For More Information

Balen, Kate. "On the Rise." *Fortune,* October 12, 1987, p. 192.

Hughes, John. "Indian Chief." *Chicago Tribune,* May 14, 1986, sec. 5, pp. 1–2.

Mankiller, Wilma, and Michael Wallis. *Mankiller: A Chief and Her People.* New York: St. Martin's Press, 1993.

"*People* Magazine's Woman of the Year." *People,* December 2, 1985, p. 91.

Reinhold, Robert. "Cherokees Install First Woman as Chief of Major American Indian Tribe." *New York Times,* December 15, 1985, sec. 1, p. 30.

Robbins, Catherine C. "Expanding Power for Indian Women." *New York Times,* May 28, 1987, sec. 3, p. 1.

Wallace, Michele. "Wilma Mankiller." *Ms.* 16, no. 7 (January 1988): p. 68–69.

Warren, James. "The Saga of Wilma Mankiller, First Female Chief of the Cherokees." *Chicago Tribune,* January 20, 1988, sec. 5, p.2.

Ben Nighthorse Campbell

1933-

Personal Background

Father. Albert Valdez Campbell was probably born July 12, 1900, at Pagosa Springs on the southern edge of Colorado near the Ute Indian Reservation. He lived there with his parents until age twelve, when he ran away from home to a Cheyenne community in Montana, hundreds of miles off. Relatives lived in the community, and Albert found a place with them. He left to serve in the United States Army. An alcoholic when his army service ended, he drifted to California and found work as an orderly in the Weimar Joint Tubercular Sanitarium. A small-town hospital, it was located in the foothills of the Sierra Nevada Mountains, about thirty miles from Sacramento.

Mother. Born in Portugal on September 6, 1898, Mary Vierra immigrated to the United States with her family in 1906. As a young adult, she was stricken with tuberculosis and became a patient at Weimar. There she met Albert, and the two were married in August 1929. They had a daughter, Roberta, in 1930. When Mary's health improved, she began working at the sanitarium. She would alternate between working and being a patient there for many years. She had her second child, Ben, at Weimar on April 13, 1933.

The Campbell family. Life was difficult for the Campbell family. Albert was frequently away from home on alcoholic binges, and

Sketches by Gary Bennett

▲ **Ben Nighthorse Campbell**

Event: Advancing Native American rights.

Role: Ben Nighthorse Campbell spent his early years with little knowledge of his heritage. As an adult, he traced his family ancestry back to the Cheyenne people of Montana. Campbell's occupations have ranged from judo champion to soldier to horse breeder to jeweler to government official. Serving as a congressman and senator, he has championed the causes of Indian peoples throughout the United States.

Mary, although still suffering from tuberculosis, had to become the chief breadwinner for the family while tending her children and home. Finally Mary made Albert leave the house altogether. She struggled to hold her family together but, unable to manage, decided to place her children in an orphanage until she regained her health and fortune.

Nearly six years old at the time, Ben found himself in St. Patrick's Orphanage in Sacramento. His mother planned to keep contact with him by traveling to Sacramento each weekend. She could not always afford to do so, however, since the bus fare cost $4. Fortunately, in a few months Mary found a woman in Weimar who would look after the children while she worked. Ben and his sister were brought home.

Early life. Albert Campbell would later give up alcohol, return to the family, and become a store owner. Meanwhile, the family continued to struggle. Ben took jobs to add income to his mother's meager earnings. Both the children raised farm products for the family's meals. Beginning at age twelve, Ben worked as a fruit packer and then as a picker. In his later teens, he began to hitchhike up the mountains for jobs in the lumber industry. An outgoing young man, he found time for friendships and games with his peers in town. He also made time for his two pets, a broken-down roan mare named Redwing and a dog named Peanuts. Mostly, though, Ben learned as a teenager to be tough. He and his friends kept getting themselves into trouble. Their adventures included stealing a car for one evening, and when he was sixteen, Ben ran away from home for a brief while. Incidents of drinking, fighting, and gun stealing sent him in and out of juvenile hall. Meanwhile, Ben developed some habits that pointed to his Indian heritage. He was always drawing pictures of Indians and, from age twelve, trying to make jewelry.

Judo champion. According to Campbell, sports and military service lifted him out of his troubled youth. In high school, he was a popular center and tight end on the varsity football team. Judo, however, was to become his major interest for many years. Sometime in the 1940s, the young, strong, and brash Campbell met a young, slender Japanese man. Somehow the two got into a quarrel, and the fragile-looking Japanese threw the much larger American with a judo move. From that time on, Campbell was a disciple of the sport. He began to take lessons wherever he could find an instructor.

Bored with school, Campbell saw a way out when the North Koreans swept over the thirty-eighth parallel into South Korea. He enlisted in the U.S. Air Force and soon found himself stationed in Japan. There, the 180-pound Campbell continued to practice judo. Released from the air force, Campbell planned to continue studying judo by enrolling in a college that had such a program. San Jose State University qualified, but Campbell lacked the grades to be admitted. So he enrolled in San Jose City College to make up his missed school work, then was admitted to the university. There he studied police science and joined the judo classes of Yosh Uchida. Campbell realized that, even at 180 pounds, he was too small for national or international judo competition. So he worked hard at the sport while building his weight up. As a rule, Campbell was determined to succeed at whatever he did, and he carried this attitude over to the judo exercises under Uchida. Campbell rose to the rank of fourth-degree black belt in the sport, becoming captain of the San Jose State judo team and winning the AAPC championship (Amateur Athletic Championship of the Pacific Coast). He had high goals, intending to beat the best that America had to offer in the sport, Kenichi Hatai and Frank Harris.

Campbell got married briefly at the age of twenty-two, but this marriage was soon annulled. Married again to Elaine Morgan at the age of twenty-seven, Campbell believed that, in order to meet his goals in judo, he would have to practice against tough competition. He and Elaine moved to Japan, where Campbell arranged to join the judo team of Mejii University, whose members were the best in Japan. Another American, Paul Maruyama, also joined the university team.

Campbell soon realized the competition would indeed be tough. It was the custom of the entire Mejii team to, one by one, challenge any newcomer to a match. No matter how good the newcomer was, he was soon worn out as fresh team members offered continuous challenges. Any beginning Mejii team member was doomed to take a severe beating. One after another, team members challenged Campbell until he was beaten so badly that he could barely drag himself out of the practice area. Campbell vowed never to be defeated that badly again and worked even harder to be the best at the sport. His dedication to judo, however, interfered with his marriage. Elaine divorced him after only a few months in Japan.

Olympics. The 1964 Olympic Games were to be held in Japan, with judo being added to the games for the first time. By now, Campbell had reached his full stature. Standing five feet eleven inches high and weighing 240 pounds (largely muscle), Campbell was of the finest at the sport in America. Four men were chosen to represent the United States in the Olympics: Frank Harris, an African American air force sergeant; Jimmy Bergman, an American Jew; Paul Maruyama, a Japanese American; and Campbell, of American Indian heritage. Looking at the ethnic mix, some competitors wondered where the "Americans" were on the American team, but Campbell thought it truly represented the range of American peoples.

During the pre-Olympic practices, Campbell established his claim to international standing by beating the captain of the Mejii team. But these practices proved costly. He injured a knee in one of the bouts. In the Olympics, Campbell easily defeated his first opponent, then faced a much larger German champion. The two fought until the weight of the challenger wore down Campbell's injured knee and he was forced to drop out of the Olympic games. His days of judo competition were over. Campbell retired at the age of thirty-one.

Judo instructor. Although he could no longer compete, Campbell was by now a symbol of the sport in America. He returned to the Sacramento area and rebuilt the Sacramento Judo Club, making it a leading center of judo in the nation. He also began to develop judo camps around the country. One of these, Camp Bushido, near Sacramento, occupied much of his time for a few years after the Olympics. The camp was to have a great influence on Campbell's life.

Remarriage. One of his efforts to advance the sport led him to the San Juan School District, where he began an experimental program to teach judo to the students. There he met Linda Price, a Colorado rancher's daughter who had taken a teaching job in the

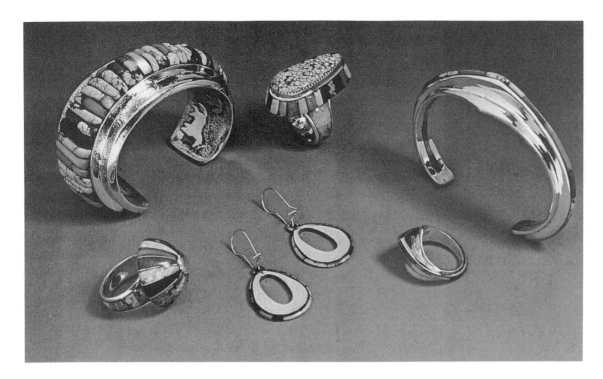

▲ **Jewelry made by Campbell**

district. In 1964 Linda enrolled in one of Campbell's classes. This led to his inviting her to help with Camp Bushido. The couple were married July 23, 1966. The family would later grow to include a daughter and son.

Teacher, jeweler, rancher, and politician. Campbell has pursued three long-term interests: sports, jewelry making, and horses. For twelve years, while he was competing in judo, he nearly abandoned his involvement with jewelry and horses. But once the challenge of judo competition was over, Campbell renewed his other interests. He and Linda acquired a quarter horse, Sailor's Night, and began breeding horses. They moved to a ranch near Montrose, Colorado, and Campbell charged into new occupations with the same determination that he had earlier shown for judo. By 1969 he was a respected rancher and had been recognized for his jewelry making as one of the outstanding Indian artists. Except for a kindly postmaster in Weimar who showed him how to whittle as a boy, he was a self-taught artist. According to Campbell, he did not

273

move to Colorado to work but rather to retire, pursue his art, and raise horses. He explained his interest in horses:

> Well, there is a strong spiritual thing about horses. The horse is one of the few domesticated animals used in Indian ceremonials. When an animal is domesticated, the Plains Indians feel the animal has lost its power. [But] the buffalo and horse are still considered to have power. (Hait, p. 45)

Participation:
Advancing Native American Rights

Albert's family. Campbell had sometimes pestered his father about his ancestry. But in those days, being Indian was not popular. Campbell's father preferred to forget about his heritage, even though he was living with the Northern Cheyenne when he enlisted in the army. Campbell would ask and his father would tell him to forget about the past. He did, however, inform Campbell that he might be related to the Black Horse family of the Cheyenne.

In 1966 Campbell's interest was sharpened by chance. He was visiting a swap meet when he saw a photograph of an elderly Cheyenne man, Wolf Voice. This encouraged him to visit the Northern Cheyenne in Montana and inquire about his ancestors. He found Wolf Voice, who knew where members of the Black Horse family lived. Campbell visited them and announced that he believed himself to be related to the family. In 1968, when he at last introduced himself to Alec Black Horse, Campbell was welcomed. Alec told him that he needed another son, accepting him as such, and Campbell easily accepted the Cheyenne way of life. Some believed that the aging Alec was the brother of Maria Ramona, Campbell's great-grandmother.

At last Campbell could guess the identity of some of his ancestors, but it took several more years and much searching to trace his ancestry with even a small degree of accuracy. Albert Campbell had thought himself a Jicarilla Apache. The Campbell family, however, had Indian heritage from several midwestern groups. Great-grandmother Maria Ramona Mestas, who married Alexander Campbell, was from the San Juan Pueblo. She seemed to have come to the pueblo as a young woman, however, and may have been Cheyenne. As Campbell continued searching out his roots, friends among the Cheyenne began helping him find traces of his family. Some thought Maria Ramona had been killed in an 1864 massacre at Sand Creek. Farther back in the family line, another ancestor had lived among the Taos pueblo people. Campbell's search confirmed that he was part Northern Cheyenne. A descendant of the Black Horse family, he was therefore given the middle name Nighthorse in an Indian naming ceremony. As he learned about his own family through frequent visits among the people, he became familiar with Cheyenne beliefs. Campbell worked them into his art pieces:

> The Indian design is based on the directions, colors, and shapes—especially circles. In the old traditional Cheyenne pieces, red stood for south; yellow, for east; blue or black for west; and white for north (Viola, p. 45).

Horses. Jewelry was not the only link to his Indian heritage. Campbell began to work with the Ute people who lived near his ranch. He eventually took a job with them managing the Ute horse-training center and race track, Ute Downs. Meanwhile, he and Linda continued to breed their own quarter horses. Campbell brought his two interests together by including horse figures in his jewelry. At the same time, he found another opportunity to help his Indian relatives.

Politics. Ben Nighthorse Campbell had long believed that education was one way to raise the standards of Indian life. In Colorado he found himself involved in trying to improve the educational system in the Ignacio School District. A popular citizen, he was elected to serve on the school board. This led to his election to the Colorado State Assembly in 1983. A year later, he was named the outstanding Colorado legislator, noted for his straight talk and honesty. He continued his efforts for Indian education through the American Indian Education Association, his fine work for the citizens of Colorado earning him election to the U.S. Congress in 1987. Campbell thought he would serve one term in Congress but remained in Washington as a congressman until 1993.

Among the issues Campbell tackled during his two terms in Congress were injustices suffered by Native Americans. Two

▲ In Cheyenne clothing, Campbell rides a horse in the 103rd Tournament of Roses Parade in Pasadena, California, January 1, 1992; Campbell was co-marshal of the parade with Cristobal Colon, a twentieth-generation descendant of Christopher Columbus

decades earlier, in 1976, Campbell had joined other Cheyenne as well as Sioux and Arapaho peoples in a celebration of prayer. The occasion was the 100-year anniversary of the Battle of Little Big Horn, in which Plains tribes defeated white army men. At the celebration, he saw firsthand the different treatment accorded to Indians. Only Indians had their cars searched and were escorted to meetings by police. Fifteen years later in Congress, Campbell won a fight over the name of a monument to this battle. He succeeded in having it changed to Little Bighorn Battlefield National Monument from Custer Battlefield National Monument. (George Armstrong Custer was the white general who died in the Battle of Little Big Horn.) To Campbell, correcting the name helps boost pride among Indians in their heritage, which helps combat major problems such as their high suicide rate.

Campbell would continue to visit the Northern Cheyenne and to speak for the rights of Indians throughout his career as a congressman. He was instrumental in getting a bill passed to settle water claims for the Ute Indians of Colorado. Through the Colorado-Ute Indian Water Rights Settlement Act of 1988, Campbell helped see that Colorado's Indians received money and water to which they were entitled. Also, he started legislation to establish a National Museum of the American Indian at the Smithsonian Institution in Washington, D.C. Important to tribes is an amendment to the act that concerns Indian remains—skulls, sacred objects, and the like—collected by U.S. officials over the years. The amendment obligates the government to let tribes reclaim their ancestors' remains and objects for sacred burial or use. Perhaps one of Campbell's most public stands for Indian rights came during Bill Clinton's inauguration as president. Dressed in Cheyenne attire, Campbell rode in the inaugural parade to influence attitudes toward Native Americans.

> ## Why Parade in Cheyenne Clothing?
>
> "I wanted to let Indian people know they're not forgotten, that ... we're still part of America. They may drive dump trucks for a living instead of chasing buffalo, they may dress in a business suit or in jeans instead of buckskins, but they have a distinct lifestyle, heritage and culture." (Brock, p. 8)
>
> "I think one of the messages ... I was trying to send was that we [Native Americans] have every right to be involved in that structure of government too, and in fact, if you're going to make changes, just complaining about it from the outside isn't going to get it done. You've got to get involved in the process." (*Good Morning America*, January 27, 1994)

Aftermath

Senator Campbell. Having served six years in the House of Representatives, Campbell was prepared to retire from politics and concentrate at age fifty on his jewelry-making and his horses. The

A Different Kind of Campaign Help

For a few weeks in his race for the Senate, Campbell was down in the election polls. Some traditional Cheyenne leaders had a vision that he was in trouble and advised that he do three things: carry an eagle feather near his heart; paint his palms, the top of his head, and the area over his heart with a sacred paint of red ochre; and smoke every morning, meaning that he should burn sweetgrass or sage or cedar. The day after Campbell followed their advice, the polls turned in his favor and campaign donations began to arrive.

citizens of Colorado had other ideas, however. In 1993 Ben Nighthorse Campbell was elected to serve as a United States senator.

Campbell became the first Native American elected to the Senate in more than sixty years. His constituency, the people who elected him, were miners and ranchers. An individual thinker and dresser, Campbell has attended Senate meetings in cowboy boots, a neck-scarf held by his own self-made jewelry, and a ponytail. He insists on doing what he thinks is right and on not being afraid of how people will react to his positions or if they will reelect him. Thoughts of young people, he says, keep him in office:

> I think government has a responsibility to make it easier on kids. I managed to make it, but think of the ones that didn't. They got sick, or couldn't emotionally put up with it, or whatever, and they ended up in prison. (Campbell in Brock, p. 13)

Among the committees on which Campbell serves is the Senate Select Committee on Indian Affairs, which deals with issues such as religious freedom for Native Americans and Indian gaming, or gambling, rights. In the senator's view, the issues all fall into one category—self-determination. The American Indians, Campbell says, want to make their own decisions, not have leaders in Washington decide for them.

For More Information

Brock, Tom. "Senator Ben Nighthorse Campbell: Interview." *Boulder Magazine,* Summer 1994, pp.6–10.

Good Morning America. New York: Columbia Broadcasting System, January 27, 1994.

Hait, Pam. "Beads, Boots and Jaguars: The Artists as They See Themselves." *Arizona Highways,* April 1979, pp.42–54.

Viola, Herman J. *Ben Nighthorse Campbell.* New York: Orion Books, 1993.

Bibliography

Chafe, William Henry. *The American Woman.* London: Oxford University Press, 1972.

Cone, James H. *Martin and Malcolm and America: A Dream or a Nightmare?* Maryknoll, New York: Orbis, 1981.

Dallek, Robert. *Lone Star Rising: Lyndon Johnson and his Times, 1908-1960.* New York: Oxford University Press, 1991.

DeCurtis, Anthony, and James Henke, eds. *The Rolling Stone Illustrated History of Rock and Roll.* New York: Random House, 1992.

Dees, Morris. *A Season for Justice: The Life and Times of Civil Rights Lawyer Morris Dees.* New York: Scribners, 1981.

Drew, Elizabeth. *Washington Journal: The Events of 1973-1974.* New York: Random House, 1975.

Friedan, Betty. *The Second Stage.* New York: Summit Books, 1981.

Gentry, Curt. *J. Edgar Hoover: The Man and His Secrets.* New York: Norton, 1981.

Goodwin, Eric Frederick. *Remembering America: A Voice from the Sixties.* Boston: Little, Brown, 1988.

Griffin, Des Martin. *Martin Luther King: The Man Behind the Myth.* New York: Emissary, 1987.

Halberstam, David. *The Unfinished Odyssey of Robert Kennedy.* New York: Random House, 1968.

Hodgson, Godfrey. *America In Our Time.* New York: Doubleday, 1976.

Howard, Craig. *Voices of the Vietnam POWs: Witnesses to Their Fight.* New York: Oxford, 1993.

Johnson, Rebecca Baines. *A Family Album.* New York: McGraw-Hill, 1965.

Johnson, Sam. *Captive Warriors: A Vietnam POW Story.* College Station: Texas A & M University Press, 1982.

King, Coretta. *The Worth of Martin Luther King.* New York: Newmarket, 1987.

King, Martin Luther. *A Testament of Hope.* San Francisco, California: Harper, 1990.

Larralde, Carlos. *Mexican American Movements and Leaders.* Los Alamitos, California: Hwong Publishing, 1976.

Lowenstein, Allard. *Brutal Mandate: A Journey to South West Africa.* New York: Macmillan, 1962.

Makos, Christopher. *Warhol: A Personal Photographic Memoir.* New York: NAL Books, 1988.

Miller, Mark. *Lyndon; An Oral Biography.* New York: Putnam's, 1980.

Mankiewicz, Frank. *U.S. vs. Richard M. Nixon: The Final Crisis.* New York: Quadrangle/New York Times, 1975.

BIBLIOGRAPHY

Nash, Jay Robert. *Citizen Hoover: A Critical Study of the Life and Times of J. Edgar Hoover.* Chicago: Nelson-Hall, 1972.

North, Mark. *Act of Treason: The Role of J. Edgar Hoover in the Assassination of President Kennedy.* New York: Carrol and Graf, 1991.

Ratcliff, Carter. *Andy Warhol.* New York: Abbeville Press, 1983.

Scaduto, Anthony. *Bob Dylan: An Intimate Biography.* New York: Grosset & Dunlap, 1971.

Schulke, Flip. *Martin Luther King, Jr.* New York: Norton, 1976.

Schulke, Flip and Penelope O. McPhee. *King Remembered.* New York: Norton, 1986.

Solder, Kenneth. *The Pentagon Papers Trial.* Cambridge, Massachusetts: Editorial Justa, 1975.

Sullivan, William C. *The Bureau: My Thirty Years in Hoover's FBI.* New York: Norton, 1979.

Summers, Anthony. *Official and Confidential: The Secret Life of J. Edgar Hoover.* New York: Putnam's, 1993.

Toledano, Ralph de. *J. Edgar Hoover, The Man In His Time.* New Rochelle, New York: Arlington House, 1973.

Van DeMark, Brian. *Into the Quagmire: Lyndon Johnson and the Escalation of the Vietnam War.* New York: Oxford University Press, 1991.

Violet, Ultra. *Famous for Fifteen Minutes: My Years with Andy Warhol.* San Diego, California: Harcourt Brace Jovanovich, 1988.

Walton, James. *The Political Philosophy of Martin Luther King.* New York: Greenwood, 1971.

Wood, Joe, editor. *Malcolm X: In Our Own Image.* New York, St. Martin's Press, 1992.

Cumulative Index

Bold denotes profiles and volume numbers.

B

M

MacArthur, Arthur **7:** 170-172
MacArthur, Arthur, III **7:** 174
MacArthur, Douglas 7: 71-73, 144-145, 153, 155-158, 167, **170-183**
MacArthur, Jean Marie Faircloth **7:** 174
MacArthur, Mary Harding **7:** 170
Macaulay, Catherine Sawbridge **2:** 104
MacKenzie, Alexander **2:** 154
Madeiros, Celestino **6:** 24-26
Madison, Dolley Payne **4:** 142
Madison, Dolley Payne 2: 13, 206, **236-249**
Madison, Fort (Iowa) **3:** 9, 16
Madison, James 1: 233; **3:** 193; **4:** 69; **2:** 3, **4-13,** 22, 28, 30, 31, 32, 39, 76, 77, 90-91, 113, 175, 205, 210-212, 232, 236, 238-242, 246-249, 254, 259
Maggie: A Girl of the Streets **5:** 177
Magnalia **3:** 252
Main Street Railroad Company 208
"The Majestic Lie" **5:** 181-182
Major Ridge (*see* Ridge [Major])
Ma-ka-tai-me-she-kia-kiak **3:** 6
Maky, Nathan C. **5:** 58
Malcolmson, Alexander **6:** 158
Malcolm X 6: 219-220; **7:** 243; **8:** 21, 6-7, 57, **60-71**
Malden, Fort **2:** 217, 230-231
Malone, Dudley Field **6:** 182, 203
Malory, Thomas **7:** 24
Malthus, Thomas Robert **6:** 268-269
Mamate **2:** 225
Manassas, Battle of (*see* Bull Run, Battles of)
Mandan **2:** 132, 135
Mandan, Fort **2:** 132-133
Mangus **6:** 126
Manhattan Project **7:** 18-19, 119, 122, 129, 220-222, 225
Manifest Destiny **4:** 40
Manila Bay, Battle of **5:** 233, 243-244, 268
Manila, Philippines **6:** 128
Mankiller, Wilma 8: 252, **256-267**
Manzzanar **7:** 105
Maps of Virginia **1:** 73

Marah **5:** 188
The Marble Faun **4:** 128
Marbury, Francis **1:** 86-87
Marbury v. *Madison* **2:** 90-91, 93
Marbury, William **2:** 90-91
March on Washington **7:** 89-90, 92-93; **8:** 18-20, 44-45, 68-69
Marcy, William L. **4:** 71
Marie Antoinette **1:** 252, 260, 261
Marilyn **8:** 149
Marne River **6:** 133
Maroons **3:** 161; **6:** 212
Marquette University **7:** 202
Marrow, Stanley **4:** 247-248
Marshall, Burke **8:** 42
Marshall Field Company **5:** 74
Marshall, George **7:** 71, 73-75, 143, 154, 168, 208
Marshall Hotel **6:** 228
Marshall, James Wilson **4:** 5, 35
Marshall, John 2: 46, **84-95**; **3:** 27
Marshall, Norma A. Williams **7:** 244-245
Marshall Plan **7:** 143-144, 161, 168-169
Marshall, Thurgood 7: 229-230, **244-255**
Marshall, Vivian Burney **7:** 246
Marshall, William **7:** 244-245
Maruyama, Paul **8:** 272
Marx, Karl **5:** 92, 94; **6:** 21; **8:** 11
Mason, Charlotte Osgood **6:** 238
Mason, Elizabeth Champlin **2:** 210
Mason, George **2:** 11
Massachusetts Bay Colony **1:** 61, 89-90
Massachusetts Fifty-fifth regiment **4:** 225, 226
Massachusetts in the Woman Suffrage Movement **3:** 81
Massachusetts State Legislature **3:** 98
Massachusetts Supreme Court **6:** 141, 142
Massacre at Wounded Knee **6:** 126
"Masters of War" **8:** 138, 142
Mather, Cotton **1:** 100, 102; **3:** 252
Matthews, Robert **3:** 245
Maury, James **1:** 186-187, 204
Mayer, H. B. **5:** 81

N

PROFILES IN AMERICAN HISTORY

Significant Events and the People Who Shaped Them